Dinosaurs

a visual encyclopedia

DK

DK PUBLISHING

DK

LONDON, NEW YORK,
MELBOURNE, MUNICH, and DELHI

Senior editors Ben Morgan, Caroline Bingham
Project designer Pamela Shiels
Editor Wendy Horobin
Senior designer Rachael Grady
US editor Margaret Parrish
Picture researcher Frances Vargo
Production editor Siu Chan
Art director Martin Wilson
Category publisher Mary Ling

Consultant Dr. Darren Naish

DK India
Managing editor Suchismita Banerjee
Managing art editor Romi Chakraborty
Senior editors Pakshalika Jayaprakash, Kingshuk Ghoshal
Consulting editor Dipali Singh
Editorial team Parameshwari Sircar, Suefa Lee
Senior designer Govind Mittal
Design team Mahua Mandal, Pooja Pawwar, Prashant Kumar
CTS manager Sunil Sharma
Creative technical support Tarun Sharma,
Saurabh Challariya, Jagtar Singh, Nand Kishor Acharya

First published in the United States in 2011 by
DK Publishing
345 Hudson Street, New York, New York 10014

14 15 10 9 8 7 6 5 4 3 2
002–179455–Jun/11

Contents

Foreword

We are surrounded by fascinating animals. Gigantic whales and sharks swim in the oceans. Spectacular large animals—such as big cats, elephants and giraffes— live on the land. Wild places everywhere are filled with insects, birds, and thousands of other living things. But Earth's fossil record shows us that these creatures are just the tips of an amazing hidden tree of life that stretches back hundreds of millions of years into the distant past. This rich fossil record tells us an incredible and complicated story of evolution and extinction. While modern animals may well be fascinating, those of the past were often bigger, stronger, or much, much weirder.

In this beautifully illustrated book, we look in detail at the huge variety of animal life that has evolved over the past 500 million years or so, from the origins of complex life in the Precambrian age to the dinosaurs of the Mesozoic Era and the mammals and birds of more modern times.

Most of the world's fossils represent the remains of small creatures like shellfish and plankton. But others show us that incredible beasts—sometimes very different from living animals—once existed as well. We know of crocodile-sized millipedes, horse-eating giant birds, monstrous sea reptiles, and bizarre mammals like ground sloths and saber-toothed cats. Figuring out what these animals looked like when alive has often been a difficult challenge, and scientists and artists have worked hard to reconstruct their appearance and behavior.

In this book you will see many spectacular illustrations of these animals and many others, all arranged in their evolutionary families and roughly in the order in which they appeared. Opening this book is like stepping back in time. Get ready to go on a spectacular visual tour of the animal life of the past, and prepare to be amazed.

Dr. Darren Naish
Science writer and honorary research associate at the University of Portsmouth, UK

PREHISTORIC LIFE

▲ THE GRAND CANYON *gives us an amazing glimpse back in time. As the river eats deeper into ancient layers of rock, it reveals fossils that formed millions or even billions of years ago.*

Prehistoric refers to the time before written records began. It covers an enormous period of history, beginning with Earth's birth 4.6 billion years ago. Enter an endlessly fascinating world.

How life began

Earth first formed about 4.6 billion years ago. When the planet was very young, life would have been impossible—the ground was blisteringly hot and there was no water in sight. So how did life begin?

EARLY EARTH
A sea of molten rock covered the newly formed Earth. In time, this cooled to solid rock, but volcanoes continued to spew out floods of lava. The volcanoes also released gases from deep inside the planet, forming Earth's atmosphere, though the air at first was poisonous.

COMETS AND ASTEROIDS
For millions of years, Earth's surface was bombarded by comets, asteroids, and even small planets. The collisions tore open the planet's newly formed crust, releasing more floods of lava. But they also delivered water.

Oceans form

As the young Earth slowly cooled, so did its atmosphere. Scalding steam released by volcanoes condensed to form liquid water that fell as rain, producing a downpour that lasted as long as a million years. Comets and asteroids brought yet more water. All the water pooled on the surface to form vast oceans.

▼ WATER *Life cannot exist without liquid water. Today water covers 71 percent of the Earth's surface.*

A watery beginning

Many scientists think life began about 3.8 billion years ago in the deep sea, which was safer than Earth's deadly surface. The first life-forms might have lived around hot volcanic vents, feeding off energy-rich chemicals dissolved in the boiling water. Special kinds of bacteria thrive in these scalding habitats even today.

Life in hot water

At Grand Prismatic Spring in Yellowstone National Park, bacteria thrive in water too hot for any other organism to bear.

Copycat molecules

The first life-form was not a whole organism or even a cell—it was just a molecule that could make copies of itself. This is what DNA does today. DNA can't copy itself outside cells, so the first living molecule must have been something different. Later on, it evolved into DNA.

— *Model of a DNA molecule*

Bacteria are single-celled organisms that are too small to see. Millions live on your skin and inside your body.

The age of bacteria

Soon after life began, the self-copying molecules built cells around themselves and became bacteria. Bacteria were the only forms of life on Earth for the next 3 billion years, a vast span of time.

A true survivor

Some of the oldest evidence of life on Earth comes from stromatolites. These are rocklike mounds formed by colonies of bacteria. Fossil stromatolites date back to 3.5 billion years ago. The bacteria in stromatolites live like plants, using the Sun's energy to make food and in doing so releasing oxygen. Billions of years ago, they made enough oxygen to transform Earth's air, paving the way for air-breathing animals to evolve.

▼ LIVING STROMATOLITES *can still be found today, such as here in Shark Bay, Western Australia.*

Stromatolite ——

9

Evolution

Fossils of prehistoric animals show us that life on Earth is always changing. Over time, old species disappear and new ones develop from them, like new relatives appearing in a family tree. These new species appear thanks to a process of gradual change we call evolution.

NATURAL SELECTION

Evolution is driven by a process called natural selection. Animals and plants produce more offspring than survive to adulthood, all of them slightly different. Nature selects those with the best characteristics, which then pass on these characteristics to the next generation.

The giraffe's neck
The giraffe's long neck evolved because natural selection weeded out individuals that couldn't reach food high in the trees. With each generation, the tallest giraffes got the most food and had the most babies. Over time, the species changed as its neck grew longer.

▲ BREEDING FROGS *lay many hundreds of eggs, but only a tiny number will survive to become adults themselves.*

 TAKE A LOOK—A STORY OF FINCHES

The most famous person to collect evidence for the idea of evolution was the English naturalist Charles Darwin. He visited the Galápagos Islands in the 1830s, where he found a range of similar finch species, each with a beak suited to its particular diet. He realized they'd all evolved from a common ancestor that had settled on the islands long ago.

Woodpecker finch
Camarhynchus pallidus

Medium ground finch
Geospiza fortis

Vegetarian finch
Platyspiza crassirostris

Warbler finch
Certhidea olivacea

An unpopular theory

People made fun of Darwin for his ideas; he was drawn with the body of a chimpanzee in 1871 when he proposed that humans were related to apes.

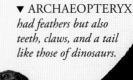

▼ ARCHAEOPTERYX *had feathers but also teeth, claws, and a tail like those of dinosaurs.*

FOSSIL EVIDENCE

One reason Darwin was ridiculed is that the fossil record is much too sparse to show a process of gradual change. However, some key fossils show clear links between related animal groups. One example is *Archaeopteryx*—a missing link between dinosaurs and birds.

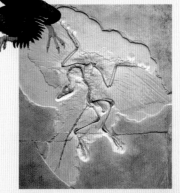

EVOLUTION OF THE ELEPHANT

In a few rare examples, we can see gradual evolution in fossils. The elephant belongs to a group of animals called proboscideans. Over time, proboscideans became larger and developed larger tusks and trunks. But the ancient animals shown here may not be direct ancestors of the elephant—they are merely glimpses of parts of the elephant's large and hidden family tree.

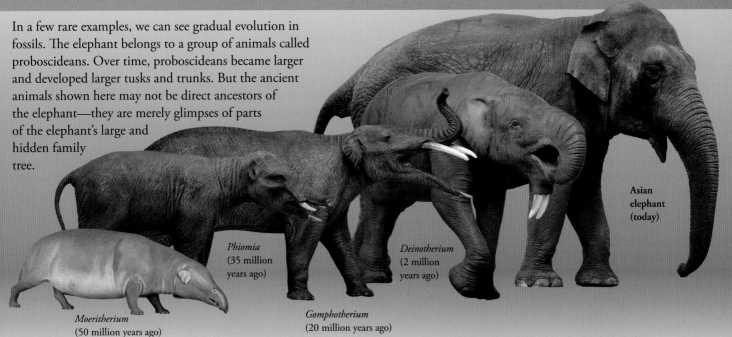

Asian elephant (today)

Phiomia (35 million years ago)

Deinotherium (2 million years ago)

Moeritherium (50 million years ago)

Gomphotherium (20 million years ago)

Artificial selection

Darwin realized that animal breeders change their breeds using a process very similar to natural selection. Instead of letting nature choose which animals will breed, breeders make the choice themselves. Darwin called this artificial selection. All dog breeds were created this way from their wild ancestor, the wolf.

Gray wolf

▼ DOGS *All domestic dogs today have a common ancestor in the wolf.*

11

Timeline of life

Earth's history stretches back 4.6 billion years to our planet's birth. Scientists divide this vast span of time into different periods, such as the Jurassic Period, when many of the dinosaurs lived. Here you can see all the periods on a timeline showing the history of life.

◄ GRAND CANYON
The different periods in Earth's history are named after the layers of rock in which fossils are found. At the Grand Canyon, you can see these ancient rock layers, which get older toward the bottom.

THE LINES TELL TALES

The past leaves clues buried in the rock below our feet. Certain types of rock build up in layers (strata) over millions of years. Each layer corresponds to one of the major periods in Earth's history.

▶ EARTH'S HISTORY *is divided into very long stretches of time called eras. These are further divided into shorter stretches called periods, such as the Jurassic and Triassic.*

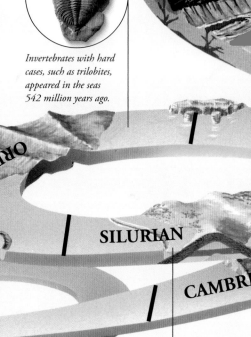

Dinosaurs died out 65 million years ago.

CRETACEOUS

Invertebrates with hard cases, such as trilobites, appeared in the seas 542 million years ago.

ORDOVICIAN

SILURIAN

CAMBRI

Life began about 3.8 billion years ago, perhaps in the deep sea.

PRECAMBRIAN

Plants spread onto land 440 million years ago.

Earth formed 4.6 billion years ago.

ERAS AND PERIODS

		PALEOZOIC ERA			
PRECAMBRIAN	CAMBRIAN	ORDOVICIAN	SILURIAN	DEVONIAN	CARBONIFEROU
4.6 billion to 542 million years ago	**542–488 million years ago**	**488–444 million years ago**	**444–416 million years ago**	**416–358 million years**	**358–299 million years a**
	Trilobites scuttled around on the seafloor (see pages 36–37).		*Pseudocrinites anchored itself to the seabed in the late Silurian.*		*Dragonflies and other insects buzzed through the air (see pages 54–55).*
		Starfish (sea stars) became common in the sea (see pages 40–41).		*Dunkleosteus, a giant predator, terrorized the seas (see page 68).*	

JURASSIC

TRIASSIC

PERMIAN

Ice age

Mammals took over about
70 million years ago, after
dinosaurs died out.

Birds evolved from dinosaurs
150 million years ago.

Dinosaurs appeared
230 million years ago.

PALEOGENE

DEVONIAN

NEOGENE

Fish (the first
vertebrates) became the
dominant form of life
in the seas 400 million
years ago.

Amphibians evolved from
fish and spread onto land
360 million years ago.

Modern humans
appeared
200,000 years ago.

MESOZOIC ERA

CENOZOIC ERA

PERMIAN	TRIASSIC	JURASSIC	CRETACEOUS	PALEOGENE	NEOGENE
299–251 million years ago	251–200 million years ago	200–145 million years ago	145–65 million years ago	65–23 million years ago	23 million years ago

Dimetrodon *was the
most fearsome predator
of its time (see page 218).*

*The first dinosaurs
appeared, one of the
earliest known being
Herrerasaurus.*

*The earliest known bird,
Archaeopteryx, appeared
(see page 208).*

*The first mammals were
small, mouselike animals
(see pages 222–223).*

*One of the earliest known
primates, Eosimias, appeared
in this period (see page 277).*

*Our apelike
ancestors began
walking (pages
278–281).*

Changing planet

Planet Earth is always changing. Areas of land (continents) move slowly around on Earth's surface, changing the map of the world. The climate swings from warm to cold, and the plants and animals change from one era to the next, sometimes dramatically. Scientists divide the age of the dinosaurs into three periods, all of which were very different from today's world.

EARTH TODAY

Today Earth's land is divided into seven major areas that we call continents: Europe, Africa, Asia, North America, South America, Antarctica, and Australasia. All the continents are still moving, but very slowly—at about the speed your fingernails grow.

Coelophysis

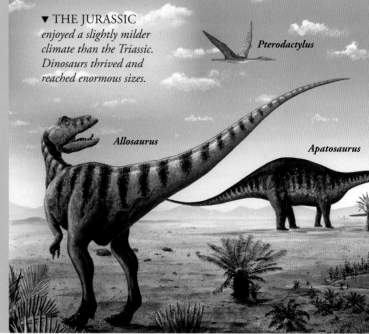

▼ THE JURASSIC *enjoyed a slightly milder climate than the Triassic. Dinosaurs thrived and reached enormous sizes.*

Pterodactylus

Allosaurus

Apatosaurus

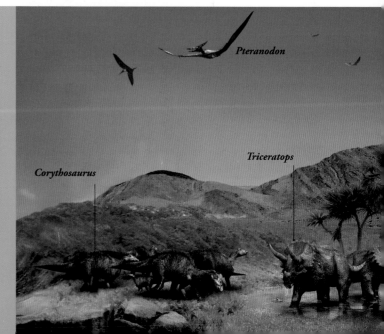

Pteranodon

Corythosaurus

Triceratops

◄ THE TRIASSIC *saw the planet's first dinosaurs, all fairly small, like this Coelophysis. They lived in a hot, largely barren world.*

Triassic life
251–200 million years ago
In the Triassic period, Earth's land formed a single continent called Pangaea. The coast and river valleys were green, but much of the interior was desert. There were no flowering plants; instead, tough-leaved plants such as cycads (a palmlike tree), ginkgos, horsetails, and conifers flourished (all of which are still with us). Early dinosaurs included *Herrerasaurus*, *Plateosaurus*, *Chindesaurus*, *Coelophysis*, and *Eoraptor*.

Cycad

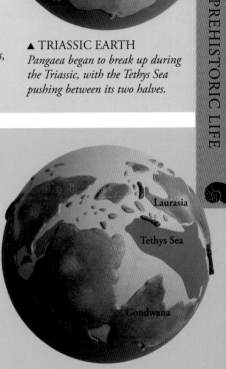

▲ TRIASSIC EARTH
Pangaea began to break up during the Triassic, with the Tethys Sea pushing between its two halves.

Brachiosaurus

Stegosaurus

Jurassic life
200–145 million years ago
Pangaea broke into two continents around 200 million years ago, with oceans spreading over what had been land to create enormous shallow seas. The Jurassic saw the emergence of giant, plant-eating sauropods (such as *Brachiosaurus* and *Diplodocus*) and large predators (such as *Allosaurus*). Lush forests spread across the land and the deserts shrank. Common plants included conifers, monkey puzzle trees, and ferns.

Fern

▲ JURASSIC EARTH
Pangaea split into Laurasia in the north and Gondwana in the south, with shallow seas between.

▼ THE CRETACEOUS *was cooler still, although it was warmer than today's world. Dinosaurs ruled the land but pterosaurs and insects ruled the air.*

Ankylosaurus

Cretaceous life
145–65 million years ago
The continents continued to break up during the Cretaceous. As a result, dinosaurs on different continents evolved in different ways, giving rise to many new species. *Tyrannosaurus* emerged, as did *Triceratops* and *Iguanodon*. Flowering plants appeared; early species included magnolias and passion flowers. Dense forests contained trees we know today, such as oak, maple, walnut, and beech.

Magnolia

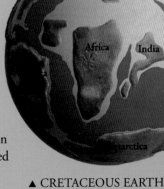

▲ CRETACEOUS EARTH
The continents began to resemble those we recognize today during the Cretaceous period.

All about fossils

Almost everything we know about prehistoric animals comes from fossils. A fossil is the preserved remains or trace of an ancient animal or plant. The word "fossil" comes from the Latin word *fossilis*. That means "dug up," and that's how some fossils are discovered, although most are exposed by erosion. Most fossilized animals have lain buried for millions of years.

A dinosaur dies and falls into the muddy bank of a river.

▲ IT'S IN THE DETAIL *Complete fossilized skeletons are rare, but when found they provide a huge amount of information for fossil hunters (paleontologists).*

DID YOU KNOW?

■ Fossils are usually found in rock but may also be found in mud or gravel.
■ The parts of an animal most likely to fossilize are the hard parts: the bones or teeth or a creature's shell.
■ Teeth are among the most commonly found fossils.
■ The oldest fossils are stromatolites (mounds of rock made by sea-dwelling bacteria). These have been dated to 3.5 billion years ago.

TYPES OF FOSSIL

Fossils can be sorted, or classified, into different types, depending on how they formed. All take millions of years to form—fossilization is not quick.

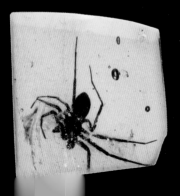

Total preservation If an insect or spider was caught in the sticky sap released by a tree such as a pine, it may be preserved complete. Creatures that are millions of years old have been preserved in fossilized tree resin (known as amber) in this way.

Mineralization Dinosaurs, like us, had hard bones, and sometimes just these parts of an animal are preserved—though not as bone, which is replaced over time with minerals to form rock. Rock has to be carefully removed to expose the fossils.

What makes a fossil?

All kinds of living things have been discovered in fossil form. We have unearthed fossilized animal skeletons, skin impressions, footprints, teeth, animal droppings, insects, and plants. The hard parts of an animal, such as the bones, are the parts that fossilize best.

TAKE A LOOK—WHAT IS A PALEONTOLOGIST?

People who study fossils are called paleontologists. Paleontologists may work in the field, digging up new fossils, or in labs or museums. They work like detectives, carefully gathering as many clues as they can to find out what happened in the past and to figure out where each new discovery fits in the tree of life.

A sea has spread over the area, and new layers of sand and mud have built up. The skeleton is slowly turning into rock.

Millions of years later, the sea is gone and the layers of rock over the fossil are slowly eroded by weather and glaciers, bringing the fossil back to the surface.

Thousands of years later, the glaciers have gone and the land is now a barren desert.

Over the years, layers of mud settle on top and bury the animal.

A SLOW PROCESS

A fossil can only form if an animal's body is buried quickly after death, so fossilized land animals are usually animals that died in a river and sank into mud, for example, or that died in a sandstorm and were buried in sand. These five diagrams show one way a dinosaur's bones—in this case a *Triceratops*—may be fossilized and found millions of years later.

The fossil has been exposed and a team of paleontologists is working to remove it.

Petrified Tree trunks, just like bones, can be turned to rock by mineralization over millions of years. Petrified trees still look like logs. Petrification means "change to stone."

External mold Sometimes the original organism dissolves completely, but leaves an impression of itself in the rock. This impression is called a mold.

Natural cast This forms just like an external mold, but the hole then fills in as minerals from water slowly crystallize inside it, forming a rock such as flint.

Trace fossil Occasionally an animal will leave a hint of its presence: a trace. This may be a footprint, a nest, tooth marks, or even droppings. These are called trace fossils.

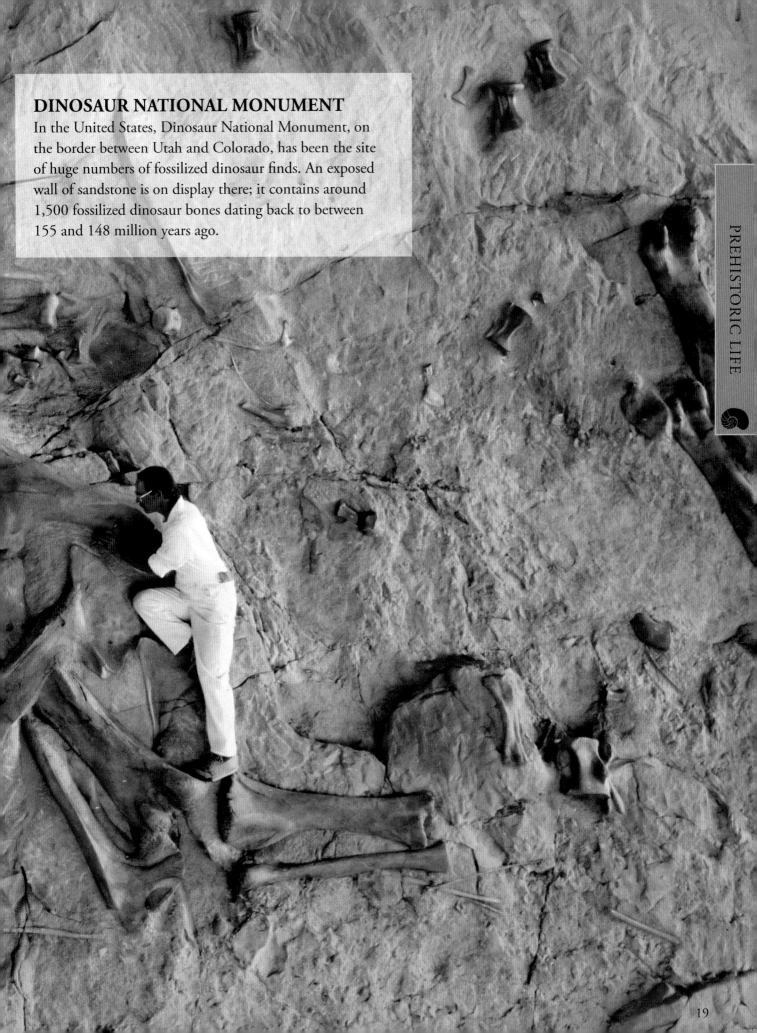

DINOSAUR NATIONAL MONUMENT

In the United States, Dinosaur National Monument, on the border between Utah and Colorado, has been the site of huge numbers of fossilized dinosaur finds. An exposed wall of sandstone is on display there; it contains around 1,500 fossilized dinosaur bones dating back to between 155 and 148 million years ago.

Fossil hunting

You may have seen a fossil hunt on television, or you may have visited a fossil site. Perhaps you have been lucky enough to find your own fossil. What happens on an organized fossil dig?

Scientists who study fossils are called paleontologists. Paleontologists use basic digging tools to remove fossils from the ground, such as hammers, chisels, and trowels. Brushes help sweep away dust.

IT WAS FOUND THERE!

Every dinosaur dig is different. Some fossils are found embedded in solid rock that needs to be chipped away bit by bit. Others fall out of soft, crumbly cliffs and can be very fragile, falling apart easily. The *Ouranosaurus* (a plant-eating dinosaur) above was found buried in the desert sand and was easy to dig out by hand.

UNCOVERING FOSSILS

Paleontologists classify the dinosaur fossils they uncover in one of four ways.

■ **Articulated skeleton.** This is a skeleton that is still joined together. It may be complete, but pieces are usually missing.

■ **Associated skeleton.** This means the bones have broken up and spread out, but they can be identified as belonging to the same dinosaur.

■ **Isolated bone**. This is a bone that has been separated from its skeleton, and fossilized alone. It may be a leg bone such as a femur (thigh bone), which is a large fossil.

■ **Float.** These are scraps of fossilized bone—the fossil has shattered, and the scraps are usually too small to be useful.

▲ A SLOW JOB *Once the paleontologists have carefully removed all dirt from around each of the fossilized bones, the position of each bone is carefully mapped on graph paper, with the help of a square grid called a quadrat.*

EXCAVATING A DINOSAUR

The excavation of two dinosaur fossils, *Afrovenator* (a theropod) and *Jobaria* (a sauropod) in Africa is shown here in a series of photographs. The bones were first discovered by local tribesmen, who found them jutting out of desert rock. It can take many months to excavate a complete dinosaur find, and this dig was no exception.

◀ MAKING A START
Painstaking work over a number of weeks to remove rock finally revealed each fossil. A large team of people worked on this dig.

◀ ON SHOW
As more soil is removed, the fossils become clear. The team was dealing with a theropod that could reach 30 ft (9 m) and a sauropod that could reach 60 ft (18 m) in length, so the bones were large.

◀ SITE MAP
One paleontologist made a final, detailed drawing of the bones in position. This showed clearly how some bones had separated from the animal over the millions of years it had lain encased in rock.

◀ WRAP IT UP!
Once the bones were ready to be removed, they were covered with bandages soaked in a plaster solution. When the plaster sets hard, this protects the fossil, ready for its removal to a museum laboratory for further study.

So many **bones**

One quarry has yielded far more dinosaur bones than any other. From 1909 to 1924, 385 tons (350 metric tons) of dinosaur fossils were removed from the Dinosaur National Monument on the Utah-Colorado border. That's a lot of bones!

A look at size

From dinosaurs the size of chickens to lumbering sauropods, the animals that have walked and swum on Earth have varied enormously in size and shape and length. Let's take a look at a few examples.

Predator X
- **Length** 49 ft (15 m)

Orca
- **Length** 30 ft (9 m)

Shonisaurus
- **Length** 66 ft (20 m)

Leedsichthys
- **Length** 30 ft (9 m)

Sperm whale
- **Length** 66 ft (20 m)

Brachiosaurus
- **Length** 75 ft (23 m)

Mammoth
- **Shoulder height** 16 ft (5 m)

Great white shark
- **Length** 20–26 ft (6–8 m)

Tyrannosaurus
- **Length** 39 ft (12 m)

Hatzegopteryx
- **Wingspan** 36 ft (11 m)

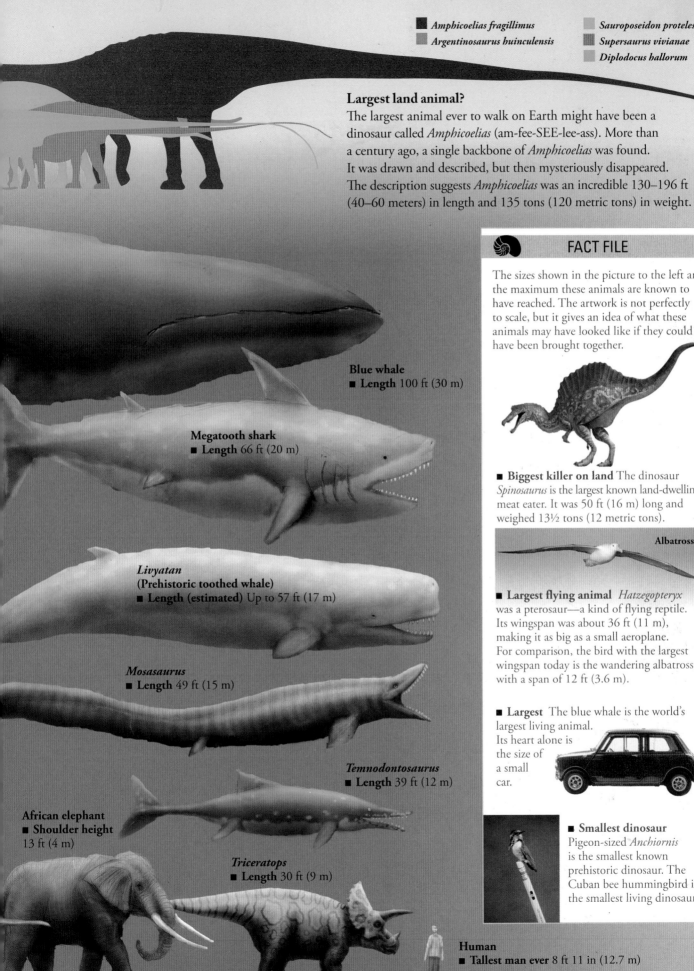

■ *Amphicoelias fragillimus*   ■ *Sauroposeidon proteles*
■ *Argentinosaurus huinculensis*   ▦ *Supersaurus vivianae*
                                       ■ *Diplodocus hallorum*

Largest land animal?

The largest animal ever to walk on Earth might have been a dinosaur called *Amphicoelias* (am-fee-SEE-lee-ass). More than a century ago, a single backbone of *Amphicoelias* was found. It was drawn and described, but then mysteriously disappeared. The description suggests *Amphicoelias* was an incredible 130–196 ft (40–60 meters) in length and 135 tons (120 metric tons) in weight.

Blue whale
■ **Length** 100 ft (30 m)

Megatooth shark
■ **Length** 66 ft (20 m)

Livyatan
(Prehistoric toothed whale)
■ **Length (estimated)** Up to 57 ft (17 m)

Mosasaurus
■ **Length** 49 ft (15 m)

Temnodontosaurus
■ **Length** 39 ft (12 m)

African elephant
■ **Shoulder height**
13 ft (4 m)

Triceratops
■ **Length** 30 ft (9 m)

Human
■ **Tallest man ever** 8 ft 11 in (12.7 m)

FACT FILE

The sizes shown in the picture to the left are the maximum these animals are known to have reached. The artwork is not perfectly to scale, but it gives an idea of what these animals may have looked like if they could have been brought together.

■ **Biggest killer on land** The dinosaur *Spinosaurus* is the largest known land-dwelling meat eater. It was 50 ft (16 m) long and weighed 13½ tons (12 metric tons).

Albatross

■ **Largest flying animal** *Hatzegopteryx* was a pterosaur—a kind of flying reptile. Its wingspan was about 36 ft (11 m), making it as big as a small aeroplane. For comparison, the bird with the largest wingspan today is the wandering albatross, with a span of 12 ft (3.6 m).

■ **Largest** The blue whale is the world's largest living animal. Its heart alone is the size of a small car.

■ **Smallest dinosaur** Pigeon-sized *Anchiornis* is the smallest known prehistoric dinosaur. The Cuban bee hummingbird is the smallest living dinosaur.

INVERTEBRATES

▲ TRILOBITES *Soft-bodied invertebrates don't usually fossilize, but those with hard shells, such as these trilobites, have left impressive fossil records. Some trilobite fossils date back more than 500 million years.*

Invertebrates are animals that have neither a backbone nor a bony internal skeleton. This is an incredibly varied group; it includes insects, spiders, mollusks, sponges, jellyfish, and worms.

What are invertebrates?

From insects to mollusks, and from worms to jellyfish, invertebrates dominate our planet in terms of their numbers: they make up around 97 percent of the animal kingdom. What features do these animals share in common? Very few! However, they are animals that possess neither a backbone, nor a bony internal skeleton.

Invertebrates are divided into about 30 groups. They include:

ARTHROPODA

The group Arthropoda includes insects, arachnids (creatures such as spiders and scorpions), and crustaceans. Arthropods make up the largest group of invertebrates, and account for about 90 percent of known animal species.

Imperial scorpion

◀ GARDEN CENTIPEDE *A centipede has at least 15 pairs of legs. Centipedes are carnivorous, hunting prey such as insects and spiders.*

▼ ROSE CHAFER BEETLE *There are more than 300,000 species of beetle, some very brightly colored.*

MOLLUSCA

From a small garden snail to a giant squid, the group that forms Molluska is incredibly varied. Most mollusks have a shell, or at least the remnants of one, but not all—octopuses have no shell, and neither do slugs.

Squid

▲ NUDIBRANCH *These marine mollusks are often called "sea slugs." The infant form (larva) has a shell.*

▶ GIANT AFRICAN SNAIL *These are large snails—they can reach 8 in (20 cm) in length.*

ANNELIDA

Annelid worms have bodies that are divided into segments. Earthworms and bristleworms are types of annelid worm. Members of this group can be found living in seawater, in fresh water, and on land. Amazingly, there are more than 12,000 recognized species of annelid worm.

Earthworm

▲ RAGWORM *These creatures have a pair of swimming legs (called parapods) on each segment of their bodies.*

▶ TIGER LEECH *Some leeches, like this one, will wait for a passing animal and feed off that animal, sucking its blood.*

TAKE A LOOK—METAMORPHOSIS

Most invertebrates leave the egg as a larva and undergo several developmental stages before reaching adult form. This is known as metamorphosis.

◀ CATERPILLAR *After hatching from an egg, a butterfly caterpillar proceeds to eat and eat and eat. Its job is to grow quickly.*

▶ TIME TO PUPATE *A tough, leathery coat forms around the caterpillar, and it becomes a pupa. After some time, a butterfly will break free.*

▼ ADULT FORM *Finally, the butterfly emerges. It has to spread out its wings to dry before it can fly. A butterfly is the adult form.*

CNIDARIA

Sea anemone

This group includes sea jellies (also known as jellyfish), corals, and sea anemones. They have stinging cells called nematocysts. Some can swim, while others remain fixed to the seabed, waiting for food to drift past.

▶ BRAIN CORAL *Many corals are named for their appearance, like this heavily wrinkled coral.*

▼ SEA NETTLES *Jellyfish, such as these sea nettles, have bodies that are largely made of water. Take a jellyfish out of water, and the shape will collapse.*

ECHINODERMATA

Many echinoderms have very spiny bodies and nearly all live on the seafloor—none can survive in fresh water. They include starfish (sea stars), sea urchins, and sea cucumbers. Most of these animals can move around, and they have up to 20 legs—but no brain.

Sunflower sea star

▶ SEA CUCUMBER *These echinoderms are found on seabeds all over the world.*

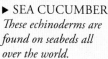

▼ CROWN-OF-THORNS SEA STAR *This is the largest starfish and a voracious predator, feeding on corals. It has needle-sharp spines, each capable of injecting a nasty venom.*

PORIFERA

Porifera are also called sponges. They were mistaken for plants until the 1700s but, in fact, are very simple animals, with no arms, legs, heads, or sense organs. Sponges have simple baglike or tubelike bodies and live stuck to the seafloor, filtering food from the water.

◀ AZURE VASE SPONGE *There are thousands of sea sponges, some very colorful.*

▼ ELEPHANT EAR SPONGE *Some sponge species can grow quite large. This one has reached 3 ft (1 m) in height and is still growing.*

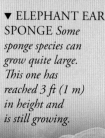

27

The first animals

Fossils tell us that animal life began about 600 million years ago. The first animals lived in darkness, rooted to the seabed, and had simple, soft bodies shaped like disks or leaves, with which they gathered nutritious chemicals or particles in the water. These strange beings seem to have had no legs, no heads, no mouths, no sense organs, and no internal organs.

FIRST LIFE

For nearly nine-tenths of the Earth's history, there were no animals or plants. During most of this early era, called the Precambrian period, the only life forms were microscopic single cells. Some grew in colonies on the sea floor, building up over time to form cushion-shaped mounds of rock – "stromatolites" – that still form today.

Living stromatolites in Australia

Charnia

CHAR-nee-a

- **When** 575–545 million years ago (Precambrian)
- **Fossil location** England, Australia, Canada, Russia
- **Habitat** Seafloor
- **Length** 6 in–6½ ft (0.15–2 m)

Discovered by a schoolboy in 1957, *Charnia* caused a sensation because it came from rocks thought far too old to contain animal fossils. It had a feather-shaped body and lived rooted to the seafloor by a stem, perhaps feeding on microbes filtered out of the water. Its main body was made of rows of branches that gave it a striped, quilted appearance. Some experts think its body might have housed algae that made it green and allowed it to gather energy from sunlight (photosynthesis).

Charnia

◀ **ANCHOR**
Some fossil of Charnia *have a stem with a disk at the base. These disks, buried in the sandy seabed, may have been anchors that held* Charnia *fixed in place while the feathery top waved about in the current.*

Spriggina

sprig-EEN-a

- **When** 550 million years ago (Late Precambrian)
- **Fossil location** Australia, Russia
- **Habitat** Seafloor
- **Length** 1¼ in (3 cm)

Spriggina may have been one of the very first animals with a front and back end. It may even have had a head with eyes and mouth, suggesting it was one of the first predators to exist. Some scientists think it may have been an early trilobite. Others liken it to worms.

▲ SEGMENTS
Fossils show that Spriggina's *body was made of segments. Most fossils are curved in different ways, suggesting it had a flexible body.*

Dickinsonia

dickin-SO-nee-a

- **When** 560–555 million years ago (Precambrian)
- **Fossil location** Australia, Russia
- **Habitat** Seafloor
- **Length** ⅜–39 in (1–100 cm)

One of most baffling Ediacaran fossils is *Dickinsonia*—a flat, round organism that appears to have had distinct front and back ends but no head, mouth, or gut. Studies suggest *Dickinsonia* lived fixed to the seafloor, perhaps absorbing food through its base.

Cyclomedusa

cy-clo-med-OO-sa

- **When** 670 million years ago (Precambrian)
- **Fossil location** Australia, Russia, China, Mexico, Canada, British Isles, Norway
- **Habitat** Seafloor
- **Length** 1–12 in (2.5–30 cm) across

Mysterious *Cyclomedusa* was originally mistaken for a jellyfish because of its circular shape, but neighboring fossils are often misshapen, as though growing around each other on the seafloor. Some scientists think *Cyclomedusa* was just a colony of microbes or the anchor for the stalk of a bigger creature.

 DID YOU KNOW...?

In 1946, a scientist named Reg Sprigg was eating a packed lunch in the Ediacara Hills of Australia when he spotted what looked like jellyfish fossils in the rocks. He'd discovered something amazing: the oldest animal fossils in the world. One was named *Spriggina*, after him, and all the fossils from the period are now called Ediacaran fossils.

▲ DICKINSONIA *fossils are usually oval, with what look like segments extending from a central groove. Hundreds of fossils have been found, with a huge variety of sizes.*

Parvancorina

PAR-van-coe-REE-na

- **When** 558–555 million years ago (Precambrian)
- **Fossil location** Australia, Russia
- **Habitat** Seafloor
- **Length** ⅜–1 in (1–2.5 cm)

Parvancorina had a shield-shaped front end that may have been a head and that faced into the current when it was alive. It also had a central ridge flanked by what look like segments. Many fossils have a well-preserved shape, suggesting that its body had a hardened outer casing.

Cambrian explosion

About 530 million years ago, a huge range of new animals appeared in the seas, including the first creatures with clear legs, heads, sense organs, skeletons, and shells. All the main categories of invertebrates (animals without backbones) known today seem to have evolved almost at once, as well as some weird creatures quite unlike anything else. Scientists call this mysterious burst of life the Cambrian explosion.

(see box)

Wiwaxia
we-WAX-ee-a

- **When** 505 million years ago (Middle Cambrian)
- **Fossil location** Canada
- **Habitat** Seafloor
- **Length** 1–2 in (3–5 cm)

Wiwaxia looked like a tiny, armored porcupine, since its body was covered with protective spines and rows of overlapping armor plates. Its flat lower surface, where the mouth was located, did not have any protection. The mouth had two or three rows of sharp, conical teeth that may have been used to scrape algae from the seabed. *Wiwaxia* had no distinct head or tail and was probably blind, relying on touch and smell to find the way.

▲ THIS WIWAXIA *fossil from the Burgess Shale fossil bed in Canada is about 500 million years old. The armorlike plates on its back are called sclerites.*

Anomalocaris
a-NOM-a-low-CAR-iss

- **When** 505 million years ago (Middle Cambrian)
- **Fossil location** Canada, S. China
- **Habitat** Oceans
- **Length** Up to 3 ft (1 m)

A little like a giant shrimp, *Anomalocaris* (below) was the largest animal found in the Burgess Shale fossil bed of Canada (see box). Experts suspect it was the top predator in Cambrian seas and used a pair of spiked claws attached to its head to grasp prey such as trilobites. It had no legs could swim by flexing its segmented body and waving the flaps on its sides. Large compound eyes indicate it had good vision and hunted by sight.

▲ FOSSILS *of* Anomalocaris *often show only a small part of the body. This is one of its feeding claws.*

Echmatocrinus

ECK-mat-oh-crine-us

- **When** 505 million years ago (Middle Cambrian)
- **Fossil location** Canada
- **Habitat** Oceans
- **Length** 1 in (3 cm) wide, below the tentacles

Echmatocrinus lived attached to the seafloor, its cone-shaped body topped by a ring of 7–9 tentacles, each bearing small side-branches. The surface of the main cone was covered with a jigsaw of hard, protective plates. When it was first discovered, scientists thought *Echmatocrinus* might be related to starfish, but it lacks the five-sided symmetry of the starfish family. Some experts think it might instead be a kind of coral.

Ottoia

ot-OY-ah

- **When** 505 million years ago (Middle Cambrian) to now
- **Fossil location** Canada
- **Habitat** Oceans
- **Length** 1½–3¼ in (4–8 cm)

Ottoia was a kind of worm that lived in U-shaped burrows, which is why its fossils are usually curved. Its mouth was covered with tiny hooks and could be turned inside out like a sock to capture small animals from the muddy seafloor. Fossilized food remains inside *Ottoia*'s gut reveal that it was a cannibal, preying on its own kind as well as devouring small shelled animals. *Ottoia* is one of the most common early Cambrian fossils, with around 1,500 known specimens.

***Ottoia* fossil**

Hallucigenia

ha-lucy-JEAN-ee-a

- **When** 505 million years ago (Middle Cambrian)
- **Fossil location** Canada, China
- **Habitat** Oceans
- **Length** Up to 1 in (2.5 cm)

Hallucigenia is one of the strangest animals from the Cambrian Period. At one end is a large blob that may be a head, but with no mouth or eyes. It may simply be a stain on the fossil and not a part of the animal. Running along the wormlike body were rows of sharp spines and rows of fleshy tentacles. Orginally the spines were thought to be legs, but scientists now think the fleshy tentacles were the legs, despite not being arranged in pairs.

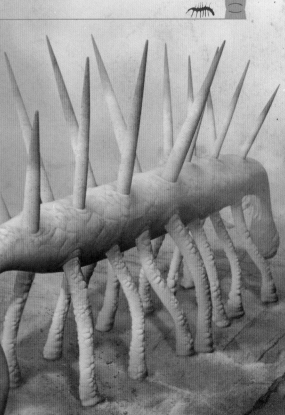

 DID YOU KNOW...?

All the fossils on these two pages come from the Burgess Shale Formation in the Rocky Mountains in Canada. Littering the ground at this famous mountaintop site are hundreds of beautifully preserved animal fossils dating back almost to the very dawn of animal life. The Burgess Shale contains imprints of soft body parts that normally don't fossilize and reveals that invertebrate life was already amazingly varied half a billion years ago.

Opabinia

One of the weirdest prehistoric animals ever
discovered, *Opabinia* had five eyes on stalks and
a long, flexible trunk (proboscis) tipped with a
grasping claw. This mouse-sized sea creature
probably used its trunk in the same way an
elephant does, picking up items of food with
the tip and then passing them to its mouth.

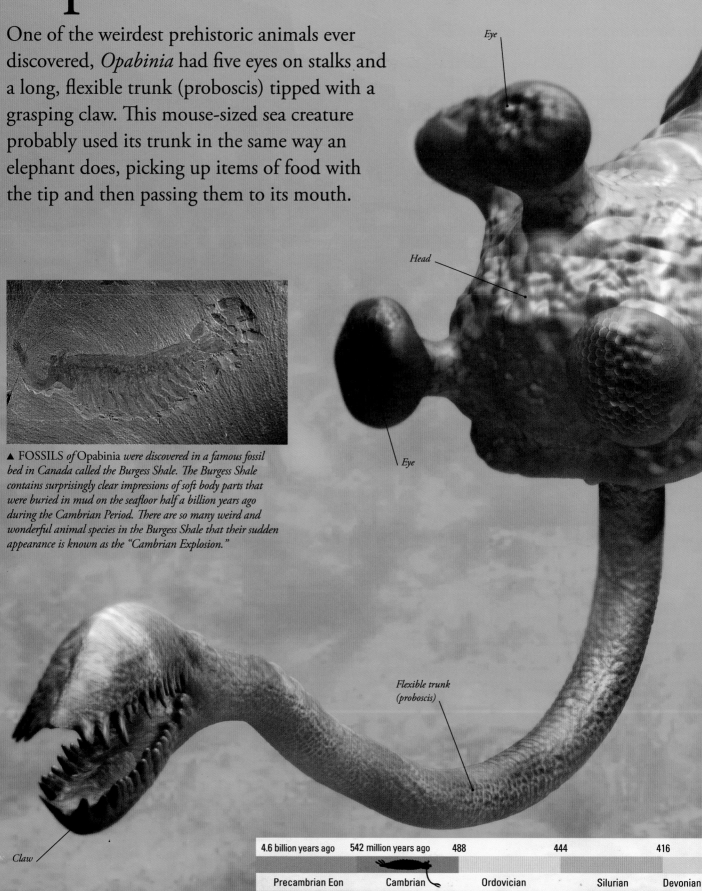

▲ FOSSILS *of* Opabinia *were discovered in a famous fossil
bed in Canada called the Burgess Shale. The Burgess Shale
contains surprisingly clear impressions of soft body parts that
were buried in mud on the seafloor half a billion years ago
during the Cambrian Period. There are so many weird and
wonderful animal species in the Burgess Shale that their sudden
appearance is known as the "Cambrian Explosion."*

Eye

Head

Eye

Flexible trunk
(proboscis)

Claw

4.6 billion years ago	542 million years ago	488		444		416
Precambrian Eon	Cambrian		Ordovician		Silurian	Devonian

Segments

OVERLAPPING FLAPS *ran along each side of Opabinia's body. Perhaps the animal swam by moving the flaps up and down in a wave pattern to push itself through the water.*

Mouth (underneath)

Tail

Opabinia

OH-pa-BIN-ee-a

- **When** 515–500 million years ago (Middle Cambrian)
- **Fossil location** Canada
- **Habitat** Near the seabed
- **Length** 2½ in (6.5 cm)

Opabinia's body consisted of 16 segments, each of which had side flaps and gills on the underside for breathing in water. Scientists think the animal lived near the seabed and used its trunk to fish around in the mud for food. It had no jaws or teeth, so it probably only ate soft items of food. Although very different from all other living or prehistoric animals, *Opabinia* is thought to be related to the arthropods (invertebrates with jointed limbs and external skeletons, such as insects, spiders, and crabs).

59		299		251		200		145		65		23		Now
Carboniferous		Permian		Triassic		Jurassic		Cretaceous		Paleogene		Neogene		

Marrella

Some 500 million years ago, the tiny, shrimplike creature *Marrella* darted around the seafloor, beating its 50 feathery legs as it swam in search of dead animals to eat. *Marrella* appeared in the "Cambrian Explosion," when a vast range of animal life evolved in a short space of time.

Shield

Antennae (feelers)

INVERTEBRATES

Marrella

ma-RELL-a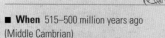

- **When** 515–500 million years ago (Middle Cambrian)
- **Fossil location** Canada
- **Habitat** Seabed
- **Length** ¾ in (2 cm)

Marrella's head was protected by a large and possibly colorful shield with four long, backward-pointing spikes. Under the shield was *Marrella*'s flexible body, which consisted of 25 segments, each with a pair of feathery legs that doubled as gills for breathing underwater. Attached to the head were two pairs of long, flexible antennae (feelers). *Marrella* was one of the first arthropods—the group that today includes insects, spiders, and other animals with external skeletons.

SEABED SEARCHER ▶
Marrella probably swam along the seabed or just above it, using its long antennae to sweep the mud in search of food.

4.6 billion years ago	542 million years ago	488	444	416	359	299	25
Precambrian Eon	Cambrian		Ordovician	Silurian	Devonian	Carboniferous	Permian

34

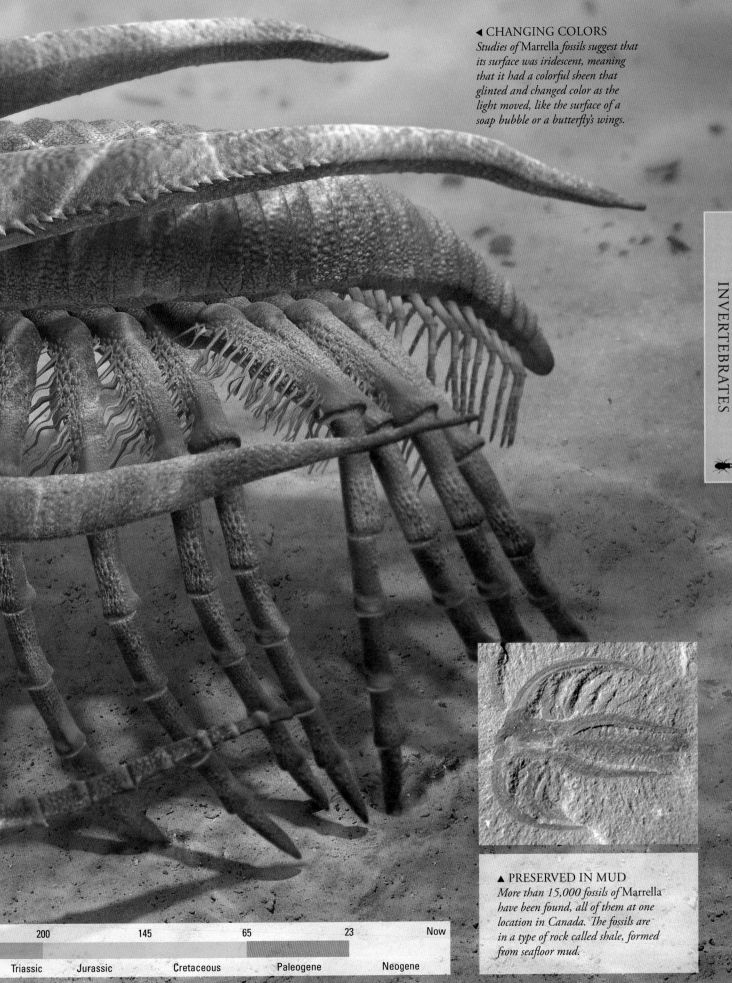

◄ CHANGING COLORS
Studies of Marrella fossils suggest that its surface was iridescent, meaning that it had a colorful sheen that glinted and changed color as the light moved, like the surface of a soap bubble or a butterfly's wings.

▲ PRESERVED IN MUD
More than 15,000 fossils of Marrella have been found, all of them at one location in Canada. The fossils are in a type of rock called shale, formed from seafloor mud.

200	145	65	23	Now
Triassic	Jurassic	Cretaceous	Paleogene	Neogene

Trilobites

For more than 250 million years, the ancient seas teemed with trilobites—prehistoric animals related to today's insects, woodlice, and crabs. There were more than 17,000 different types of trilobite, ranging from the flea-sized to monsters twice the size of this book. Most crawled along the ocean floor in search of food, but a few were swimmers or floaters that drifted through the water.

Ditomopyge
DIT-o-mo-PY-gee

- **When** 300–251 million years ago (Late Carboniferous to Late Permian)
- **Fossil location** N. America, Europe, Asia, W. Australia
- **Habitat** Seafloor
- **Length** 1–1¼ in (2.5–3 cm)

Ditomopyge lived toward the end of the trilobites' reign, just before the age of the dinosaurs. It had a hard outer skeleton (exoskeleton) made up of overlapping plates covering its body segments. Underneath, each segment had a pair of wriggling legs. The head was protected by a large shield with backward-pointing spines and would have sported a pair of flexible antennae (feelers) for finding the way and tasting food.

FAMILY FACT FILE

Key features
- Head shield
- Segmented, three-lobed body
- Many had compound eyes
- External skeleton (exoskeleton)

When
Trilobites appeared in the Cambrian Period, 526 million years ago, and disappeared at the end of the Permian Period, 250 million years ago, when the last species was wiped out.

Eodalmanitina

EE-o-dal-man-ee-tee-na

- **When** 465 million years ago (Middle Ordovician)
- **Fossil location** France, Portugal, Spain
- **Habitat** Seafloor
- **Length** Up to 1½ in (4 cm)

Like many trilobites, *Eodalmanitina* had large eyes and good vision. Trilobites were among the first animals to evolve sophisticated eyes. These consisted of many tiny, crystalline lenses packed together in a honeycomb pattern, like the compound eyes of insects. *Eodalmanitina* had distinctive bean-shaped eyes. Its long body tapered toward the tail, which was tipped by a short spine.

Eye

Ceratarges

SER-a-tar-gees

- **When** 380–359 million years ago (Middle to Late Devonian)
- **Fossil location** Morocco
- **Habitat** Seafloor
- **Length** 2½ in (6.6 cm)

Ceratarges was one of many trilobites with spectacular spines and horns. These prickly weapons may have been used to ward off predators. Another theory, however, is that they evolved as a result of battles between rival trilobites fighting over mates, like the antlers of modern stag beetles.

Spine

Encrinurus

EN-crine-yoo-rus

- **When** 444 million years ago (Silurian)
- **Fossil location** Worldwide
- **Habitat** Seafloor
- **Length** Up to 2 in (5 cm)

This small trilobite had many berry-shaped bumps on the shield protecting its head. *Encrinurus*'s eyes were probably situated at the end of short stalks. It may have spent a lot of time hiding in the mud on the seabed, with only its eyes above the surface.

Phacops

FAY-cops

- **When** 380–359 million years ago (Middle to Late Devonian)
- **Fossil location** Worldwide
- **Habitat** Seafloor
- **Length** Up to 2¼ in (6 cm)

Named for its keen sense of sight, *Phacops* ("lens eye"), like *Eodalmanitina*, had bulging eyes that gave it good vision, suggesting it lived in well-lit areas such as shallow seas. One of the most common and widespread trilobites, *Phacops* has been found in Europe, Afric, Australia, and North America. Geologists even use its fossils as a handy way to estimate the age of a rock.

Lenses in eye

▶ ROLLING UP
Phacops could curl up in a tight ball to protect its softer undersides when attacked, much like some modern woodlice.

Selenopeltis

INVERTEBRATES

The common trilobite *Selenopeltis* lived in cool waters along the coast of Gondwana, a mighty prehistoric continent that later broke apart to form South America, Africa, and Australia. It had long, sweeping spines that give its fossils a graceful appearance, making them a favorite among fossil collectors.

Selenopeltis
se-LEE-no-pel-tiss

- **When** 471–445 million years ago (Early to Late Ordovician)
- **Fossil location** British Isles, France, Iberia, Morocco, Czech Republic, Turkey
- **Habitat** Ocean waters
- **Length** Up to 4½ in (12 cm)

Selenopeltis had a wide skeleton and a distinctive squarish head. Spines extended backward from its cheeks and the sides of each body segment. Unlike most other trilobites, it had small eyes.

4.6 billion years ago	542 million years ago	488		444		416
Precambrian Eon	Cambrian		Ordovician		Silurian	Devonian

◄ SPINY TRILOBITES
This amazing slab of rock
contains more than just
Selenopeltis *fossils. There are
two other types of trilobite (a
large one without spines and
a small one with a tail spine)
and lots of starfish—see if
you can find them all.*

359	299	251	200	145	65	23	Now
Carboniferous	Permian	Triassic	Jurassic	Cretaceous	Paleogene	Neogene	

Echinoderms

The starfish and sea urchins we see at the beach belong to an ancient group of sea-dwelling animals known as echinoderms ("ee-KYE-no derms"). Echinoderms have round or star-shaped bodies and feet like tiny suckers, but no heads or brains. Fossils reveal that echinoderms of the distant past were much like those we see today.

Encrinus fossil

Encrinus trapped food with its sticky arms. The arms could close tightly for protection from predators.

FAMILY FACT FILE

Key features
- Body divided into five equal parts arranged in a circle around a central disk
- Rows of small, suckerlike feet on base
- No front or back and no head or brain

When
Echinoderms first appeared at the start of the Cambrian Period, about 530 million years ago. Over 7,000 species are found in oceans across the world today.

Encrinus
EN-crine-us

- **When** 235–215 million years ago (Middle Triassic)
- **Fossil location** Europe
- **Habitat** Shallow seas
- **Size** Cup 1½–2¼ in (4–6 cm) long

Attached to the seafloor by a stalk, *Encrinus* used a ring of 10 feathery arms to catch tiny organisms floating past. The organisms, trapped in a sticky fluid, were then swept by tiny hairs toward a central mouth. *Encrinus* belonged to a class of echinoderms known as crinoids or sea lilies that still exists today.

Clypeus
CLY-pee-us

- **When** 176–135 million years ago (Middle to Late Jurassic)
- **Fossil location** Europe, Africa
- **Habitat** Burrows on the seafloor
- **Size** 2–4½ in (5–12 cm) across

Clypeus was a type of sea urchin. Like a modern sea urchin, it had a hard, rounded shell made up of five parts arranged in a star pattern. The shell was covered by spines, but unlike the stiff, pointed spines of many sea urchins, these were soft and hairlike. *Clypeus* found food by burrowing and eating its way through the mud on the seafloor.

Spine bases

Pentasteria
PEN-ta-STEER-ee-a

- **When** 203–100 million years ago (Early Jurassic to Early Cretaceous)
- **Fossil location** Europe
- **Habitat** Sand beds
- **Size** Up to 4½ in (12 cm) across

Pentasteria was a starfish that lived during the age of the dinosaurs. It was much like a modern starfish, with five arms, a mouth in the middle of its underside, and two rows of tubelike feet along each arm. Unlike modern starfish, however, it couldn't use its feet as suckers to prize open shells.

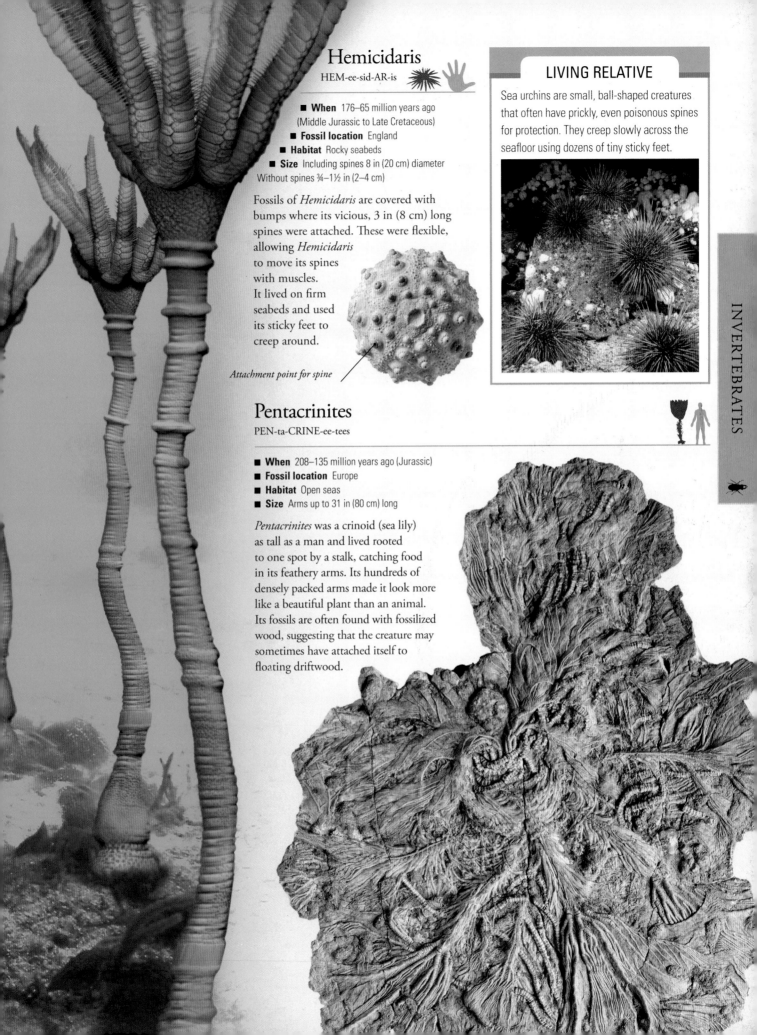

Hemicidaris

HEM-ee-sid-AR-is

- **When** 176–65 million years ago (Middle Jurassic to Late Cretaceous)
- **Fossil location** England
- **Habitat** Rocky seabeds
- **Size** Including spines 8 in (20 cm) diameter Without spines ¾–1½ in (2–4 cm)

Fossils of *Hemicidaris* are covered with bumps where its vicious, 3 in (8 cm) long spines were attached. These were flexible, allowing *Hemicidaris* to move its spines with muscles. It lived on firm seabeds and used its sticky feet to creep around.

Attachment point for spine

LIVING RELATIVE

Sea urchins are small, ball-shaped creatures that often have prickly, even poisonous spines for protection. They creep slowly across the seafloor using dozens of tiny sticky feet.

Pentacrinites

PEN-ta-CRINE-ee-tees

- **When** 208–135 million years ago (Jurassic)
- **Fossil location** Europe
- **Habitat** Open seas
- **Size** Arms up to 31 in (80 cm) long

Pentacrinites was a crinoid (sea lily) as tall as a man and lived rooted to one spot by a stalk, catching food in its feathery arms. Its hundreds of densely packed arms made it look more like a beautiful plant than an animal. Its fossils are often found with fossilized wood, suggesting that the creature may sometimes have attached itself to floating driftwood.

Brittle stars

Look at any part of the seabed and you are likely to find star-shaped creatures with long, slender arms wriggling across the bottom. These are not fish, but invertebrates called brittle stars, and they are relatives of starfish and sea urchins. They are also known as snake stars because of the way they move their arms. *Palaeocoma* was an early kind of brittle star. Wary of predators, *Palaeocoma,* like modern brittle stars, may have hidden in cracks in rocks and corals, coming out only at night to feed.

Palaeocoma

pale-ee-oh-COAM-ah

- **When** Nearly 200 million years ago (Early Jurassic)
- **Fossil location** Europe
- **Habitat** Seafloor
- **Size** 2–4 in (5–10 cm) across
- **Diet** Remains of plants and animals

Palaeocoma had a flat, central disklike body. Extending from it were five long, spiny arms, with which it moved swiftly along the seabed. When disturbed, it could escape quickly, pulling and pushing its body using the muscles in its arms. On the underside of its body was a star-shaped mouth containing five toothed jaws. When feeding, it used the tiny, muscular tube feet underneath its arms to sweep food into its mouth. It had no eyes, but may have been able to sense light through its feet.

4.6 billion years ago	542 million years ago	488		444		416		359	2
Precambrian Eon		Cambrian		Ordovician		Silurian		Devonian	Carboniferous

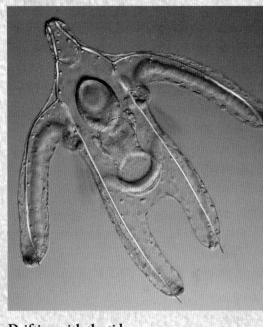

Drifting with the tide

Like many sea creatures, brittle stars live on the seafloor as adults but spend the early part of their lives as plankton—tiny organisms that float freely in the sunlit upper waters of the ocean. They drift with the currents for weeks, traveling hundreds of miles before finally sinking to the seafloor, where they change into adult brittle stars.

LIVING RELATIVE

Around 2,000 species of brittle star exist today, in icy seas and warm waters all over the world. These, often brilliantly colored, creatures—some with patterned bodies—have five snakelike arms. When attacked, they shed an arm, which wriggles for a while, confusing the predator. Brittle stars quickly regrow the lost arm.

251	200	145	65	23	Now
Permian	Triassic	Jurassic	Cretaceous	Paleogene	Neogene

Spiders and scorpions

Spiders and scorpions belong to an ancient family of predatory animals called chelicerates ("kell-ISS-er-ates"), all of which have special mouthparts that they use either as pincers or fangs. Modern chelicerates are small, but their earliest ancestors grew to gigantic sizes and were among the top predators of their time. The biggest of these prehistoric monsters were the sea scorpions.

Pterygotus
terry-GOAT-us

- **When** 400–380 million years ago (Late Silurian to Middle Devonian)
- **Fossil location** Europe, N. America
- **Habitat** Shallow seas
- **Length** Up to 7 ft 4 in (2.3 m)

Pterygotus was a sea scorpion that grew larger than a fully grown man. Using its colossal eyes, it scanned the water for prey such as fish and trilobites. Perhaps it hid half-buried in sand until victims wandered close by, before lashing its tail to produce a violent burst of speed and snatching up the animal in its claws. Fossils have been found worldwide, and some experts think *Pterygotus* not only terrorized the seas but swam up rivers and into lakes as well.

 **FAMILY FACT FILE**

Key features
- Segmented bodies and jointed limbs
- Hard external skeleton (exoskeleton)
- Pincerlike feeding claws or fangs
- Four pairs of walking legs

When
The chelicerates appeared late in the Ordovician Period, about 445 millon years ago. Over 77,000 identified species exist today.

DID YOU KNOW...?

Animals with jointed legs and external skeletons (such as insects, spiders, and scorpions) are called arthropods. Sea scorpions were the largest arthropods that ever lived—giant versions of the ones we find today in the yard. Today, arthropods are small but in the distant past they grew to greater sizes, perhaps because the Earth's air contained more oxygen, making it easier for arthropods to breathe and grow.

Eurypterus

you-RIP-terruss

- **When** 420 million years ago (Late Silurian)
- **Fossil location** United States
- **Habitat** Shallow seas
- **Length** Up to 4 in (10 cm)

This small sea scorpion was less well armed than the fearsome *Pterygotus*. It used prickly legs to pull tiny animals toward its fangs, which it then used to tear the victim to shreds. *Eurypterus* hunted on the muddy floors of shallow seas.

Mesolimulus

mee-zo-LIM-you-luss

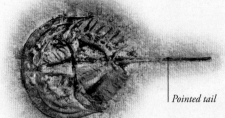

Pointed tail

- **When** 162–145 million years ago (Late Jurassic)
- **Fossil location** Germany
- **Habitat** Shallow ocean waters
- **Length** Up to 3¼–3½ in (8–9 cm), without tail

Mesolimulus is also called a horseshoe crab (though it's more closely related to spiders and scorpions than crabs). It had a huge shell, small, widely spaced eyes, and a stiff tail with a sharp tip, like a spear. It lived on the seafloor, where it hunted worms and shellfish.

LIVING RELATIVE

Modern horseshoe crabs such as *Limulus* are almost exactly like their prehistoric cousins from the Jurassic Period. *Limulus* lives in shallow water off the eastern coast of North America. It swims upside down, as its ancient relative probably did.

Limulus

Spider

SPY-der

- **When** 400 million years ago (Late Silurian) to now
- **Fossil location** Worldwide
- **Habitat** All land
- **Size** Up to 12 in (30 cm) across

Although the soft and delicate bodies of spiders do not fossilize well, thousands of species have been found, many of them preserved in pebbles of amber—a clear, golden material formed from fossilized pine-tree resin. Spiders are specialized hunters that often use silk traps to capture prey before killing victims with a lethal injection of venom from their fangs. The oldest fossilized spider's web is 100 million years old.

Spider in amber

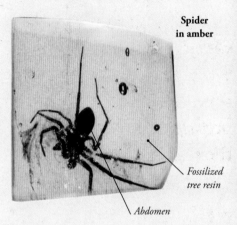

Fossilized tree resin

Abdomen

Proscorpius

pro-SCOR-pee-us

- **When** 400–300 million years ago (Silurian – Carboniferous)
- **Fossil location** Worldwide
- **Habitat** Uncertain
- **Length** 1½ in (4 cm)

The first scorpions lived in the sea rather than on land and breathed through gills. One of the oldest fossils is *Proscorpius* from the Late Silurian Period. This creature's mouth was under its head like that of a horseshoe crab, rather than at the front like a modern scorpion's. It isn't clear whether it lived on land or in water.

Giant millipede

Millipedes were among the first animals to walk on Earth. They took their first steps at least 428 million years ago, venturing onto land to eat the few simple, mosslike land plants that existed back then. By 350 million years ago, the plants had evolved into trees and the millipedes had become giants, too. Biggest of all was *Arthropleura*. As big as a crocodile, it was the largest invertebrate ever to live on land.

▲ THIS FOSSIL, *measuring 3 in (7.1 cm) long, shows just a part of one of* Arthropleura's *legs.*

4.6 billion years ago	542 million years ago	488	444	416	359
Precambrian Eon	Cambrian	Ordovician	Silurian	Devonian	Carboniferous

Arthropleura

arth-row-PLOO-ra

- **When** 350 million years ago (Early Carboniferous)
- **Fossil location** Scotland
- **Habitat** Forests
- **Length** Up to 8½ ft (2 m)
- **Diet** Unknown

Arthropleura lived on the dark, damp floor of tropical jungles during the Carboniferous Period. Fossils of its mouth have not been found, making its diet a mystery, but traces of ferns in its gut suggest it was a plant-eater. Although able to breathe out of water, it probably stayed in damp places and may have had to return to water to shed its skin as it grew. Some scientists think it could also swim under water.

▲ CREEPY CREATURE Arthropleura's *body consisted of 30 segments, each with a pair of legs. Fossilized footprints show it swerving around obstacles and suggest it could move quickly, lengthening its stride to speed up.*

LIVING RELATIVE

Millipede means "a thousand feet," but most millipedes have only 100–300 legs. Despite all the legs, they are slow walkers, their tiny feet swinging forward in waves. They feed on rotting plant matter, burrowing into soil to find it. Centipedes, in contrast, are fast-moving hunters that kill with venomous claws.

251	200	145	65	23	Now
Permian	Triassic	Jurassic	Cretaceous	Paleogene	Neogene

Insects

Long before dinosaurs evolved, Earth was already buzzing with insects. The first insects were tiny, wingless creatures that lived on the ground about 400 million years ago. Later they evolved wings and became the world's first flying animals. Mastering flight made them incredibly successful and they evolved into thousands of new species. Today, they make up three-quarters of all animal species on Earth.

Ants

- **When** 110–130 million years ago (Cretaceous Period) to now
- **Number of species today** More than 12,000 known
- **Diet** Everything from seeds and leaves to fungi and flesh

Ants evolved from wasps that began living in the ground in colonies. They were rare in the age of the dinosaurs but became very common later. Their huge colonies have a single breeding queen and hundreds of workers and soldiers, all of which are wingless females—daughters of the queen.

Bees

- **When** 100 million years ago (Early Cretaceous) to now
- **Number of species today** Nearly 20,000
- **Diet** Nectar, pollen

After flowering plants appeared 125 million years ago, some prehistoric wasps began to feed on flowers instead of preying on other insects, and these became bees. There are now thousands of different types of bee. Some are solitary, but many live in colonies with a single queen. Worker bees rear the young and collect nectar from flowers to store as honey.

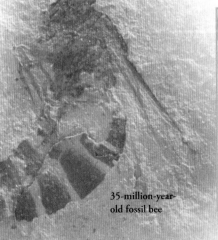

35-million-year-old fossil bee

DID YOU KNOW...?

When a bee feeds on a flower, a yellow dust called pollen sticks to its body. When it lands on another flower, the pollen rubs off and causes that flower to produce seeds. This process is known as pollination.

FAMILY FACT FILE

Key features
- Three main body parts: head, thorax (chest), and abdomen (belly and tail)
- A hard, protective external skeleton (exoskeleton)
- Three pairs of legs with joints
- Two antennae (feelers)
- Usually two pairs of wings

When
The first insects appeared in the Devonian Period, 396 million years ago.

Flies

- **When** 230 million years ago (Triassic) to now
- **Number of species today** About 240,000
- **Diet** Fly larvae (maggots) mostly eat rotting matter and flesh. Adults eat various liquid foods from nectar to blood.

Many insects can fly, but true flies are a particular family of insect that have two wings rather than four. Instead of a second pair of wings, they have two tiny knobs that flick back and forth to stabilize flight. Flies appeared at the same time as dinosaurs. Some of the early fly species almost certainly pestered the dinosaurs, sucking their blood and feeding on their eyes.

March fly

Beetles

- **When** 260 million years ago (Late Permian) to now
- **Number of species today** Up to 1 million
- **Diet** Anything from pollen and nectar to fruit, flesh, other insects, rotting bodies, wood, and animal dung

Beetles evolved from flying insects that once had two pairs of wings. The front pair turned into hard, protective cases that folded down over the rear wings to form a shield. The first flowering plants were probably pollinated by beetles. As flowering plants spread and evolved into new forms, so did the beetles. Today, there are so many species of beetle that they may well outnumber all other existing animal species combined.

▲ THE BEST *insect fossils are found in amber – a hard, golden material formed of ancient tree resin. Tree resin is a thick, sticky liquid that oozes out of wounded trees, often trapping insects such as these ants.*

Hydrophilus
(water beetle)

Cockroaches

- **When** 300–350 million years ago (Carboniferous Period) to now
- **Number of species today** Over 4,500
- **Diet** Rotten plant material

The first cockroaches looked much like those alive today. They scurried around on prehistoric forest floors, searching with their antennae (feelers) for dead plants. Termites evolved from wood-eating cockroaches that began living in colonies.

Archimylacris, a prehistoric cockroach

Butterfly

The delicate wings of butterflies do not fossilize easily, making butterfly fossils rare. Even so, a few amazingly well-preserved specimens have been found in very fine-grained rock or amber (fossilized tree resin). The oldest known butterflies date back to about 65 million years ago. By 30 million years ago, butterflies were common and very much like those we see flying today.

DID YOU KNOW...?

Amazingly, a butterfly cannot taste food with its mouth or antennae (feelers). Its taste buds are on its feet, so it needs to stand on food to taste whether it's delicious or not.

Lethe corbieri

LEE-thee cor-bee-AIR-ee

- **When** 30 million years ago (Paleogene)
- **Fossil location** France
- **Habitat** Woodland

This species was a member of a family of butterfly known as the browns, which still exists today. Its wings had bold circular marks and were probably brown underneath and orangey-brown on top. The caterpillars would have fed on grass or palm leaves, while the adults sucked nectar from flowers using a coiled feeding tube (proboscis). Like other browns, but unlike other insects, *Lethe* walked on four legs rather than six.

INVERTEBRATES

4.6 billion years ago	542 million years ago	488	444	416	359
Precambrian Eon	Cambrian	Ordovician	Silurian	Devonian	Carboniferous

LIVING RELATIVE

This peacock butterfly has eyespots like those of *Lethe*. Eyespots defend butterflies from predators such as birds, which peck at eyes in order to strike the head. Eyespots cause birds to peck the wings and miss the head, allowing the insect to escape with only a torn wing.

251	200	145	65	23	Now
Permian	Triassic	Jurassic	Cretaceous	Paleogene	Neogene

FOSSILIZED IN AMBER

Millions of years ago, these insects were trapped in a honey-colored goo: pine tree resin. Over time, the resin hardened into amber, preserving the insects so well that even the fine veins in their wings are visible. They look as if they lived yesterday, but these fossilized insects are thought to be around 38 million years old.

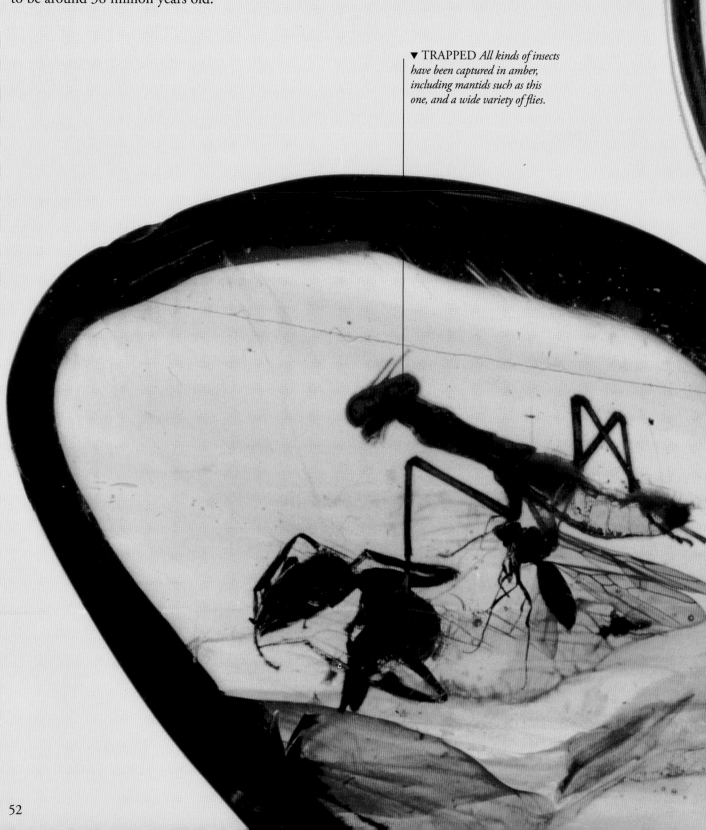

▼ TRAPPED *All kinds of insects have been captured in amber, including mantids such as this one, and a wide variety of flies.*

▲ A WINDOW THROUGH TIME *The insects found in amber prove that the insects we see today date back millions of years. Some amber fossils are more than 100 million years old!*

◄ GOLDEN GLOW *Amber is a hardened, fossilized material that forms from pine tree resin. Pine trees produce resin from wounds in the trunk. The resin flows, but as it dries it hardens to seal a cut in the tree's trunk.*

Meganeura

Possibly the largest insect that has ever lived, *Meganeura* looked like a gigantic dragonfly. Its wingspan was 2½ ft (75 cm)—12 times greater than that of common dragonflies today. This monster insect used its giant wings to hunt other insects in midair. Insects and other invertebrates grew to a great size in the lush forests of the Carboniferous Period, perhaps because Earth's air was richer in oxygen than today, making breathing easier.

4.6 billion years ago	542 million years ago	488		444		416		359		299		25
Precambrian Eon		Cambrian		Ordovician		Silurian		Devonian		Carboniferous		Permian

Meganeura
MEGA-new-ra

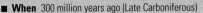

- **When** 300 million years ago (Late Carboniferous)
- **Fossil location** Europe
- **Habitat** Tropical swamp forests
- **Wingspan** Up to 30 in (75 cm)

Meganeura was not a true dragonfly but a member of a closely related family called griffinflies. It had stronger legs than modern dragonflies and a simpler pattern of veins in its wings. It flew quickly through tropical forests, using its huge compound eyes to spot prey. It could snatch flying insects in midair, grabbing them with its legs and bringing them up to its mouth to devour as it flew.

▲ VEINS IN WINGS
Meganeura means "large-veined." This fossil, found in France, shows the thick veins that acted as struts to stiffen the large, delicate wings.

▲ WINGED WONDER
Like modern dragonflies, Meganeura *flapped its front and rear wings separately and perhaps at different speeds, giving it a fine control of flight. Dragonflies are amazingly agile, able to hover, fly backward, and change direction in an instant.*

LIVING RELATIVE

One of the world's largest dragonflies today is the giant dragonfly (*Petalura gigantea*), which is found in New South Wales, Australia. Despite having a wingspan of almost 5½ in (14 cm), it is actually quite a poor flyer, and rarely moves far from its area. Like its ancestors, it eats flying insects.

INVERTEBRATES

200	145	65	23	Now
ssic	Jurassic	Cretaceous	Paleogene	Neogene

Ammonites

Ammonite fossils are unmistakeable, thanks to their beautiful coiled shapes. These sea creatures were close relatives of today's octopuses and squids but lived inside a shell, which they enlarged with new chambers as they grew, forming a spiral. They lived throughout the seas and swam by squirting water, the hollow inner chambers of their shells acting as air tanks to help them float.

FAMILY FACT FILE

Key features
- Coiled shell divided into chambers
- Soft body inside the outermost chamber
- Large head and well-developed eyes
- Long tentacles for capturing prey

When
Ammonites appeared 425 million years ago and were very common in the oceans throughout the age of the dinosaurs. They perished at the same time as the dinosaurs, 65 million years ago.

Scaphites

scaff-EYE-tees

- **When** 144–65 million years ago (Late Cretaceous)
- **Fossil location** Europe, Africa, India, N. America, S. America
- **Habitat** Shallow seas
- **Size** Up to 8 in (20 cm) across

Scaphites was an unusual ammonite. Instead of forming a neat spiral, its shell grew in a crooked shape. As a result, the opening for its head would have gotten tighter and tighter as *Scaphites* grew, eventually starving the animal to death. Perhaps *Scaphites* only lived long enough to lay its eggs, dying soon after, as happens in octopuses.

The shell's outermost chamber housed the ammonite's soft body.

Scaphites fossil

Promicroceras

pro-my-CROSS-e-ras

- **When** 200 million years ago (Early Jurassic)
- **Fossil location** Worldwide
- **Habitat** Seas
- **Size** Up to ¾ in (2 cm) across

Vast numbers of *Promicroceras* died at the same time, carpeting the seafloor with shells. Over time, these turned into fossils, forming an amazing type of rock called Marston marble, which consists of almost nothing but ammonites. The cause of the mass death is a mystery, but one possibility is poisoning of seawater by algae (microscopic plants).

Marston marble

Echioceras

ECK-ee-oh-se-ras

- **When** 200 million years ago (Early Jurassic)
- **Fossil location** Worldwide
- **Habitat** Seas
- **Size** Up to 2½ in (6 cm) across

Echioceras had a tightly coiled shell, which may have made it difficult to move rapidly. It preyed on other slow-moving creatures in the Jurassic seas.

Rib

Because the shell's air-filled inner chambers floated upward, ammonites swam with their heads beneath their bodies.

Bifericeras

BYE-fuh-ih-suh-ras

- **When** 200 million years ago (Early Jurassic)
- **Fossil location** Europe
- **Habitat** Open seas
- **Size** 1¼ in (3 cm) across

Bifericeras fed on small invertebrates that lived in the seas. The larger shells ("macroconches") belonged to the females and the smaller ones ("microconches") to the males. Females needed larger body sizes for producing and protecting their eggs.

Microconch (male) fossil formed of the mineral iron pyrite ("fool's gold").

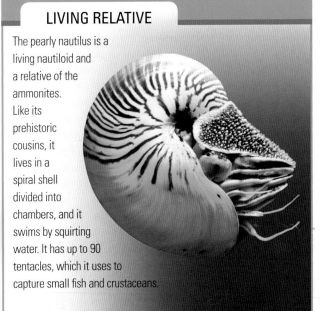

Macroconch (female)

Aturia

ay-TOO-ree-a

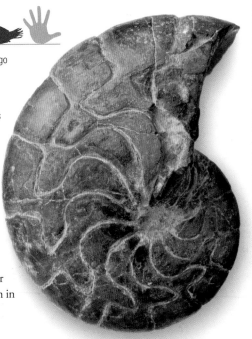

- **When** 65–23 million years ago (Paleogene to Early Neogene)
- **Fossil location** Worldwide
- **Habitat** Open waters
- **Size** Up to 6 in (15 cm) across

Although the ammonites died out at the same time as the dinosaurs, closely related animals called nautiloids survived. *Aturia* was a fast-swimming nautiloid that probably preyed on fish and shrimp. Its shell was smooth and streamlined for speed, without the ribs seen in many ammonites.

LIVING RELATIVE

The pearly nautilus is a living nautiloid and a relative of the ammonites. Like its prehistoric cousins, it lives in a spiral shell divided into chambers, and it swims by squirting water. It has up to 90 tentacles, which it uses to capture small fish and crustaceans.

Fossil gems

Ammonite fossils can be as beautiful as jewels. Some look like glass ornaments when they are cut open and polished, their once-hollow shells having filled up with crystalline minerals over millions of years. Others have a pearly surface that shimmers with color, forming one of the world's most precious gemstones.

▼ AMMONITES GREW in a spiral shape, adding new chambers to their shell as they got bigger. This fossil of the ammonite Desmoceras is about 100 million years old.

Rare jewels

In 1981, the World Jewellery Confederation gave official gemstone status to a brightly colored mineral found only on the surface of certain ammonite fossils. It is thought to be one of the rarest gemstones on the Earth, rivaling red diamond. It is found only in a few parts of the Rocky Mountains in North America and used to make exclusive luxury jewelry.

PEARLY AMMONITES

Ammonites made their shells from the mineral aragonite – the shiny mineral from which pearls form. In most fossils the shell has entirely disappeared and all that remains is a mould of its hollow interior. However, some ammonite fossils retain a pearly film of aragonite on the surface. In the best specimens, this delicate layer produces shimmering colours by splitting reflected light, a phenomenon known as iridescence.

Fossil seashells

The seashells on these pages might look like a collection found on a beach, but these are all fossil shells and are millions of years old, some dating back to before the dinosaurs. Seashells fossilize well because they are so hard. They are among the easiest fossils to find. Most are shells of mollusks—soft-bodied invertebrates such as snails and clams.

Carrier shell (*Xenophora*)
Pliocene

Scallop (*Oxytoma*)
Early Jurassic

Fan mussel
(*Pinna*)
Jurassic

Giant cerith (*Campanile*)
Eocene

Saltwater clam
(*Gervillaria*)
Cretaceous

Nut clam (*Nuculana*)
Eocene

Beak shell
(*Rimella*)
Eocene

Bubble shell (*Bulla*)
Pleistocene

Wentletrap
(*Cirsotrema*)
Pliocene

FAMILY FACT FILE

Gastropods
All the spiral shells on these pages were made by sea-dwelling gastropods (the class of mollusks that includes snails, slugs, and limpets). Just like garden snails, shelled gastropods can hide inside or under their shells for protection. The soft body within consists mainly of a single large muscular foot.

Snail

Bivalves
These mollusks have two shells joined by a hinge so they can snap shut. Cockles, clams, scallops, mussels, and oysters are all bivalves.

When
Mollusks date back some 500 million years to the Cambrian Period.

Top shell
(*Calliostoma*)
Eocene

Comb shell (*Murexsul*)
Pliocene

Basket shell (*Fimbria*)
Eocene

Scallop (*Pecten*)
Miocene

Jewel-box shell (*Chama*)
Eocene

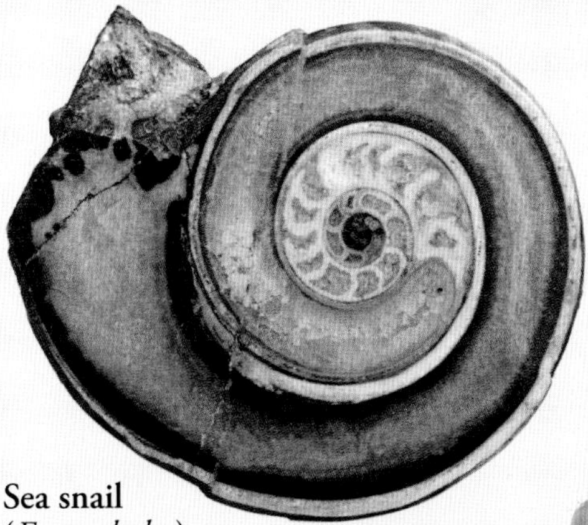

Sea snail (*Euomphalus*)
Carboniferous

Sea snail (*Clavilithes*)
Eocene

Horse mussel (*Modiolus*)
Cretaceous

Cockscomb oyster (*Rastellum*)
Cretaceous

Venus shell (*Chione*)
Miocene

Cone shell (*Conus*)
Eocene

Nerite (*Velates*)
Eocene

Cockle (*Acrosterigma*)
Pliocene

Hooded ark shell (*Cucullaea*)
Cretaceous

Sea snail (*Ecphora*)
Pliocene

Sundial shell (*Granosolarium*)
Eocene

Sundial shell (*Granosolarium*)
Eocene

Fig shell (*Ficopsis*)
Eocene

Whelk (*Neptunea*)
Pliocene

EARLY VERTEBRATES

▲ PHLEGETHONTIA *This early vertebrate may look like a snake, but it was a legless amphibian. It grew to lengths of about 28 in (70 cm) and hunted small prey using spiked teeth.*

Vertebrates are animals with backbones. Fish were the first vertebrates; they appeared in Earth's oceans more than 500 million years ago. These first fish were jawless and very different from today's fish.

What are vertebrates?

A donkey, a crocodile, a fish, a parrot, and a frog all have one thing in common. They all have a backbone, or vertebral column, connected to a supporting bony skeleton inside their bodies. They are all vertebrates.

FAMILY TREE OF VERTEBRATES

Although vertebrates are the animals we know most about, they actually make up just a tiny part of the animal kingdom. Vertebrates with limbs—tetrapods—are all descended from fish.

Fish

Tetrapods

Amphibians

Mammals and relatives

Reptiles

Turtles and tortoises

Ichthyosaurs

Plesiosaurs (marine reptiles)

Lizards and snakes

Archosaurs

Crocodiles and relatives

Pterosaurs (flying reptiles)

Dinosaurs and birds

Vertebrates can be divided into five groups: mammals, birds, reptiles, amphibians, and fish.

MAMMALS

Mammals can be divided into three groups, depending on their means of reproduction. Placental mammals give birth to well-developed young. Marsupials give birth to undeveloped young. Monotremes (there are just five living species) lay eggs.

Chimpanzee

◀ GERBIL *Rodents are a large group of mammals, characterized by large incisors, perfect for gnawing.*

▼ AFRICAN ELEPHANT *The largest living land mammal in the world, a male African elephant can stand 13 ft (4 m) at the shoulder.*

BIRDS

There are almost 10,000 species of bird. They are the living descendants of dinosaurs, but they developed the ability to fly. Feathers help them to fly, but also keep them warm.

Budgerigar

▶ COMMON RHEA *Not all birds can fly. In fact, more than 40 species of bird, like this rhea, have lost the ability to fly.*

▲ PEREGRINE FALCON *This is one of the fastest of all animals.*

TAKE A LOOK—A PEEP INSIDE

Vertebrates have a backbone and internal bony skeleton. They also have a highly developed nervous system, and a larger brain for body size than invertebrates. Blood is pumped around the body by the heart, supplying the vertebrate's body with food and oxygen and removing waste products. They breathe using lungs.

▶ BONE *is a lightweight, living organ, and it is found only in vertebrates. Because it is supplied with blood vessels, it can grow (unlike the hard casing of an invertebrate such as a crab, which has to be shed to allow growth).*

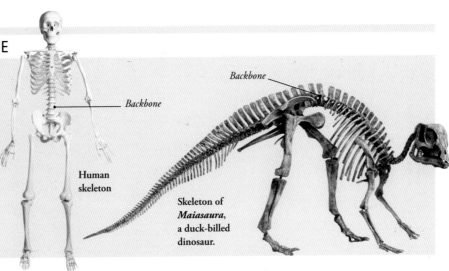

Backbone

Backbone

Human skeleton

Skeleton of ***Maiasaura***, a duck-billed dinosaur.

REPTILES

Along with some amphibians, reptiles were the first vertebrates to live entirely on land. Their skin is dry and covered in scales to help retain water, a necessary adaptation, since many reptiles live in warm areas with limited access to water.

Parson's chameleon

▶ MILK SNAKE
Some species of reptile have to shed their skin as they grow. They do this between four and eight times a year.

▼ CAIMAN
Crocodilians, such as the caiman below, have thrived since they appeared with early dinosaurs, some 200 million years ago.

AMPHIBIANS

Modern amphibians have moist, soft skin, and most amphibians can absorb oxygen through this skin in addition to having lungs. They largely live on land but require damp conditions. Most have to return to water to lay eggs.

◀ CHINESE GIANT SALAMANDER *(the world's largest living amphibian).*

▶ FIRE SALAMANDER
This salamander will curl up underground in colder, winter months. Its bright color warns predators it is poisonous.

▼ POISON DART FROG *There are some 4,500 species of frog and toad, including about 120 species of poison dart frog.*

FISH

Earth's first vertebrates—fish—now form more than half of all vertebrate species. Gills allow them to breathe underwater.

Spiny puffer fish

▼ WHALE SHARK *This is the world's largest fish. Despite its size, it feeds on plankton—tiny organisms that drift in water.*

▼ STAYING TOGETHER *Many fish swim in schools, finding safety in numbers.*

65

Jawless fish

The first vertebrates were fish, but they were very different from today's fish. The early fish couldn't bite, since jaws were yet to evolve. Instead, they fed by sucking or scraping. With few or no fins, they swam by waggling their tails like tadpoles. They had no internal bones, but some had wide, bony shields covering their heads—protection from predators such as giant sea scorpions.

Drepanaspis
DREP-an-ASP-iss

- **When** 410 million years ago (Early Devonian)
- **Fossil location** Europe
- **Habitat** Ocean floor
- **Length** 14 in (35 cm)

With its flat, paddle-shaped head and narrow body, *Drepanaspis* was a strangely shaped fish. It hunted for food near the bottom of Devonian seas. *Drepanaspis*'s feeding methods are a mystery, since its jawless mouth faced upward instead of downward, a curious feature that would have made it difficult to scoop in food. Like many other jawless fish, *Drepanaspis* had bony armor to protect it from attack.

LIVING RELATIVE

Two groups of jawless fish still exist today: hagfish and lampreys. Both are eel-shaped creatures with no bones, scales, or fins. Hagfish feed on worms or dead sea animals. Some lampreys are parasites – they use their circular, jawless mouths to latch on to fish so they can feed on their blood.

Toothed mouth of a lamprey

FAMILY FACT FILE

Key features
- Mouths but no jaws
- Many species lacked paired fins
- Usually no stomach
- Swam by beating a muscular tail

When
Some jawless fish fossils have been dated to the Cambrian Period, more than 500 million years ago. Many jawless fish died out at the end of the Devonian Period, almost 350 million years ago.

Birkenia
bir-KEEN-ee-a

- **When** 425 million years ago (Middle Silurian)
- **Fossil location** Europe
- **Habitat** Freshwater pools and streams
- **Length** 4 in (10 cm)

Although *Birkenia* did not have fins, it was still an active swimmer in the pools and streams in which it lived. It fed on the remains of dead plants and animals, probably sucking in scraps with its gaping mouth. Unlike many other jawless fish that had bony head-shields, *Birkenia*'s head was covered in small scales.

Sacabambaspis
SAC-a-bam-BASP-iss

- **When** 490 million years ago (Early Ordovician)
- **Fossil location** Bolivia
- **Habitat** Coastal waters
- **Length** 12 in (30 cm)

This fish had a broad head-shield and a body that narrowed to end in a small fin. With this shape, it probably swam very much like a tadpole, sucking in scraps of food through its ever-open mouth. *Sacabambaspis* had sense organs that helped it to feel movement in the water, allowing it to judge the distance to its prey—and avoid predators.

Zenaspis
zen-ASP-iss

- **When** 410 million years ago (Early Devonian)
- **Fossil location** Europe
- **Habitat** Shallow seas and river mouths
- **Length** 10 in (25 cm)

Eye

Zenaspis had a horseshoe-shaped head protected by an armored shield, while the rest of its fairly flat body was protected by scales. Its eyes were placed close together on top of its head (a perfect position for spotting predators for a bottom-dwelling fish). Like lots of jawless fish, *Zenaspis* did not have teeth. Instead, its mouth, located on the underside of the body, was lined with bony plates. It probably fed on small creatures found on the seafloor or in river mouths.

Cephalaspis
SEFF-a-LASP-iss

- **When** 410 million years ago (Early Devonian)
- **Fossil location** Europe
- **Habitat** Freshwater pools and streams
- **Length** 9 in (22 cm)

This small fish lived at the bottom of pools or streams. Perhaps it moved its broad head-shield from side to side, stirring up mud as it searched for hidden worms and other creatures. It may also have fed on the waste of other animals that lived in the water. Pairs of scaly flaps balanced its body, and a fin on its back prevented it from rolling over.

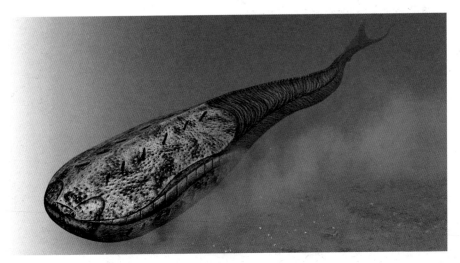

Armored fish

Also known as placoderms, the armored fish were the first fish to grow to a monstrous size, some reaching the size of modern sharks. They were also among the first fish with biting jaws, which they used as lethal weapons. For protection from each other, these prehistoric fish evolved suits of armor made of overlapping plates of bone.

Gemuendina
JEM-yoo-en-DEE-na

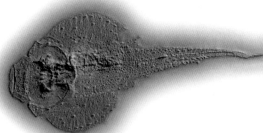

- **When** Almost 410 million years ago (Early Devonian)
- **Fossil location** Germany
- **Habitat** Shallow seas
- **Length** 10–12 in (25–30 cm)

A small, flat-bodied fish with a narrow tail, *Gemuendina* looked similar to the modern stingray except that its mouth was on top of its head. Unlike other armored fish, it did not have plates of bone in its mouth. Instead, it used star-shaped scales to grasp prey.

Dunkleosteus
DUN-kell-OSS-tee-us

- **When** Nearly 380 million years ago (Late Devonian)
- **Fossil location** USA, Europe, Morocco
- **Habitat** Shallow seas
- **Length** 20 ft (6 m)

Sometimes described as the *Tyrannosaurus* of the seas, *Dunkleosteus* was one of the largest armored fish. It was as big as an elephant and a vicious hunter, with the most powerful bite of any fish (except perhaps the megatooth shark). Instead of teeth, *Dunkleosteus* had a kind of beak formed of bony plates with sharp points. Some *Dunkleosteus* fossils have bite marks matching these jaws, suggesting the killer was also a cannibal.

▲ MONSTER JAWS Dunkleosteus *had a massive head and large, scissorlike jaws with razor-sharp bony plates that formed a "beak." Its bite was powerful enough to crack concrete.*

Coccosteus

cock-oh-STEE-us

- **When** 380–350 million years ago
(Middle to Late Devonian)
- **Fossil location** N. America, Europe
- **Habitat** Shallow waters
- **Length** 16 in (40 cm)

Although quite small in size, *Coccosteus* was an effective predator. It hunted other fish, perhaps lying in wait on the seabed for its prey before ambushing. Like *Dunkleosteus,* it had a beaklike mouth, with sharp, bladelike edges to tear flesh off larger animals. Its fossils show that it had a powerful tail, suggesting that it was a strong swimmer.

Rolfosteus

ROLL-foss-tee-us

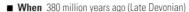

- **When** 380 million years ago (Late Devonian)
- **Fossil location** Australia
- **Habitat** Reefs
- **Length** 12 in (30 cm)

Rolfosteus was quite bizarre to look at, with a long, tubelike snout like a unicorn's horn. Scientists are puzzled over the use of the snout. *Rolfosteus* may have used it to dig through the sandy seabed to look for hidden prey, or it may have been a male ornament used to attract females. Like other armored fish, this creature had no teeth. Instead, it had flattened plates of bone at the back of its mouth. These may have been used to crush the shells of crabs and other crustaceans.

FAMILY FACT FILE

Key features
- Armor-plated bodies
- Jaws with bony plates that served as teeth
- Joints between armor plates allowed the jaws to open and the body to bend

When
Armored fish lived from the Late Silurian Period, nearly 430 million years ago, to the end of the Devonian Period, 359 million years ago.

Sharks and rays

Fossil teeth reveal that killer sharks have been cruising the seas for more than 400 million years—an astonishing length of time. Along with their flat-bodied relatives the rays, sharks belong to a truly ancient class of animals known as cartilaginous fish. These fish have no bones; instead, the skeleton is made of a rubbery material called cartilage.

Dorsal fin

Spine

Gill slits

 FAMILY FACT FILE

Key features
- Teeth are continuously shed and replaced
- Skeleton made of cartilage
- No ribs whatsoever
- No air bladder for controlling buoyancy
- Sharks must keep swimming or they will sink
- Fins in pairs for steering, unlike earlier fish

When
The earliest known fossils of sharks and rays date back to the Late Silurian, almost 420 million years ago.

Hybodus
hy-BODE-us

- **When** Late Permian to Late Cretaceous
- **Fossil location** Europe, N. America, Asia, Africa
- **Habitat** Oceans
- **Length** 6 ft (2 m)
- **Diet** Small marine animals

Hybodus looked as fierce as any modern shark and had the classic streamlined shape, but its teeth and fins were different from today's sharks. It had two types of tooth: sharp ones at the front for seizing slippery prey such as fish, and flatter, more blunt teeth at the back of the mouth for crushing shells. In front of *Hybodus*'s dorsal fin (the fin on its back) was a long, bladelike spine. This may have helped the fin to cut through the water more easily or it may have been used for defense.

Heliobatis
he-lee-oh-BAT-iss

- **When** 54–38 million years ago (Early to Middle Paleogene)
- **Fossil location** USA
- **Habitat** Freshwater streams and lakes
- **Length** 3 ft (1 m)
- **Diet** Crayfish, shrimp, and other invertebrates

Heliobatis may have been a relative of the stingray.

Its tail contained up to three needlelike stingers that may have been able to inject venom. It lived at the bottom of lakes and possibly rivers, where it hunted for crayfish, small fish, and possibly snails. It was named *Heliobatis* ("Sun ray") because of the way its fins fan out around it like rays of sunlight.

Huge pectoral fin

Notorynchus

no-toe-RIN-cuss

- **When** 56 million years ago to now
- **Fossil location** Worldwide
- **Habitat** Cool, shallow marine waters
- **Length** 10 ft (3 m)
- **Diet** Sharks, rays, fish, seals, and dead animals

Also known as the seven gill shark, *Notorynchus* had seven gill slits (unlike the five seen in most sharks). Its strange teeth were each made up of many small points (cusps), creating a jagged, sawlike edge ideal for slicing flesh. *Notorynchus* is still found today and is common in cooler seas worldwide.

Single *Notorynchus* tooth

Cusp

Squalicorax

SKWA-lih-CORE-ax

- **When** 105–65 million years ago (Mid to Late Cretaceous)
- **Fossil location** Worldwide
- **Habitat** Oceans
- **Length** 15 ft (4.5 m)
- **Diet** Marine creatures

Fossilized shark teeth are common, since sharks shed thousands of teeth during their lives. Many *Squalicorax* teeth have been found, including one embedded in the foot of a hadrosaurid dinosaur. The rare find shows that *Squalicorax* sometimes scavenged from carcasses washed into the sea.

Stethacanthus

steth-a-CAN-thus

- **When** Late Devonian to Early Carboniferous
- **Fossil location** N. America, Scotland
- **Habitat** Oceans
- **Length** 5 ft (1.5 m)
- **Diet** Marine animals

One of the oddest of all prehistoric fish, *Stethacanthus* had a dorsal fin shaped like an ironing board, with a cluster of toothlike scales (denticles) on top. It had more toothlike scales on its head, and its side fins had long, pointed rods called whips trailing behind them. These features may have been present only in males and were perhaps important in mating. *Stethacanthus* usually lurked in shallow, coastal waters, where it nosed around for small fish and shellfish.

Dorsal fin

Denticles

Whip

Helicoprion

HELL-ee-coe-PRY-on

- **When** Early Permian
- **Fossil location** Worldwide
- **Habitat** Oceans
- **Length** 18 ft (5.5 m)
- **Diet** Marine animals

This bizarre shark was named *Helicoprion* ("spiral saw") because the teeth of its lower jaw grew in a spiral, forming a disk as big

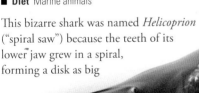

as a dinner plate. Only *Helicoprion*'s teeth have been found. The disk is known to be from the lower jaw, but how the shark used it to feed is a mystery.

Old teeth in middle of spiral

New teeth grew on the outside

71

Megatooth shark

The megatooth shark may have been the most terrifying and ferocious predator of all time—and possibly the biggest. This gigantic beast was a close cousin of today's great white shark but was far larger: the height of its tail fin alone was equal to the length of a great white. The megatooth terrorized the seas for more than 20 million years, preying on whales, dolphins, and seals. It attacked at speed, seizing victims in its vast jaws and crushing them or shaking them to pieces.

Record Breaker
A fully grown megatooth was more than times heavier than the great white, the largest shark alive today.

4.6 billion years ago	542 million years ago	488	444	416	359	299	25
Precambrian Eon	Cambrian	Ordovician	Silurian	Devonian	Carboniferous	Permian	

Megatooth shark

MEG-a-tooth shark

- **When** 25–1.5 million years ago (Late Paleogene to Early Neogene)
- **Fossil location** Europe, N. America, S. America, Africa, Asia
- **Habitat** Warm oceans
- **Length** 67 ft (20 m)

Only teeth and spine bones of the megatooth shark have been found. By comparing these with modern sharks, scientists estimate the megatooth shark may have weighed as much as 100 tonnes—as much as 30 elephants. Its fossil teeth are common in sites rich in sea mammals such as seals and dolphins, suggesting these were the megatooth's prey.

BIG TOOTH

Megatooth means "big tooth." This shark certainly lived up to its name, with more than 250 teeth, each of which grew up to 7 in (17 cm) long. The teeth had sharp, serrated edges like the cutting side of a saw—ideal for slicing through flesh.

▲ FOSSIL JAWS *of the megatooth shark have never been found, but scientists built the model above by scaling up a great white shark's jaws (in center). The megatooth's bite was five times more powerful than that of* Tyrannosaurus—*it could have crushed prey to death with a single bite.*

200	145	65	23	Now
Triassic	Jurassic	Cretaceous	Paleogene	Neogene

Bony fish

About 400 million years ago, a new family of fish began swimming in the seas. Unlike the sharks that had ruled the waters for millions of years, the new fish had skeletons hardened with calcium to form bone, earning them the name "bony fish." The bony fish evolved into a huge range of new species and make up more than 95% of fish species alive today.

Xiphactinus
zye-FAC-tee-nus

- **When** 112–70 million years ago (Middle to Late Cretaceous)
- **Fossil location** N. America
- **Habitat** Shallow waters of N. America
- **Length** 20 ft (6 m)

Xiphactinus was a powerful swimmer with a long, muscular body. It had a huge mouth and could swallow large prey whole. One fossil was found to contain the remains of a 7 ft (2 m) fish in its stomach—perhaps the prey was too big for *Xiphactinus* and killed it by thrashing around inside.

Leedsichthys
LEEDS-ick-thiss

- **When** 176–161 million years ago (Middle Jurassic)
- **Fossil location** Europe, Chile
- **Habitat** Oceans
- **Length** 30 ft (9 m)

Perhaps the largest bony fish that ever lived, *Leedsichthys* was bigger than a killer whale. Despite its fearsome size, it was a harmless filter feeder rather than a hunter—it gulped huge volumes of water into its mouth and then squirted it out while sifting shrimp and other tiny animals with its gills. Bite marks on one fossil show that *Leedsichthys* was hunted by gigantic marine reptiles called pliosaurs.

FAMILY FACT FILE

Key features
- A skeleton made of bone
- Most have ray fins (fins supported by long rays of bone that give these fish fine control of movement)
- Swim bladders (air-filled sacs) to help these fish stay buoyant in water

When
Bony fish first appeared in the Devonian Period, almost 395 million years ago, and remain very common today.

Diplomystus

DIP-low-MISS-tus

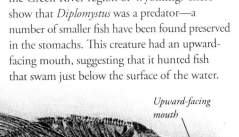

- **When** 55–34 million years ago (Middle to Late Paleogene)
- **Fossil location** USA, Lebanon, Syria, S. America, Africa
- **Habitat** Lakes
- **Length** 26 in (65 cm)

A relative of herrings and sardines, *Diplomystus* lived in freshwater rivers and lakes. Many of the best-preserved fossils have been found in the Green River region of Wyoming. These show that *Diplomystus* was a predator—a number of smaller fish have been found preserved in the stomachs. This creature had an upward-facing mouth, suggesting that it hunted fish that swam just below the surface of the water.

Upward-facing mouth

Priscacara

PRISS-ca-carr-a

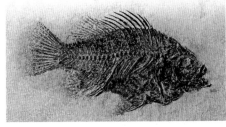

- **When** 55–33 million years ago (Middle to Late Paleogene)
- **Fossil location** N. America
- **Habitat** Freshwater streams and lakes
- **Length** 6 in (15 cm)

Priscacara lived in deep lakes in North America, where its fossils formed in mud on the lake floor, preserved in beautiful detail. The stiff spines of its fins may have been defensive weapons—they would probably have stabbed the mouth of any predator that tried to swallow *Priscacara*.

Naso

NAY-zoe

- **When** 56–49 million years ago (Paleogene)
- **Fossil location** Italy
- **Habitat** Oceans
- **Length** 3 in (8 cm)

This fossil fish is a very close relative of modern unicorn fish, which are so named because they have a spike on the forehead like a unicorn's horn. Like its modern relatives, this prehistoric species may have lived in shoals on coral reefs.

Knightia

NITE-ee-ah

- **When** 55–34 million years ago (Middle to Late Paleogene)
- **Fossil location** USA
- **Habitat** Rivers and lakes of N. America
- **Length** 10 in (25 cm)

Scientists have discovered skeletons of *Knightia* in the stomachs of many larger fish. Huge shoals must have crowded the ancient seas, making them easy prey. Hundreds of well-preserved *Knightia* fossils have been found in the Green River region of Wyoming. The State of Wyoming declared *Knightia* as its state fossil in 1987.

Perca

PER-ca

- **When** 55–37 million years ago (Middle to Late Paleogene)
- **Fossil location** USA
- **Habitat** Shallow waters
- **Length** 12 in (30 cm)

This ancient fish of the perch family looked just like its modern relative. Its body was covered in scales. On its humped back were two fins bearing sharp spines that it raised to scare away predators. Like many perches today, it may have had a striped body that helped it blend in with the reeds and bulrushes among which it hid from predators. It moved in shoals, feeding on insects, fish eggs, and small fish.

Mioplosus

MY-oh-PLOH-sus

- **When** 55–40 million years ago (Middle Paleogene)
- **Fossil location** USA
- **Habitat** Oceans
- **Length** 10 in (25 cm)

This incredible fossil shows a *Mioplosus* caught in the act of devouring its prey. The victim must have become lodged in the predator's mouth, killing it. *Mioplosus* was a hunter that preyed on fish up to half its size, using pointed teeth to trap them in its jaws.

Lepidotes

This bony fish appears to have been a food choice of a ferocious dinosaur called *Baryonyx*, as a number of *Lepidotes* scales and bones have been found in the fossilized stomach area of this dinosaur. It was quite big itself, reaching lengths of up to 6 ft (1.8 m), and it was widespread— fossil remains have been found all over the world.

▲ TEETH
Looking like little stones when fossilized, Lepidotes's teeth were once known as "toadstones" and were thought to have magical properties.

Lepidotes

leppy-DOE-tees

- **When** 199—70 million years ago (Jurassic to Early Cretaceous)
- **Fossil location** Worldwide
- **Habitat** Lakes of the northern hemisphere
- **Length** 6 ft (1.8 m)

Fabulous *Lepidotes* fossils have been found, with clear skin impressions. *Lepidotes* had thick, diamond-shaped scales. In life, this fish would have had a glossy appearance, thanks to a hard coating over the scales that reflected light.

4.6 billion years ago	542 million years ago	488	444	416	359	299
Precambrian Eon	Cambrian	Ordovician	Silurian	Devonian	Carboniferous	

Sucker lips

Lepidotes had a trick when it came to feeding. It could push out its jaw, in the same way a carp does today, and would then suck in prey such as shellfish. Shells proved no barrier to this fish's hard, peglike teeth.

Today's carp are able to push forward their jaws, just as Lepidotes *once did.*

DID YOU KNOW...?

Our teeth and the teeth of all vertebrates evolved from the scales of prehistoric fish. The scales of *Lepidotes* were covered in dentine and coated with enamel, the same material that makes up our teeth. Even the structure of these scales looks similar to human teeth.

EARLY VERTEBRATES

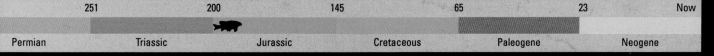

251	200	145	65	23	Now
Permian	Triassic	Jurassic	Cretaceous	Paleogene	Neogene

Lobe-finned fish

Instead of using their fins for steering, the members of this fish family began using them to "walk" into crevices in reefs and to push themselves along the seafloor. As the years passed, their fins became stockier and muscular—they were beginning to turn into legs. Called the "lobe-finned fish," these fish were the first vertebrates to crawl out of water and begin to live on land.

FAMILY FACT FILE

Key features
- Stocky, rounded (lobe-shaped) fins supported by bones
- Gills to breathe in water
- Some also had lunglike air chambers to breathe air

When
These fish appeared in the Ordovician Period (505–440 million years ago). Many died out at the end of the Cretaceous Period, 65 million years ago, but lobe-finned fish still exist today.

Eusthenopteron

YOOS-then-OP-ter-on

- **When** 385 million years ago (Late Devonian)
- **Fossil location** N. America, Greenland, Scotland, Latvia, Estonia
- **Habitat** Oceans
- **Length** 5 ft (1.5 m)

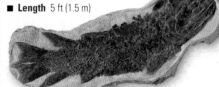

Like most fish, *Eusthenopteron* was covered in scales and had fins. However, the bones supporting its fins were similar to those of the first amphibians (animals that live partly in water and partly on land). A predator, *Eusthenopteron* may have lurked in clumps of seaweed, waiting to ambush passing prey.

Panderichthys

PAN-der-ICK-thiss

- **When** 400 million years ago (Late Devonian)
- **Fossil location** Latvia, Lithuania, Estonia, Russia
- **Habitat** Oceans
- **Length** 5 ft (1.5 m)

Even though *Panderichthys* (right) was a fish, it may have been able to climb on to land, propping itself on its front fins for just a moment. It had fins in pairs and scales all over its body, like fish today. However, its fins were supported by bones similar to those of an amphibian's. It breathed through its gills underwater, but an opening on top of its head, probably connected to a lunglike air chamber, allowed it to breathe on land as well.

▲ FISH OUT OF WATER
Panderichthys *was like an amphibian in some ways. Although its body was long and slender, its head was wide and flattened with large eyes on top, giving it a froglike face.*

Tiktaalik

tik-TAA-lick

- **When** Nearly 380 million years ago (Late Devonian)
- **Fossil location** Canada
- **Habitat** Shallow seas
- **Length** 3 ft (1 m)

This strange creature (right) was like a cross between a fish and a salamander. It had a flat head with eyes on top—perhaps for peeping above the water's surface—and a neck joint that allowed it to turn its head. Its "fins" had wrist and shoulder joints and even simple fingers. *Tiktaalik* couldn't truly walk, but it could probably wriggle out of water and use the fins to prop itself up.

Dipterus
DIP-ter-us

- **When** 370 million years ago (Late Devonian)
- **Fossil location** Scotland, N. America
- **Habitat** Rivers and lakes
- **Length** 14 in (35 cm)

Dipterus was a lungfish and a close relative of modern lungfish (strange fish that can breathe air and hibernate in burrows to survive droughts). A large plate over its gill chamber suggests *Dipterus* relied more on its gills than lungs. It had tough teeth, perhaps to crack shellfish, and bony armor plates on its head.

Osteolepis
OST-ee-oh-LEEP-iss

- **When** 390 million years ago (Devonian)
- **Fossil location** Scotland, Latvia, Lithuania, Estonia
- **Habitat** Shallow lakes
- **Length** 20 in (50 cm)

Large, square scales on its body gave *Osteolepis* its name (meaning "bony scale"). The scales and the skull bones were covered with a glossy substance rather like the enamel of human teeth. It lived in the northern lakes of Scotland in the Devonian Period.

Macropoma
mack-roe-POME-ah

- **When** 70 million years ago (Late Cretaceous)
- **Fossil location** England, Czech Republic
- **Habitat** Oceans
- **Length** 22 in (55 cm)

Macropoma belonged to the family of ancient fish known as coelacanths, which had fleshy fins that they could move in a similar fashion to our arms and legs. Coelacanths were once believed to be an evolutionary link between fish and land animals. However, scientists now think that they were not the direct ancestors of land animals.

LIVING RELATIVE

In 1938, fishermen in South Africa found a strange fish in a shark net and showed it to a local scientist. To everyone's astonishment, it turned out to be a coelacanth ("SEE-la-canth")—a type of fish thought to have been extinct since the age of dinosaurs. This "living fossil" was the zoological find of the century.

Conquering land

We know that land animals today evolved from creatures that lived in water millions of years ago. To move onto land, certain barriers had to be overcome—after all, a fin or flipper is not much use on land. Let's take a look at some of the changes that took place.

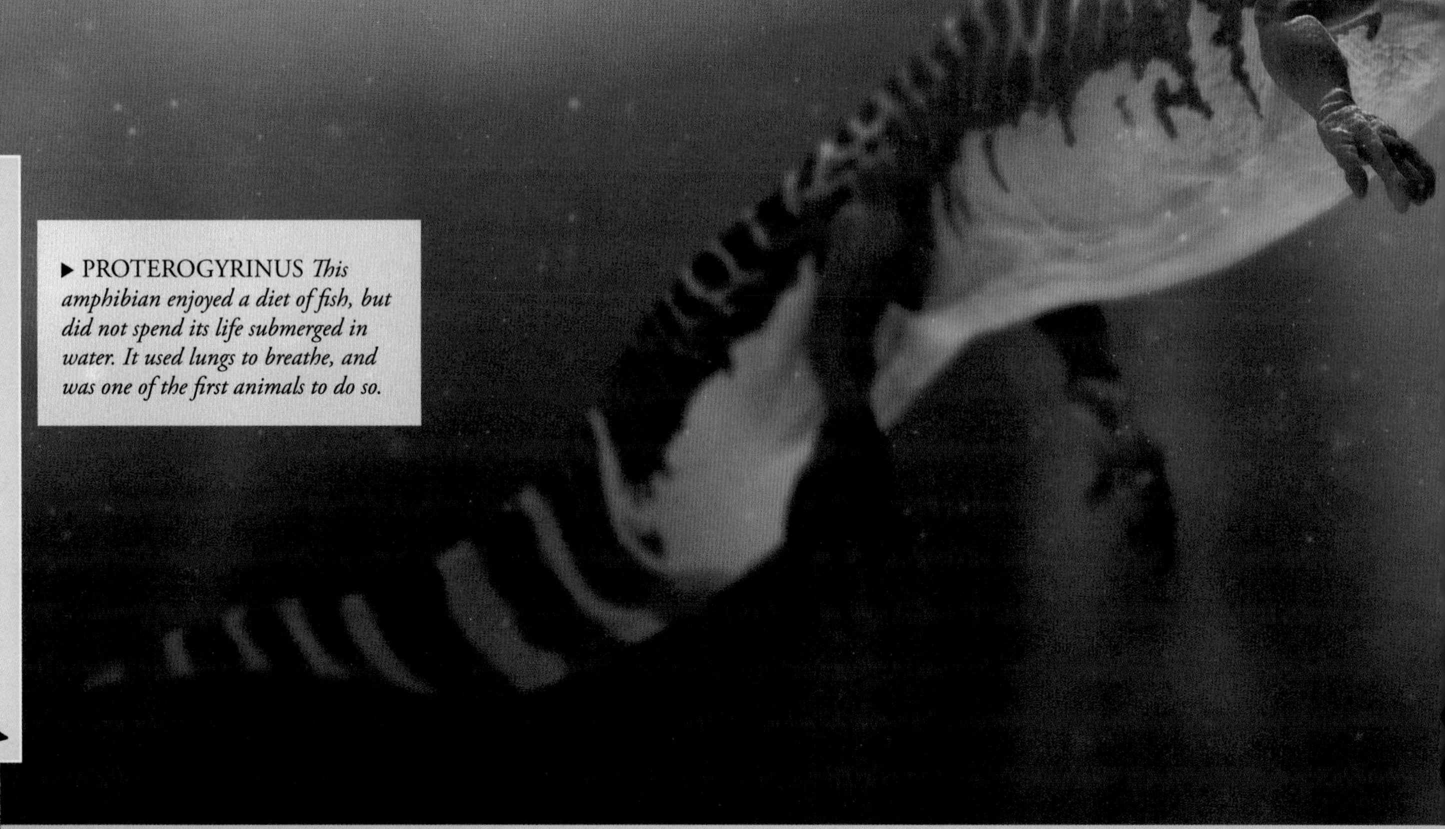

▶ PROTEROGYRINUS *This amphibian enjoyed a diet of fish, but did not spend its life submerged in water. It used lungs to breathe, and was one of the first animals to do so.*

FROM FINS TO LEGS

Legs evolved from the fins of fish. The first animals to develop legs—the tetrapods—had four legs with digits at the end of each one. Some had up to eight digits.

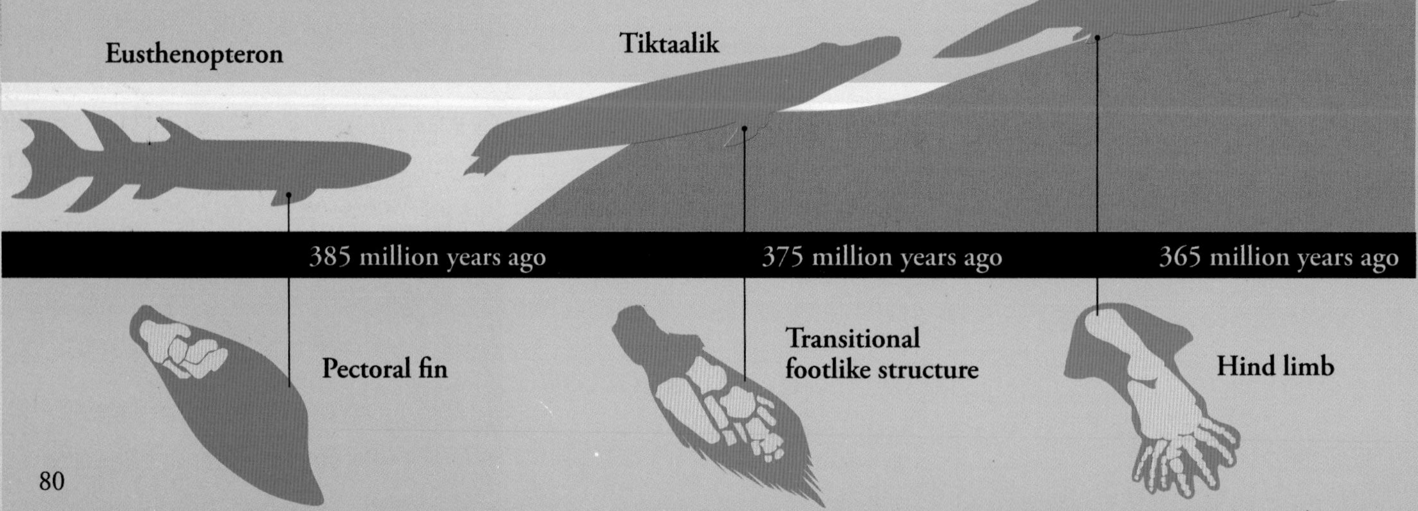

Ichthyostega

Tiktaalik

Eusthenopteron

385 million years ago 375 million years ago 365 million years ago

Pectoral fin

Transitional footlike structure

Hind limb

PROTECT THE YOUNG!

One of the most important steps in freeing animals from a dependence on water was the evolution of eggs that could be laid on land. Most amphibians have to return to water to breed, but the first reptiles had eggs with lots of membranes, and later shells, to help the egg withstand dry conditions.

▲ NO NEED FOR WATER
A tortoise's eggs do not dry out due to their shells and internal membranes.

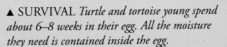

▲ SURVIVAL *Turtle and tortoise young spend about 6–8 weeks in their egg. All the moisture they need is contained inside the egg.*

▼ ANCIENT *Turtles and tortoises date back some 220 million years.*

A bit about digits

Nearly all land-dwelling vertebrates have five digits (fingers or toes) in each foot, and the same arrangement of bones in each limb. That's because they all evolved from the same ancestor—one of the early land pioneers, which happened to have five-fingered feet.

Breathing air

Land animals take oxygen from air and have no need for the gills that fish use to extract oxygen from water. Lungs evolved in some early fish to help them gulp air at the water's surface. One group of fish retained lungs, which were crucial when they began clambering onto land. Among the first fish to clamber onto land and breathe out of water were the lungfish, some 400 million years ago.

Prehistoric lungfish were found all over the world in the Devonian Period, some 400 million years ago.

▲ FIRST TRACKS *These fossilized tracks were found in 2010 in Canada. They are around 318 million years old and are believed to be evidence of some of the oldest reptiles.*

Amphibians

Amphibians are animals that spend their lives partly in water and partly on land. They evolved from fish about 370 million years ago as fins slowly turned into fully formed legs that allowed them to walk on land. Amphibians were the first four-legged animals ("tetrapods") and the ancestors of all four-legged animals alive today, from frogs and mice to elephants and humans.

Ichthyostega
ICK-thee-oh-STAY-gah

- **When** 370 million years ago (Late Devonian)
- **Fossil location** Greenland
- **Habitat** Shallow northern seas
- **Length** About 5 ft (1.5 m)

Ichthyostega's head, body, and tail fin were like those of a fish, but it had webbed feet like a frog's. It used lungs to breathe on land and had strong shoulder muscles that supported its weight out of water and helped it to crawl around. It hunted for fish and other prey in shallow pools.

Fossilized foot

Seymouria
see-MORE-ee-ah

- **When** 290 million years ago (Early Permian)
- **Fossil location** USA, Germany
- **Habitat** Swamps of N. America and western Europe
- **Length** About 2 ft (60 cm)

For many years *Seymouria* was believed to have been an early reptile because it had sturdy legs and was well suited to life on land. However, scientists discovered that a close relative of *Seymouria* had external gills in early life, like a tadpole, which suggests *Seymouria* did too. Although adults lived on land, youngsters probably lived entirely in water. The adult males had thick skulls that may have been used to butt rivals in mating contests.

Phlegethontia
FLEH-geh-THON-tee-ah

- **When** 300 million years ago (Late Carboniferous to Early Permian)
- **Fossil location** USA, Czech Republic
- **Habitat** Swamps of N. America and western Europe
- **Length** About 3 ft (0.9 m)

Phlegethontia belonged to a group of amphibians that had evolved snakelike bodies and lost their legs. It had rows of small, spiked teeth similar to those found in some nonvenomous snakes.

Microbrachis
MY-crow-BRACK-iss

- **When** 300 million years ago (Early Permian)
- **Fossil location** Czech Republic
- **Habitat** Swamps of eastern Europe
- **Length** Almost 6 in (15 cm)

Microbrachis (below) looked like a tiny salamander with puny limbs. It had gills for breathing in water and probably swam like a fish, propelling itself forward by swishing its flattened tail from side to side. It seems to have spent most of its time in swamps, rivers, lakes, and ponds, where it hunted for prey such as small fish and shrimp.

Microbrachis

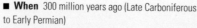

Eryops

EH-ree-ops

- **When** 295 million years ago (Early Permian)
- **Fossil location** N. America
- **Habitat** Swamps of N. America and western Europe
- **Length** About 6 ft (1.8 m)

One of the largest land animals of its time, *Eryops* looked like a fat crocodile. It had a long snout (its name means "drawn-out face"), and its huge, strong jaws were lined with sharp fangs. It couldn't chew and so would have flung its head up and backward, tossing prey further into its mouth just as crocodiles and alligators do today. *Eryops* had sturdy limbs but moved slowly on land because of its bulky body and short legs.

Acanthostega

ah-CAN-tho-STAY-gah

- **When** 365 million years ago (Late Devonian)
- **Fossil location** Greenland
- **Habitat** Northern rivers and swamps
- **Length** About 2 ft (0.6 m)

This is believed to have been the first tetrapod capable of briefly climbing out of water. It had lungs but also gills and is thought to have lived largely in shallow swamps. Unlike its fish relatives, *Acanthostega* had eight webbed digits on its forelimbs.

Crassigyrinus

CRASS-ee-jih-RYE-nuss

- **When** 350 million years ago (Early Carboniferous)
- **Fossil location** Scotland and USA
- **Habitat** Shallow waters of northern Europe
- **Length** About 5 ft (1.5 m)

This bizarre creature probably lived in water, since its tiny limbs would have made walking on land impossible. It was a large and powerful predator, with two rows of sharp teeth lining a huge mouth that it used to catch prey with a snapping motion. Large eyes suggest it could have hunted well in murky water, or perhaps at night.

FAMILY FACT FILE

Key features
- Four limbs with wrist and elbow joints
- Distinct fingers and toes
- Eggs laid in water
- Fishlike larvae (babies)

When
Amphibians evolved from fish during the Devonian Period, 370–400 million years ago.

Amphibamus

Lush tropical forests and swamps covered the land in the Late Carboniferous Period. Giant insects buzzed around, and the newly evolved amphibians chased after them (see previous page). Some were as big as alligators, but tiny *Amphibamus* was the size of a newt. It had many of the features of modern frogs and salamanders and may have been their ancestor.

▲ SKELETON
More than 350 million years old, this fossil of Amphibamus *was found in Ohio. The wide head and large eye sockets are clearly visible.*

Amphibamus

AM-fee-bah-muss

- **When** 300 million years ago (Late Carboniferous)
- **Fossil location** USA
- **Habitat** Swamps of N. America and western Europe
- **Length** 6 in (15 cm)
- **Diet** Probably insects

Amphibamus had large eyes for spotting prey. Perhaps it hunted by standing still and snatching insects that came close, as frogs do. Like most modern amphibians, it may have had to return to water to breed and lay eggs.

SKIN BREATHER

Amphibamus fossils come from a site that was a river delta in the Carboniferous Period. Perhaps the animal lived in creeks or swamps near the river. Like most amphibians it might have been able to breathe through its moist skin, but it would have had to stay in damp places so its skin didn't dry out.

4.6 billion years ago	542 million years ago	488		444		416
Precambrian Eon	Cambrian		Ordovician		Silurian	Devonian

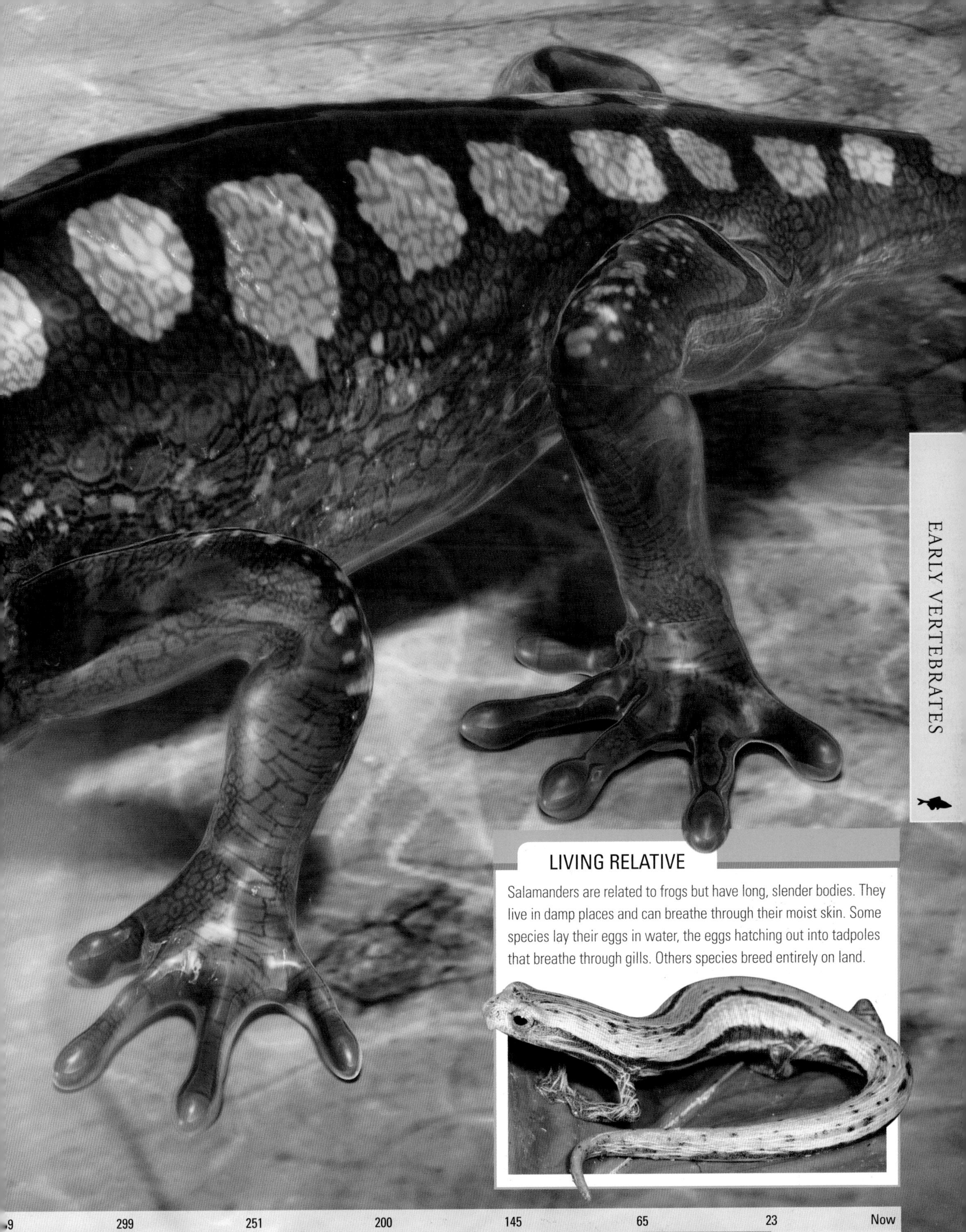

LIVING RELATIVE

Salamanders are related to frogs but have long, slender bodies. They live in damp places and can breathe through their moist skin. Some species lay their eggs in water, the eggs hatching out into tadpoles that breathe through gills. Others species breed entirely on land.

.9	299	251	200	145	65	23	Now
Carboniferous	Permian	Triassic	Jurassic	Cretaceous	Paleogene	Neogene

Early plants

Plants can be divided into spore-producing plants, such as mosses and ferns, and seed-bearing plants, such as flowering plants. There are now thought to be more than 400,000 identified species. But where did they first come from?

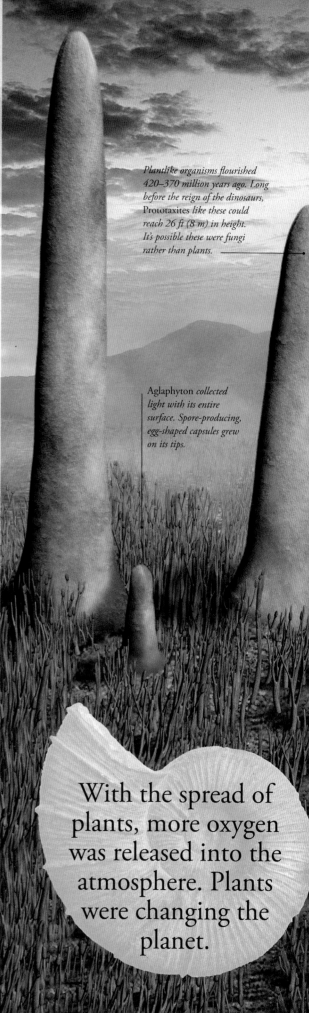

Plantlike organisms flourished 420–370 million years ago. Long before the reign of the dinosaurs, Prototaxites like these could reach 26 ft (8 m) in height. It's possible these were fungi rather than plants.

Aglaphyton collected light with its entire surface. Spore-producing, egg-shaped capsules grew on its tips.

The beginnings
Plants originated as algae—simple organisms that live in water and feed off the Sun's energy. The first algae lived in the sea. Over time, they spread into fresh water habitats and into damp places on land.

Moving onto land
More than 400 million years ago, plants started to grow on land. The first land plants were small, mosslike organisms and had no true leaves, roots, or flowers.

An unusual "seed"
Plants such as mosses and ferns have capsules that hold spores. Spores are a bit like seeds, but microscopic and not as hardy. Spores were a good means for early plants to reproduce, because an organism can produce millions of spores.

Spore-producing plants need damp conditions in which to reproduce.

With the spread of plants, more oxygen was released into the atmosphere. Plants were changing the planet.

Cooksonia, *one of the first upright plants, appeared 425 million years ago. It was just 4 in (10 cm) tall and could support itself with branching stems.*

▼ WILLIAMSONIA *These stocky trees would have been familiar to Jurassic and Cretaceous dinosaurs throughout the world. This plant had flowerlike parts. Learn more about the emergence of flowers on pages 224–225.*

Land plants spread out

When plants such as *Cooksonia* evolved sturdier stems, plants began to grow taller and spread farther across land. Later, plants evolved the ability to produce seeds, which can sprout in much drier places than spores. Dense forests then sprang up, turning the land green.

Early seeds

This plant may look as if it's producing fruits, but actually it is bearing seeds, each the size of an egg. *Medullosa* was the size of a small tree. It appeared about 350 million years ago.

A helping hand

As forests flourished, plants began to compete to reach the light. Woody stems evolved, allowing plants to reach higher. Plants similar to those we know today began to appear. Tree ferns, for instance, would have been familiar to the dinosaurs.

Conifer forests

During the dinosaur era, forests were dominated by towering conifer trees. These have thin, needlelike leaves, which cope well with hot, dry climates. The monkey puzzle tree is a type of conifer that still survives from this period.

Postosuchus

Before dinosaurs became widespread, other enormous reptiles ruled the land. One of the top predators in North America during the Triassic Period was *Postosuchus*, a close cousin of the crocodile family. This fearsome beast lived alongside the first small dinosaurs and probably ate them, too.

Fiery end
Postosuchus belonged to a reptile family that died out at the end of the Triassic, perhaps because of climate change caused by volcanic eruptions. The extinction allowed dinosaurs to become the top predators in the Jurassic.

4.6 billion years ago	542 million years ago	488	444	416	359	299
Precambrian Eon	Cambrian	Ordovician	Silurian	Devonian	Carboniferous	

Postosuchus

POST-oh-SOOK-us

- **When** 230–200 million years ago (Mid to Late Triassic)
- **Fossil location** USA
- **Habitat** Woodlands of N. America
- **Size** 15 ft (4.5 m)
- **Diet** Meat, smaller reptiles

Postosuchus belonged to a family of reptiles called rauisuchians. Unlike lizards, which have sprawling legs, the rauisuchians had pillarlike, upright legs—a sign that they were agile, active predators like the giant predatory dinosaurs that evolved later. Their hip joints were very different from those of dinosaurs, however, and their ankles were similar to those of crocodiles. *Postosuchus* had wickedly curved, daggerlike teeth that it used to tear prey to bits. One fossil was found with the remains of four different animals in its belly.

▲ NOSY CREATURE

Postosuchus *had a huge skull and large nostrils. Perhaps it had a very keen sense of smell for sniffing out its prey.*

Two legs or four?

Postosuchus had large hind legs and small arms, suggesting it walked on its hind legs like a dinosaur. However, some scientists believe it always walked on all fours. Others think it used two legs only to sprint.

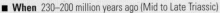

Permian	Triassic	Jurassic	Cretaceous	Paleogene	Neogene
251	200	145	65	23	Now

Effigia

It looked like a dinosaur, ran like a dinosaur, and probably fed like a dinosaur, too—but *Effigia* was no dinosaur. This Triassic reptile belonged to the same part of the reptile family tree as crocodiles and alligators but evolved a body shape remarkably similar to that of the ostrich dinosaurs (ornithomimids), which were not to appear until 80 million years later.

Effigia

eff-IJ-ee-ah

- **When** 210 million years ago (Late Triassic)
- **Fossil location** USA
- **Habitat** Woodlands of western N. America
- **Length** 5–10 ft (1.5–3 m)
- **Diet** Unknown but possibly omnivorous

Effigia walked on its hind legs, holding up its long tail for balance, and had very tiny arms. It had large eyes and a small, birdlike skull. Reptiles like *Effigia* were common in the Late Triassic but seem to have been killed by a change in climate caused by volcanic eruptions.

Modern pine cones

▲ WHO NEEDS TEETH?
Effigia *had a beak but no teeth, which makes its diet hard to guess. Perhaps it used its beak to crack pine seeds or eggs. It may also have preyed on small animals.*

4.6 billion years ago	542 million years ago	488	444	416	359	299
Precambrian Eon	Cambrian	Ordovician	Silurian	Devonian	Carboniferous	

Long tail

Long neck

Long hind legs

Crocodile-like ankle

Toothless beak

Small arms

▲ LIKE A DINOSAUR
Effigia *shared many features with dinosaurs, from large eyes and small arms to a toothless beak. Its ankles, however, were much more like those of a crocodile.*

DID YOU KNOW...?

Effigia (which means "ghost" in Greek) was named after the Ghost Ranch Quarry in New Mexico, where its fossil was found in 1947. *Effigia* has lived up to its name—the fossil lay hidden from sight for nearly 60 years, trapped inside an unopened slab of rock in an American museum. That is, until 2006, when the rock was cracked open and *Effigia* was discovered.

251	200	145	65	23	Now
Permian	Triassic	Jurassic	Cretaceous	Paleogene	Neogene

Crocodylomorphs

Crocodylomorphs (which means having a crocodile-like shape) were part of the archosaur, or "ruling reptile" group, along with dinosaurs and pterosaurs. Some were small, others gigantic, and they lived both on land and in the sea. Like their modern relatives—crocodiles and alligators—most were active hunters, always ready to ambush passing fish or land animals.

EARLY VERTEBRATES

Sphenosuchus
SFEN-oh-soo-kuss

- **When** 200 million years ago (Early Jurassic)
- **Fossil location** S. Africa
- **Habita** Land
- **Length** 3–5 ft (1–1.5 m)
- **Diet** Small land animals

Sphenosuchus was one of the earlier crocodylomorphs. It had long and slender legs—a sign it could run fast when chasing prey or fleeing from predators. Only a skull and a few leg bones have been found. Air-filled spaces in parts of the skull resemble those found in birds, hinting at an evolutionary link between crocodylomorphs and birds.

Geosaurus
GEE-oh-SORE-us

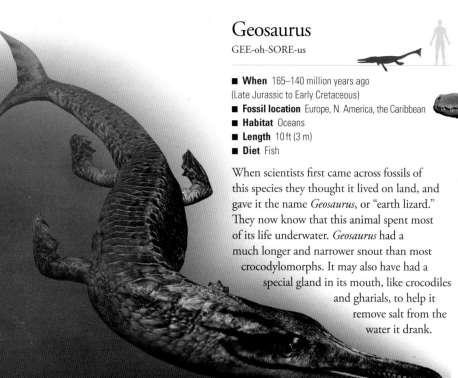

- **When** 165–140 million years ago (Late Jurassic to Early Cretaceous)
- **Fossil location** Europe, N. America, the Caribbean
- **Habitat** Oceans
- **Length** 10 ft (3 m)
- **Diet** Fish

When scientists first came across fossils of this species they thought it lived on land, and gave it the name *Geosaurus*, or "earth lizard." They now know that this animal spent most of its life underwater. *Geosaurus* had a much longer and narrower snout than most crocodylomorphs. It may also have had a special gland in its mouth, like crocodiles and gharials, to help it remove salt from the water it drank.

🐟 FAMILY FACT FILE

Key features
- Long bodies
- Short, strong limbs
- Powerful jaws
- Sharp teeth

When
Crocodylomorphs first appeared 225 million years ago, in the Late Triassic and were the ancestors of modern crocodiles and alligators.

Platelike scales made of bone

Dakosaurus

DACK-oh-SORE-us

- **When** 165–140 million years ago (Late Jurassic to Early Cretaceous)
- **Fossil location** Worldwide
- **Habitat** Shallow seas
- **Length** 15 ft (4–5 m)
- **Diet** Fish, squid, and marine reptiles

Dakosaurus was a fierce marine predator. With a skull like that of a carnivorous dinosaur and large, jagged teeth, it had a powerful bite that could slice through the flesh of other marine reptiles and crunch the shells of ammonites. Its legs had become paddles that helped it steer as its fishlike tail propelled it through the water. It could chase and overcome animals much bigger than itself.

Simosuchus

SIGH-moe-SOO-kuss

- **When** 70 million years ago (Late Cretaceous)
- **Fossil location** Madagascar
- **Habitat** Forests
- **Length** 4 ft (1.2 m)
- **Diet** Plants, maybe some insects

Simosuchus was an unusual crocodylomorph because it had a short skull and blunt face. In fact, its name means "pug-nosed crocodile." Even more unusually, this reptile's teeth show that it was probably a vegetarian that occasionally ate insects. New research suggests that its tail may have been much shorter than that shown in the illustration below.

Deinosuchus

DIE-no-SOO-kuss

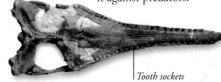

- **When** 70–65 million years ago (Late Cretaceous)
- **Fossil location** USA, Mexico
- **Habitat** Swamps
- **Length** 33 ft (10 m)
- **Diet** Fish, medium to large dinosaurs

Deinosuchus was one of the largest prehistoric alligators, nearly five times bigger and heavier than any found today. This alligator may have preyed on dinosaurs as big as itself—fossils of certain tyrannosaurs show *Deinosuchus* bite marks. It may have hunted by waiting patiently at the water's edge to pounce on passing fish, marine reptiles, or land animals. Small victims were swallowed whole. Larger prey were ripped apart into bite-sized chunks.

Steneosaurus

STEN-ee-oh-SORE-us

- **When** 200–145 million years ago (Early Jurassic to Early Cretaceous)
- **Fossil location** Europe, Africa
- **Habitat** Estuaries and coastal waters
- **Length** 3–13 ft (1–4 m)
- **Diet** Fish

Steneosaurus was probably an estuary-living crocodylomorph that ventured out onto land to lay its eggs. Although its long body was adapted for swimming, its limbs had not changed into flippers. It had a thin snout full of sharp teeth for eating fish, and its body was heavily armored to protect it against predators.

Tooth sockets

Long, powerful jaws with large, sharp teeth

▲ **UNDERWATER TERROR**
Deinosuchus *killed its prey as modern alligators do—by dragging its victims underwater and drowning them.*

93

Pterosaurs

The skies above the dinosaurs were alive with flying reptiles. These were the pterosaurs. They were not dinosaurs, but they were close relatives. One of the largest pterosaurs was *Quetzalcoatlus*. This colossal animal was easily the size of a fully grown giraffe—but with a wingspan that would have stretched across a tennis court.

Quetzalcoatlus

KWETS-ul-coe-AT-luss

- **When** 70–65 million years ago (Cretaceous)
- **Fossil location** USA
- **Habitat** Plains and woodlands
- **Size** 33–36 ft (10–11 m) wingspan

This pterosaur had a larger wingspan than a small plane, yet light bones meant that it only weighed around 550 lb (250 kg). During the day it soared over great distances, looking for small or baby dinosaurs to snap up in its giant, toothless jaws. It was one of the largest flying animals of all time.

FAMILY FACT FILE

Key features
- Each wing formed from skin stretched between an extra-long finger and the leg.
- Some pterosaurs had head crests.
- Large eyes
- Long, narrow jaws
- Hollow bones
- Pterosaurs flapped their wings

When
Pterosaurs first appeared in the late Triassic, 215 million years ago, and survived until the end of the Cretaceous Period, 65 million years ago.

Pterodactylus

TEH-roe-DACK-till-us

- **When** 150–144 million years ago (Jurassic)
- **Fossil location** Germany
- **Habitat** Coastal
- **Size** 12 in (30 cm) long

Many complete skeleton finds have ensured that *Pterodactylus* has become one of the best known of pterosaurs. This animal had a very short tail and a longer neck than earlier pterosaurs, making it a better flyer.

Pterodactylus

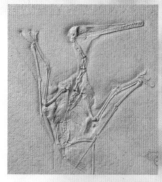

▲ PTERODACTYLUS *This fossil discovered in Germany is one of the most complete and best-preserved pterosaur fossils known.*

Pteranodon

teh-RAN-oh-don

- **When** 88–80 million years ago (Cretaceous)
- **Fossil location** North America
- **Habitat** Coastal
- **Size** 23–30 ft (7–9 m) wingspan

This creature's name means "wings and no teeth." It was one of the largest pterosaurs. *Pteranodons* lived in huge flocks and cruised over the ocean looking for fish to scoop up in their slender, pointed beaks. A large head crest may have been used for display.

▶ PTERANODON *probably flew like an albatross, using its huge wings to soar and flapping them only occasionally.*

Dimorphodon

die-MORE-foe-don

- **When** 200–180 million years ago (Jurassic)
- **Fossil location** British Isles
- **Habitat** Coastal woodlands
- **Size** 24 in (60 cm) long

Dimorphodon's head was almost a third of its body length and contained two types of teeth, which was unusual for a pterosaur. (Its name actually means "two-form tooth.") It probably hunted small vertebrates, such as lizardlike reptiles, snapping its jaws closed with immense speed to trap them.

▼ WINGS *A pterosaur's wing was made of skin stretched between an extremely long finger bone and the leg.*

Rhamphorhynchus

ram-foe-RINK-us

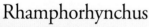

- **When** 150 million years ago (Jurassic)
- **Fossil location** Europe, Africa
- **Habitat** Coastal and riverside
- **Size** 16 in (40 cm) long

With its slim, spiked teeth, throat pouch, and long, narrow jaw, *Rhamphorhynchus* was perfectly adapted for the coastal environment in which it lived. Its long tail had a diamond-shaped flap of skin at the end and was perhaps used to help this pterosaur steer.

Eudimorphodon

Gliding on its leathery wings, *Eudimorphodon* was one of the first pterosaurs to take to the skies. Its front limbs had grown very long, its fourth fingers had stretched out, and together they formed the front edges of a pair of wings. Thin membranes of skin and muscle stretched back toward its hind legs. Powered by strong chest and arm muscles, these reptiles became masters of the air.

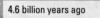

TOOTHY FISH-EATER

Eudimorphodon had more than 100 teeth packed into a jaw that was as short as a human finger. The front teeth were like fangs and faced outward, making it easier to catch slippery fish. The rear teeth had many little points, like human cheek teeth, that helped *Eudimorphodon* to chew its food.

4.6 billion years ago	542 million years ago	488	444	416	359	299
Precambrian Eon	Cambrian	Ordovician	Silurian	Devonian	Carboniferous

Eudimorphodon

YOU-die-MORE-fo-don

- **When** 210 million years ago (Late Triassic)
- **Fossil location** Italy, Greenland
- **Habitat** Coasts
- **Length** 3 ft (1 m)
- **Diet** Fish

This small reptile is one of the earliest pterosaurs. It had a long tail and a short neck, features that were lost in later species of pterosaur. *Eudimorphodon* glided through the skies, snatching fish near the surface of the water and probably insects, too. A diamond-shaped flap at the end of its bony tail helped it to steer while in flight.

The body and wings were covered in a hairy fuzz that helped Eudimorphodon *to keep warm.*

Sharp, pointed teeth were good for spearing fish.

	251	200	145	65	23	Now
Permian	Triassic	Jurassic	Cretaceous	Paleogene	Neogene	

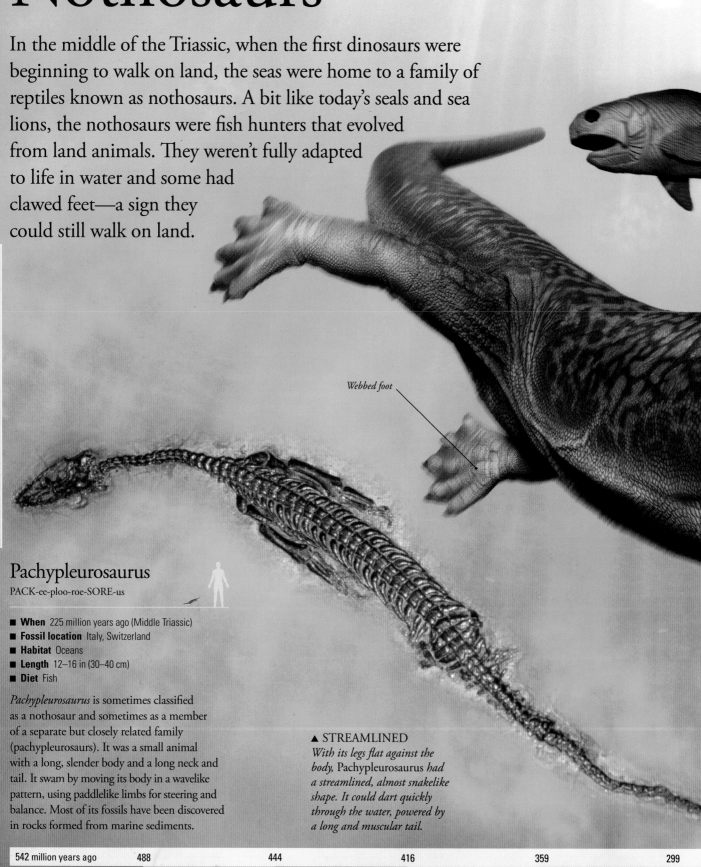

Nothosaurs

In the middle of the Triassic, when the first dinosaurs were beginning to walk on land, the seas were home to a family of reptiles known as nothosaurs. A bit like today's seals and sea lions, the nothosaurs were fish hunters that evolved from land animals. They weren't fully adapted to life in water and some had clawed feet—a sign they could still walk on land.

Webbed foot

Pachypleurosaurus
PACK-ee-ploo-roe-SORE-us

- **When** 225 million years ago (Middle Triassic)
- **Fossil location** Italy, Switzerland
- **Habitat** Oceans
- **Length** 12–16 in (30–40 cm)
- **Diet** Fish

Pachypleurosaurus is sometimes classified as a nothosaur and sometimes as a member of a separate but closely related family (pachypleurosaurs). It was a small animal with a long, slender body and a long neck and tail. It swam by moving its body in a wavelike pattern, using paddlelike limbs for steering and balance. Most of its fossils have been discovered in rocks formed from marine sediments.

▲ STREAMLINED
With its legs flat against the body, Pachypleurosaurus *had a streamlined, almost snakelike shape. It could dart quickly through the water, powered by a long and muscular tail.*

542 million years ago	488	444	416	359	299
Cambrian	Ordovician	Silurian	Devonian	Carboniferous	Permian

◀ SWIMMING Nothosaurus *probably swam like an otter, waving its long, powerful tail to drive itself through the water. The webbed feet were better suited to walking on land than swimming, but they may have helped* Nothosaurus *make sharp twists and turns as it chased its prey.*

Nothosaurus

NO-tho-SORE-us

- ■ **When** 240–210 million years ago (Early to Late Triassic)
- ■ **Fossil location** Europe, N. Africa, Russia, China
- ■ **Habitat** Oceans
- ■ **Length** 4–13 ft (1.2–4 m)
- ■ **Diet** Fish

Like a seal, *Nothosaurus* hunted in the water but probably came ashore to rest. It had amazingly long and needle-sharp teeth to seize fish. The teeth interlocked to form a cage, trapping prey in the mouth. *Nothosaurus* had a long and muscular neck. Some experts think it could twist its head sideways like a crocodile to grab passing fish—a trick known as "snap feeding."

251	200	145	65	23	Now
Triassic	Jurassic	Cretaceous	Paleogene	Neogene	

Plesiosaurs

During the Jurassic and Cretaceous periods, when dinosaurs ruled the land, the oceans were ruled by gigantic carnivorous reptiles called plesiosaurs. There were two main types: long-necked plesiosaurs, which had long, snakelike necks and small, dainty heads; and short-necked plesiosaurs (pliosaurs), which had huge heads and enormous, fang-filled jaws.

Small head

Sharp, pointed teeth

Elasmosaurus
el-LAZZ-moe-SORE-us

- **When** 99–65 million years ago (Late Cretaceous)
- **Fossil location** USA
- **Habitat** Oceans
- **Length** 45 ft (14 m)
- **Diet** Fish, squid, shellfish

Elasmosaurus's neck was as long as the rest of its body. After its discovery in 1868, the first scientists to study this animal thought the long neck was its tail and so put the head at the wrong end. This long neck came in handy—as *Elasmosaurus* swam slowly over the seabed, it would reach down to pick prey off the bottom.

▲ EXPERTS ARGUE *over how flexible the long neck of* Elasmosaurus *was. Some think it was as flexible as a snake's body and could be coiled up or held right out of the water. Others think it was stiffer but with enough flexibility to bend down and reach far to each side.*

FAMILY FACT FILE

Key features
- Plesiosaurs had long necks and small skulls; pliosaurs were short-necked, with enormous skulls
- Four large flippers
- Many pointed teeth

When
Plesiosaurs appeared in the Early Jurassic, 200 million years ago. They died out at the end of the Cretaceous Period, 65 million years ago.

Plesiosaurus
PLEE-see-oh-SORE-us

- **When** 200 million years ago (Early Jurassic)
- **Fossil location** British Isles, Germany
- **Habitat** Oceans
- **Length** 10–15 ft (3–5 m)
- **Diet** Fish, squidlike mollusks

Plesiosaurus was a long-necked aquatic reptile with a wide, turtlelike body. Like a turtle, it pushed itself through the water using its flippers, as the tail was too short to be of much use. It hunted by swimming among shoals of fish, swinging its long neck from iside to side to snatch its prey. *Plesiosaurus* had U-shaped jaws, which it could open wide, trapping prey with its conical teeth.

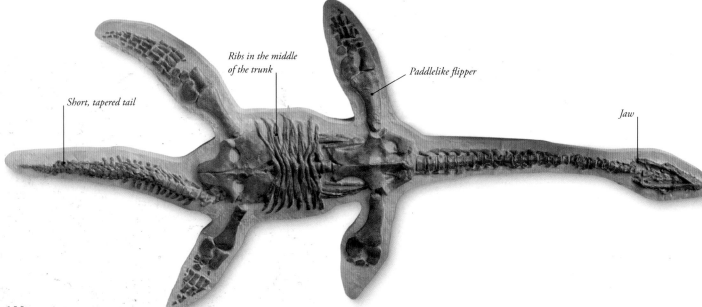

Ribs in the middle of the trunk

Paddlelike flipper

Short, tapered tail

Jaw

Liopleurodon

LIE-oh-PLOOR-oh-don

- **When** 165–150 million years ago (Mid to Late Jurassic)
- **Fossil location** British Isles, France, Russia, Germany
- **Habitat** Oceans
- **Length** 16–23 ft (5–7 m)
- **Diet** Large squid, ichthyosaurs

Each of the bones in Liopleurodon's *spine was the size of a dinner plate.*

One of the most powerful carnivores of all time, *Liopleurodon* had massive jaws and probably a stronger bite than *Tyrannosaurus*. It could easily have held a medium-sized car in its mouth and bitten it in half. Scientists believe it had a strong sense of smell, which helped it to hunt in deeper waters where prey was difficult to spot.

Kronosaurus

crow-no-SORE-us

- **When** 65 million years ago (Late Cretaceous)
- **Fossil location** Australia, Colombia
- **Habitat** Oceans
- **Length** 33 ft (10 m)
- **Diet** Marine reptiles, fish, mollusks

Kronosaurus was one of the largest sea reptiles. Even its head, at almost 10 ft (3 m) long, was bigger than a man. This monster could open its jaws wide like a crocodile and grasp prey with teeth as big as bananas. Fossilized stomach remains show that it ate other marine reptiles, including other plesiosaurs. Like all plesiosaurs, it had to rise to the surface to breathe air.

The Loch Ness monster

Does a plesiosaur survive to this day? There have long been stories of a mysterious prehistoric monster living in Loch Ness, a huge lake in Scotland. Scientific evidence that "Nessie," as the monster is more familiarly known, exists has never been found, but many people believe they have seen it and a few claim to have photographed it. Could there be any truth in the rumors?

EXCLUSIVE REPORT!

The famous photo below was first published in an English newspaper in 1934. It was said to be the first photo of the Loch Ness monster, and it caused a great deal of excitement. However, in 1994 the monster was revealed as a fake, made from a toy submarine attached to a neck and head sculpted from wood filler.

▲ THE FAMOUS SHOT *of "Nessie" is called the "surgeon's photograph" because it was supposedly taken by a London doctor, Robert K. Wilson.*

▲ LOCH NESS *is a 23-mile- (37-km-) long lake in Scotland. Despite its size, scientists think there are not enough fish in the lake to support a predator the size of the Loch Ness monster.*

Computer generated artwork of the Loch Ness monster.

WHY A PLESIOSAUR?

Pictures such as the surgeon's photograph show a long-necked creature like a plesiosaur. They inspired theories that Loch Ness's hidden depths might harbor creatures that survived from the age of the dinosaurs. But the water is probably too cold for giant reptiles, and Loch Ness was frozen solid during the last ice age.

Plesiosaur fossil

◄ FOSSILIZED PLESIOSAUR SKELETON *Plesiosaurs had long necks and small heads, just like images of the Loch Ness monster. But their necks were probably too weak to raise the head high above the surface.*

Rhomaleosaurus

In 1848, miners in a quarry in Yorkshire, England, were astonished when they discovered the skeleton of a huge creature buried in the rock. It was *Rhomaleosaurus*, one of the most fearsome predators of the Jurassic seas. At the time, the seas were ruled by two kinds of marine reptile—the dolphinlike ichthyosaurs and lizardlike creatures with long necks known as plesiosaurs. *Rhomaleosaurus* belonged to the plesiosaur family.

4.6 billion years ago	542 million years ago	488		444		416		359		299		251
Precambrian Eon		Cambrian		Ordovician		Silurian		Devonian		Carboniferous		Permian

KILLER GRIP

Rhomaleosaurus used its cone-shaped fangs to attack large prey. Like a crocodile, it may have twisted its victims around violently to tear their bodies apart and make them easier to swallow.

CAMOUFLAGE

Like large sea animals today, *Rhomaleosaurus* may have had a pale belly and a dark back. This pattern, known as countershading, is a type of camouflage—it makes marine animals harder to see both from above and below.

Rhomaleosaurus
ROME-alley-oh-SORE-us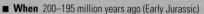

- **When** 200–195 million years ago (Early Jurassic)
- **Fossil location** England, Germany
- **Habitat** Coastal waters
- **Length** 15–21 ft (5–7 m)
- **Diet** Fish, squid, and ocean reptiles

Rhomaleosaurus was a pliosaur—a type of plesiosaur with a short neck. It hunted by sight and smell, perhaps allowing seawater to flow through its mouth and out of its nostrils so it could pick up the scent of prey. Fossilized remains of food in the bellies of pliosaurs reveal that their diet included squid, fish, and other plesiosaurs.

▶ FLIPPER
Rhomaleosaurus *swam by beating its four powerful flippers, using them like wings to "fly" through the water in the same way as penguins move underwater today.*

200	145	65	23	Now
Triassic	Jurassic	Cretaceous	Paleogene	Neogene

Ichthyosaurs

The ichthyosaurs were the largest sea-dwelling reptiles of all time. They evolved from land-living reptiles that adapted so well to life in the sea that some species came to resemble dolphins. Like dolphins, they fed, bred, and gave birth in water but had to return to the surface to breathe air.

FAMILY FACT FILE

Key features
- Large eyes for good underwater vision
- Flippers for steering and balance
- Vertical tail fin
- Gave birth to live babies rather than laying eggs
- Lungs for breathing air

When
Ichthyosaurs lived from about 245 million years ago (Triassic Period) to nearly 90 million years ago (Cretaceous Period).

Shonisaurus

SHON-ee-sore-us

- **When** 225–208 million years ago (Late Triassic)
- **Fossil location** N. America
- **Habitat** Oceans
- **Length** Up to 70 ft (20 m)
- **Diet** Fish, squid

Shonisaurus was like a cross between a whale and a dolphin, with an enormous body but a long, slender snout. Giant eyes and toothlessness in adults suggest it was a deep-diving squid hunter. One whale-sized specimen found in Canada was 70 ft (20 m) long—the largest marine reptile ever found.

Ophthalmosaurus

off-THAL-mo-SORE-uss

- **When** 165–150 million years ago (Late Jurassic)
- **Fossil location** Europe, N. America, Argentina
- **Habitat** Oceans
- **Length** 16 ft (5 m)
- **Diet** Fish, squid, mollusks

Rounded, streamlined shape

Eye socket

Flat, broad paddle

Ophthalmosaurus means "eye lizard." This ichthyosaur had the largest eyes relative to body size of any prehistoric animal. The eyes were as big as grapefruits and almost filled the skull. *Ophthalmosaurus* could probably see well in the dark and may have used its extraordinary vision to hunt in the depths of the sea. If so, it must also have been good at holding its breath for long periods on its trips into the deep.

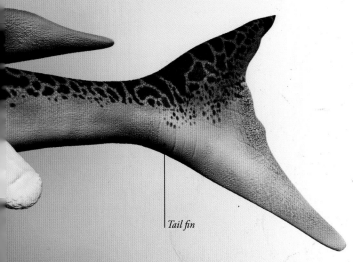

Tail fin

Mixosaurus

MIX-oh-SORE uss

- **When** 230 million years ago (Middle Triassic)
- **Fossil location** N. America, Europe, Asia
- **Habitat** Oceans
- **Length** Up to 3 ft 3 in (1 m)
- **Diet** Fish

Mixosaurus was one of the smallest ichthyosaurs. It swam by beating its tail from side to side, perhaps using bursts of speed to take shoals of fish by surprise. It caught prey in a long, narrow snout, which was lined with sharp teeth. Fossils of *Mixosaurus* have been found all over the world, indicating that the species lived throughout the oceans.

Ichthyosaurus

ICK-thee-oh-SORE-uss

- **When** 190 million years ago (Early Jurassic)
- **Fossil location** British Isles, Belgium, Germany
- **Habitat** Oceans
- **Length** 6 ft (1.8 m) long
- **Diet** Fish

Ichthyosaurus was a small, slim-snouted ichthyosaur. It had dozens of sharp, needlelike teeth and used them to catch squid or other kinds of mollusks. Studies of the ear bones of *Ichthyosaurus* show that it didn't have the highly sensitive hearing that dolphins have and couldn't detect objects in the water by using echoes (echolocation).

Stenopterygius

Long before dolphins first appeared, the seas of the Jurassic were home to reptiles that had evolved a remarkably similar body shape and lifestyle. These were the ichthyosaurs. One type of ichthyosaur, *Stenopterygius*, spent its life in the open ocean, where it hunted fish, cephalopods, and other marine animals.

Dorsal fin

In most large fossils only bones are visible, but in this remarkable Stenopterygius fossil, the fins, tail, and other soft tissues can be seen.

Backbone bends downward to support the tail.

Short hind limb

Stenopterygius

sten-OP-terr-idge-ee-us

- **When** Early to mid Jurassic
- **Fossil location** Argentina, UK, France, Germany
- **Habitat** Shallow oceans
- **Size** 13 ft (4 m) long

Like its close relative *Ichthyosaurus*, *Stenopterygius* was a dolphinlike reptile adapted to catching fish in its tooth-filled snout. Its streamlined shape and muscular fins suggest it could achieve a top speed of perhaps 60 mph (100 kph), enabling it to blast into shoals of fish like a torpedo and snatch prey in the resulting confusion.

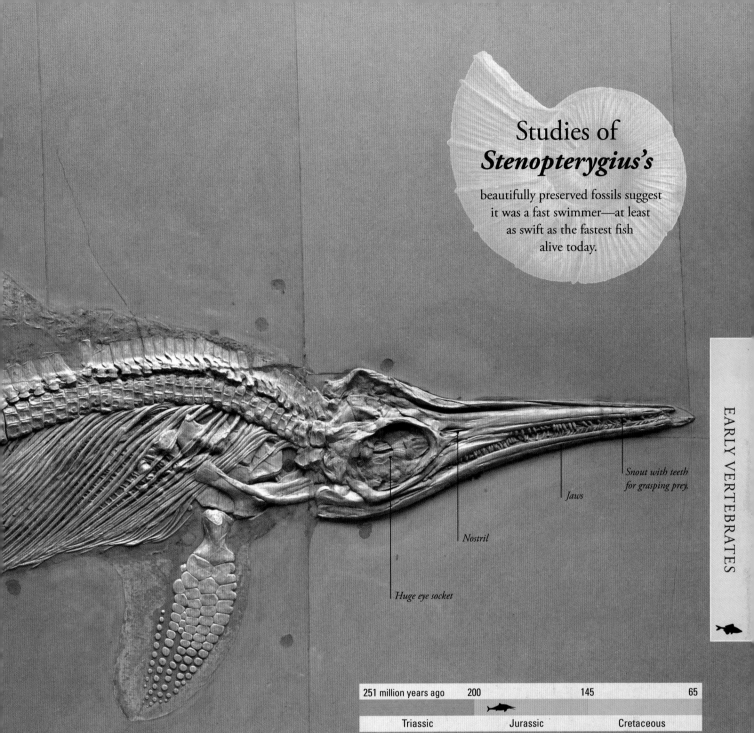

Studies of
Stenopterygius's

beautifully preserved fossils suggest
it was a fast swimmer—at least
as swift as the fastest fish
alive today.

Snout with teeth
for grasping prey.

Jaws

Nostril

Huge eye socket

251 million years ago	200		145	65
Triassic		Jurassic		Cretaceous

Birth of young

Although ichthyosaurs lived millions of years ago,
we know that these marine animals gave birth to
live young rather than laying eggs. How do we
know? It's because fossils have been discovered
that show females giving birth (always tail first).
However, it's highly unlikely that the parent cared
for its young after birth.

▶ ICHTHYOSAUR YOUNG,
such as this Stenopterygius,
*were probably self-sufficient
soon after birth.*

A young fossil hunter

In 1830, English geologist Henry De la Beche painted a curious watercolor with the intention of selling copies to raise money for a friend. The friend was Mary Anning, and the painting was the first time anyone had tried to draw a realistic picture of prehistoric life. Most amazing of all, Mary had discovered every animal in it.

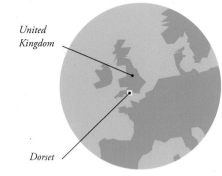

United Kingdom

Dorset

A look back in time
De la Beche called his painting *Duria Antiquior,* or "A more ancient Dorset." It featured animals that Mary had found as fossils on the coast of Dorset in England. Prints of this painting were passed around scientific circles in the 1800s, and influenced thinking on prehistoric life.

The painting showed an ichthyosaur capturing a plesiosaur.

WHAT WAS IT?

Anning spent months uncovering the body of her first fossil. It was later named *Ichthyosaurus*, which means "fish lizard." This marine reptile swam in the time of the dinosaurs.

▲ WHAT BIG EYES! *Huge eye sockets suggest that ichthyosaurs depended on their vision to hunt. They may even have hunted at night or in deep, dark waters.*

◀ HIDDEN TREASURES
The cliffs at Lyme Regis bay, where Anning hunted for fossils, are still an exciting place for fossil hunters.

WHO WAS MARY ANNING?

Mary Anning (1799–1847) was just 11 years old when her brother found the head of a large fossil on a beach. She was to become one of the most famous of all fossil hunters. Anning was never taken as seriously as she should have been because she was a woman and from a poor background, whereas most scientists of the time were men from wealthy families.

More amazing finds

The cliffs near where Anning lived are rich in fossils from the Jurassic Period. She found the first plesiosaur there in 1823 and the first pterosaur in 1828. She carefully recorded each find, before selling the fossils.

A precious notebook

Anning's life was not easy and was largely spent in poverty. She and one brother were the only survivors of 10 children, and she lacked an education. However, she managed to teach herself about the fossils she found and kept careful notes and sketches detailing each find. Over the years, her fossil-hunting successes would bring her huge recognition.

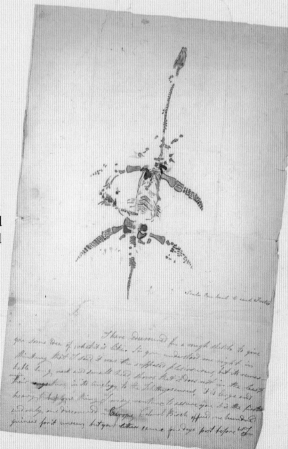

Plesiosaur sketch by Mary Anning

Mosasaurs

Just before the end of the Cretaceous Period, the seas were home to gigantic lizards as terrifying and as huge as any mythological sea serpent. Called mosasaurs, these monsters were close relatives of today's lizards and snakes. They evolved from small, land-living lizards that took to the water in search of food. As the lizards adapted to life in the sea, their legs turned into flippers and their bodies, supported by water, became enormous.

Mosasaurus

MOSE-ah-saw-rus

- **When** 70–65 million years ago (Late Cretaceous)
- **Fossil location** USA, Belgium, Japan, Netherlands, New Zealand, Morocco, Turkey
- **Habitat** Oceans
- **Length** About 50 ft (15 m)
- **Diet** Fish, squid, and shellfish

Mosasaurus was one of the largest mosasaurs. It looked a bit like a crocodile with flippers, and swam by moving its long body in slow waves. As a result, it couldn't swim fast over long distances, but might have been capable of sudden bursts of speed. Scientists think *Mosasaurus* lived in the well-lit surface waters of oceans, hunting slower-moving prey. Bite marks left by its huge, conical teeth have been found on turtle shells and ammonites. *Mosasaurus* survived to the end of the Cretaceous, when it vanished with the dinosaurs.

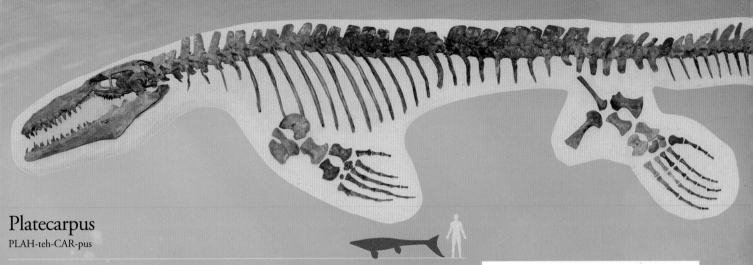

Platecarpus

PLAH-teh-CAR-pus

- **When** 85–80 million years ago (Late Cretaceous)
- **Fossil location** Worldwide
- **Habitat** Oceans
- **Length** 14 ft (4.2 m)

Platecarpus was not the largest mosasaur but it was certainly was one of the most abundant. Its fossils have been found worldwide, most commonly in the Niobrara chalk beds of North America. Like other mosasaurs, *Platecarpus* used its long, muscular tail to drive itself through water in a zigzag, snakelike manner. It had fewer and smaller teeth than other mosasaurs, suggesting a diet of softer prey such as fish and squid. The belly of one specimen was found to contain fish scales and fish bones—the remains of one of its last meals.

FAMILY FACT FILE

Key features
- Lizardlike bodies with flippers
- Powerful jaws lined with sharp teeth
- Breathed air at the water surface

When
Mosasaurs lived in the Cretaceous Period, between 85 and 65 million years ago. They were killed along with dinosaurs and most other large reptiles in the mass extinction at the end of the Period.

In the Cretaceous, an ocean ran down the middle of North America, cutting the continent in two. Its muddy bed has now turned to rock, forming the Niobrara chalk of North America. Niobrara chalk contains a wealth of amazing fossils, including mosasaurs and plesiosaurs.

DINOSAURS and BIRDS

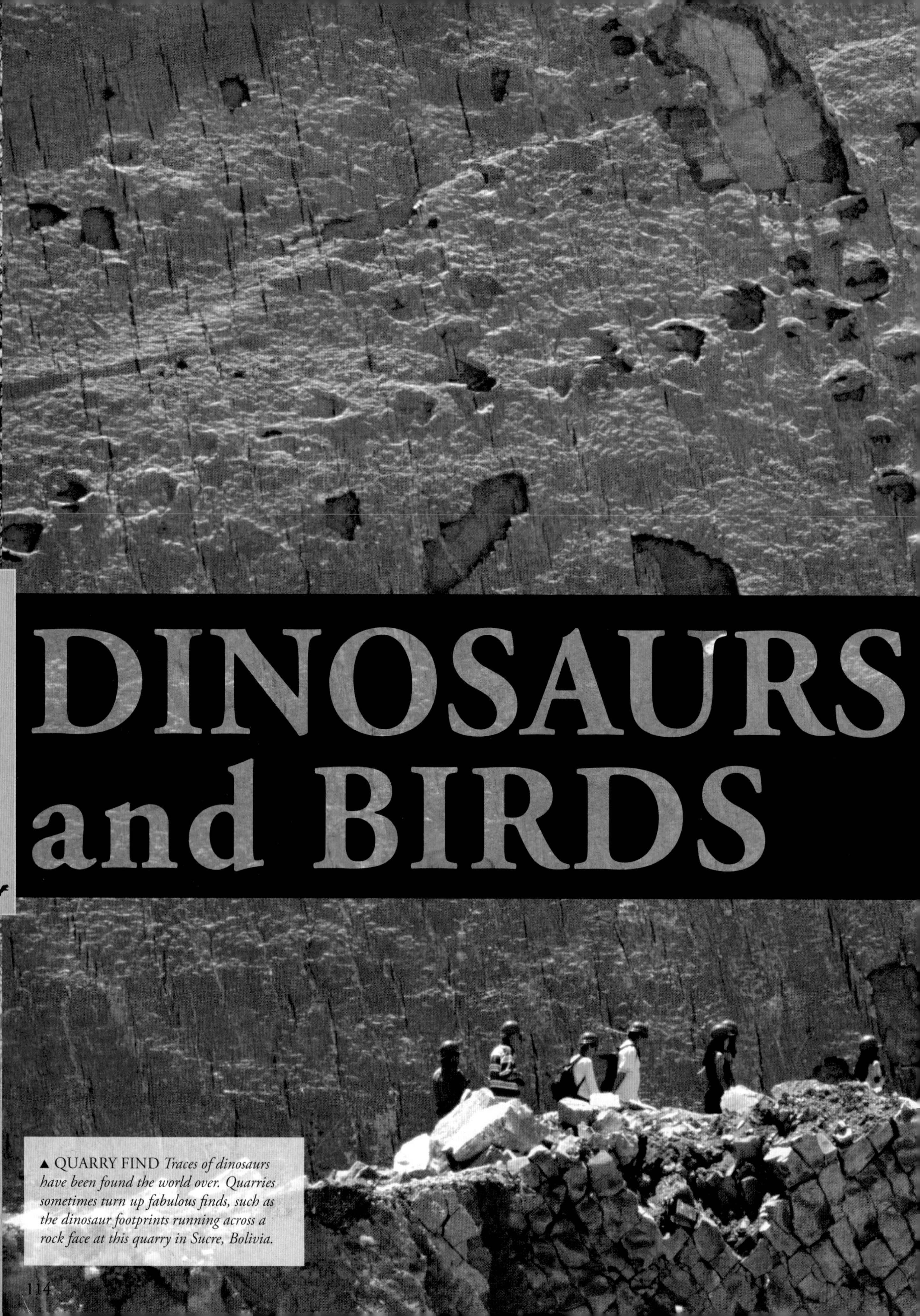

▲ QUARRY FIND *Traces of dinosaurs have been found the world over. Quarries sometimes turn up fabulous finds, such as the dinosaur footprints running across a rock face at this quarry in Sucre, Bolivia.*

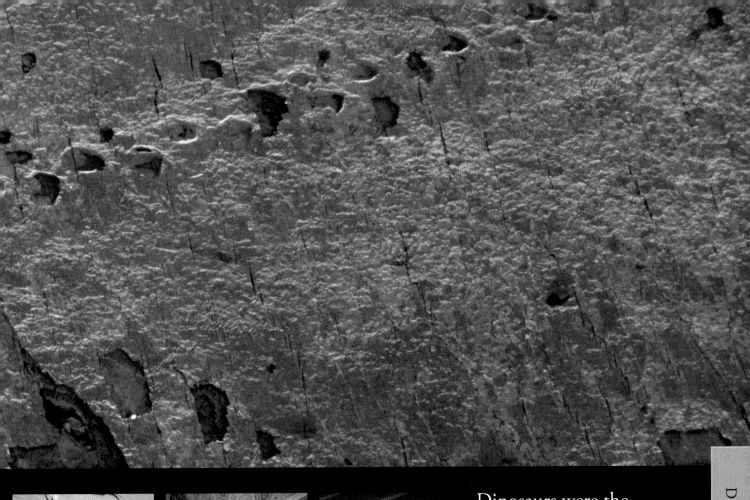

Dinosaurs were the dominant land animals on Earth for an unimaginably vast span of time: 160 million years. They were not entirely wiped out, and their descendants the birds survive to this day.

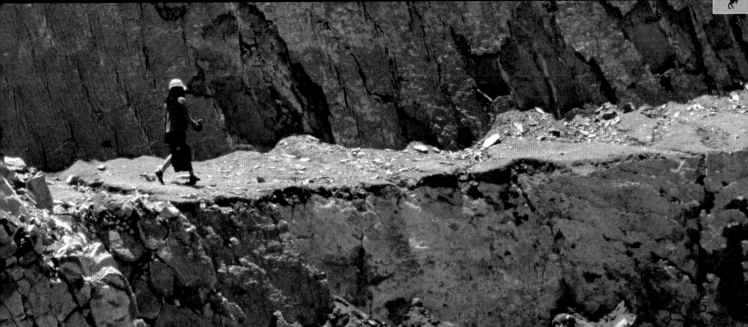

KILLER JAWS

Vast jaw muscles gave *Tyrannosaurus* possibly the most powerful bite of any animal in history. Its teeth were rock-solid spikes of enamel, able to puncture bone, hide, and muscle to inflict horrible injuries on animals

What are dinosaurs?

Dinosaurs survived for an astounding 160 million years (humans, in contrast, have existed for less than one million years). Ranging in size from animals no bigger than pigeons to lumbering giants the size of a truck, they were reptiles, but very different from modern-day reptiles.

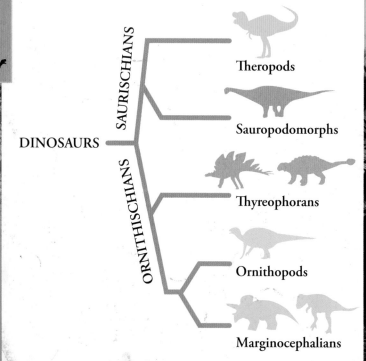

◀ WE'RE STILL HERE! *Most scientists believe that birds are the living descendants of small, meat-eating dinosaurs.*

FAMILY TREE

Dinosaurs can be split into two groups: the saurischians (or lizard-hipped dinosaurs) and the ornithischians (or bird-hipped dinosaurs). These can be split further, as shown below.

DINOSAURS

SAURISCHIANS
- Theropods
- Sauropodomorphs

ORNITHISCHIANS
- Thyreophorans
- Ornithopods
- Marginocephalians

FACT FILE

Key features
- Lived on land
- Built nests and laid eggs
- Most had scaly skin (some had feathers)
- Long tails, held off the ground
- Walked on upright, pillarlike legs.
- Holes ("windows") in the skulls of larger dinosaurs, making them lighter. (Only the armored dinosaurs had solid skulls.)
- Walked on their toes
- Claws on fingers and toes

One way in which dinosaurs differed from today's reptiles and lizards is that they could stand with their legs straight, in the same way as mammals. Some dinosaurs walked on two legs, some on four. Some may have done both.

▲ **DINOSAURS** *walked on upright, pillarlike legs.*

▲ **CROCODILES** *walked with knees and elbows bent.*

▲ **LIZARDS** *hold their legs at right-angles to the body.*

THYREOPHORANS (THIGH-ree-OFF-oh-rans)

Also called armored dinosaurs, members of this group of plant-eaters were large, walked on four feet, and had armor plates and spikes that protected them from attack. Some of these dinosaurs even had armored eyelids!

◀ KENTROSAURUS *had a double row of bony plates running along the center of its back.*

THEROPODS (THERRO-pods)

All meat-eating dinosaurs were saurischians, and they formed a group called the theropods. This is the group from which birds are descended. They ranged in size from the chicken-sized *Compsognathus* to monsters such as the mighty *Spinosaurus*.

SAUROPODOMORPHS (SORE-oh-POD-oh-morfs)

This group contained the heaviest and longest animals ever to walk on Earth. They were herbivores (plant-eaters) and would have had to graze constantly to obtain the energy they needed.

◄ SPINOSAURUS *had a massive skin "sail" that ran the length of its back.*

▲ BRACHIOSAURUS *Sauropods had tiny heads compared to their bodies.*

ORNITHOPODS (OR-nith-oh-pods)

These plant-eaters all roamed on two legs, so were able to use their forelimbs to grasp their food. They were immensely successful and very common. Fossils of these types of dinosaur have been found all over the world.

MARGINOCEPHALIANS (MAR-jee-no-sa-FAY-lee-ans)

This group of plant-eaters had heads that sported bony frills. (Marginocephalian means "fringed head.") Some walked on two legs, some on four. They were common dinosaurs in the Cretaceous and included the well-known *Triceratops*.

▲ IGUANODON, *an ornithopod, was the second dinosaur to be named.*

▲ EINIOSAURUS *had a forward-curving horn.*

Small ornithischians

The dinosaur family tree is split into two halves: saurischians and ornithischians. The ornithischians were plant-eaters with beaked jaws for plucking leaves and large bellies for digesting them. Though some ornithischians were huge, four-footed giants, many were small, two-footed herbivores that scurried about nervously in forests and scrublands, searching for food and trying to avoid predators.

FAMILY FACT FILE

Key features
- Plant-eaters
- Beaked jaws
- Back-pointing pubis bone
- Large belly for digesting vegetation

When
Ornithischians lived from the beginning of the Jurassic Period, 200 million years ago, to the end of the Cretaceous Period, 65 million years ago.

Heterodontosaurus

HET-er-oh-DON-toe-SORE-us

- **When** 200–190 million years ago (Early Jurassic)
- **Fossil location** S. Africa
- **Habitat** Scrubland
- **Length** 3 ft (1 m)
- **Diet** Plants, tubers, possibly insects

Unlike most dinosaurs, which had one type of tooth, *Heterodontosaurus* ("different-toothed lizard") had three types. Its sharp front teeth snipped off tough vegetation, which was then mashed to a pulp with its cheek teeth. It also had large, fanglike teeth to defend itself against enemies. The jaws were tipped with a horny beak that was probably used for plucking leaves.

◄ FOSSIL
Heterodontosaurus's *complete skeleton was found in 1976 with every bone in place.*

Hypsilophodon

HIP-sih-LOAF-oh-don

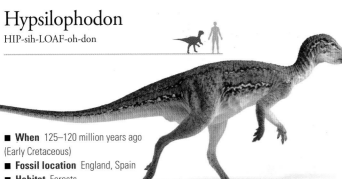

- **When** 125–120 million years ago (Early Cretaceous)
- **Fossil location** England, Spain
- **Habitat** Forests
- **Length** 7 ft (2 m)
- **Diet** Plants

Hypsilophodon was much like a modern deer, grazing on tender plants with its small, leaf-shaped teeth. Fossil footprints grouped together hint that these creatures roamed in herds like deer, though this is far from certain. Its stiff tail and long legs and feet show it was a fast-running ground animal, able to flee swiftly from predators on its hind legs while using its tail for balance.

Leaellynasaura

lee-ELL-in-ah-SORE-ah

- **When** 105 million years ago (Early Cretaceous)
- **Fossil location** Australia
- **Habitat** Forests
- **Length** 7 ft (2 m)
- **Diet** Plants

Leaellynasaura lived near the South Pole. Although it was less cold here during the Cretaceous Period than it is today, *Leaellynasaura* would have had to live without sunlight for several months of the year during polar winters. It had large eyes, which helped it see better in the dark and avoid predators. It was probably warm-blooded.

Lesothosaurus

li-SUE-too-SORE-us

- **When** 200–190 million years ago (Early Jurassic)
- **Fossil location** S. Africa
- **Habitat** Desert plains
- **Length** 3 ft (1 m)
- **Diet** Leaves, perhaps dead animals and insects

This dinosaur was named after Lesotho, the south African country where its fossils were first found in 1978. Scientists think *Lesothosaurus* was similar to a modern gazelle, grazing on low-lying plants and running away quickly at the first sight of predators. Its upper and lower teeth were small and shaped like arrowheads.

Othnielosaurus

oth-nee-ELL-oh-SORE-us

- **When** 155–145 million years ago (Late Jurassic)
- **Fossil location** USA
- **Habitat** Plains
- **Length** 7 ft (2 m)
- **Diet** Plants

Othnielosaurus moved swiftly on its strong back limbs, which were built for running. Its front limbs were short and weak, and its hands and fingers were small. Fossils show that its teeth were edged with many small ridges, making them well-suited for shredding leaves. Its vertebrae show that it had a short neck.

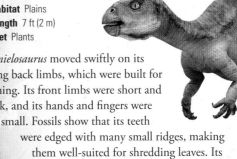

Pachycephalosaurus

This herbivore had a mysterious dome of solid bone at the top of its skull, but what for? One old theory is that males had head-butting contests like rams—but their curved necks might not have been able to take the force. Another theory is that they swung their heavy heads sideways at each other like giraffes. Or perhaps their fancy heads merely served to impress mates and rivals.

Last of the dinosaurs

Pachycephalosaurus lived at the end of the Cretaceous Period and was one of the species wiped out in the dinosaurs' mass extinction.

🦖 DID YOU KNOW...?

Pachycephalosaurus is known only from one complete skull (a replica of which is shown below) and a few skull fragments. The dome of thick bone on its skull was fringed by bony knobs and spikes, which may have been used for display. Its teeth were tiny and its eyes large.

Dome

Large eye sockets

Small teeth

251 million years ago	200		145		65
	Triassic		Jurassic		Cretaceous

Pachycephalosaurus
PACK-ee-sef-ah-low-SORE-us

- **When** 65 million years ago (Late Cretaceous)
- **Fossil location** N. America
- **Habitat** Forests of N. America
- **Length** 16 ft (5 m)
- **Diet** Plants, soft fruit, seeds

By comparing *Pachycephalosaurus*'s few fossils with those of its relatives, scientists figure that this dinosaur was about as long as a station wagon. It probably had a bulky body but the long, slender hind legs of a fast runner. Its small teeth suggest a diet of easily digested plants or, perhaps, a mixture of plants and animal foods such as eggs.

Ceratopsians

The plant-eating ceratopsians varied from sheep-sized animals to sturdy giants that were bigger than elephants. They grazed in the forests and plains of North America and Asia, perhaps in herds. They had huge, parrotlike beaks that they used to grasp and rip up plants. With their towering horns and huge neck frills, they must have been a spectacular sight.

FAMILY FACT FILE

Key features
- Massive hooked beaks for grasping plants
- Hundreds of chisel-edged teeth for slicing through leaves like scissors
- Large horns and neck frills, mainly for display
- Short legs
- Hooflike bones on fingers and toes

When
These dinosaurs thrived in the Cretaceous Period, around 80 million years ago. The last of the ceratopsians died out in the mass extinction at the end of the Cretaceous Period, 65 million years ago.

Einiosaurus

ie-nee-o-SAWR-uss

- **When** 74–65 million years ago (Late Cretaceous)
- **Fossil location** USA
- **Habitat** Woodland
- **Length** 20 ft (6 m)
- **Diet** Plants

In 1985, scientists found fossils of 15 *Einiosaurus* individuals in the same site in the USA—perhaps they were members of a herd that died together in a flood or landslide. *Einiosaurus* had an impressive frill with a wavy margin and two long horns that pointed upward. The horns were probably used for both display and fighting.

Chasmosaurus

KAS-mo-SAWR-uss

- **When** 74–65 million years ago (Late Cretaceous)
- **Fossil location** N. America
- **Habitat** Woodland
- **Length** 16 ft (5 m)
- **Diet** Palms and cycads

Chasmosaurus's neck frill has huge holes that would have been covered by skin. The frill could have been tilted upright to attract attention or startle enemies and may have been brightly colored.

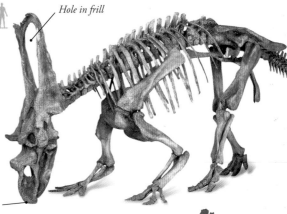

Hole in frill

Parrotlike beak

Styracosaurus

sty-RACK-oh-SORE-uss

- **When** 74–65 million years ago (Late Cretaceous)
- **Fossil location** N. America
- **Habitat** Open woodland
- **Length** 17 ft (5.2 m)
- **Diet** Ferns and cycads

Styracosaurus's magnificent frill sported six spikes up to 2 ft (60 cm) long that may have served as decoration to attract mates. *Styracosaurus* had a large, deep snout with huge nostrils, and a short, blunt horn. Its sharp teeth could cut through thick vegetation and were constantly replaced.

Pentaceratops

PEN-ta-SERRA-tops

- **When** 74–65 million years ago (Late Cretaceous)
- **Fossil location** USA
- **Habitat** Wooded plains
- **Length** 16–26 ft (5–8 m)
- **Diet** Plants

A huge head was the most remarkable feature of this dinosaur. One fossil skull, built from broken fragments, is more than 10 ft (3 m) long, making it the longest skull of any land animal in history. *Pentaceratops* means "five-horned face"—the dinosaur had one horn on the snout, two curved horns on the brow, and a small horn on each cheek.

Sturdy leg

Protoceratops

PRO-toe-SERRA-tops

- **When** 74–65 million years ago (Late Cretaceous)
- **Fossil location** Mongolia
- **Habitat** Desert
- **Length** 6 ft (1.8 m)
- **Diet** Desert plants

Tiny horn between eyes

Many well-preserved fossils of this small ceratopsian have been found in Mongolia's Gobi Desert. *Protoceratops* had a wide neck frill at the back of its skull that expanded with age and was larger in males. It also had broad, spadelike claws, perhaps for digging burrows.

Triceratops

As heavy as a 10-ton truck, *Triceratops* was built like a huge rhinoceros. It gets its name ("three-horned face") from the short nose horn and two longer brow horns. *Triceratops* used its horns and frills like deers use their antlers—to attract mates.

BATTLE SCARS

Bite marks left by the ferocious *Tyrannosaurus* on some *Triceratops* skulls suggest there were fierce clashes between the two species millions of years ago. One *Triceratops* even seems to have had a brow horn snapped off.

251 million years ago	200	145	65
Triassic	Jurassic	Cretaceous	

Brow horn over 3 ft (1 m) long

Single row of teeth on each side of lower jaw

Triceratops

try-SERRA-tops

- ■ **When** 70–65 million years ago (Late Cretaceous)
- ■ **Fossil location** N. America
- ■ **Habitat** Woodland
- ■ **Length** 30 ft (9 m)
- ■ **Diet** Forest plants

Triceratops's neck was probably quite flexible, helping it to feed not only on tree leaves but also on low-growing plants. Its powerful parrotlike beak helped it pluck tough forest vegetation, such as palms, ferns, and cycads. Its teeth were like scissors—shredding and snipping the plants.

Torosaurus skull

Window in frill

▶ FRILL

Around the back of *Triceratops's skull was a huge frill made of bone. The horns and frill were once thought to be used for defence, but many experts now believe they were used to attract females during the mating season.*

▶ TOROSAURUS

The dinosaur Torosaurus *was very much like* Triceratops *but had a larger frill with windows in it. Some scientists are unsure whether* Torosaurus *was a separate species and wonder if it may simply have been a mature* Triceratops *in which the shield had developed windows.*

127

Iguanodontians

The iguanodontians were among the most common and widespread dinosaurs of the Late Jurassic and the Cretaceous. They varied from small, nondescript dinosaurs to giants with horselike faces and huge sails on their backs, but all had beaked mouths for eating plants. The iguanodontian group also includes the large duck-billed dinosaur family (next page).

(next page).

FAMILY FACT FILE

Key features
- Toothless beaks for clipping plants
- Hooflike claws
- Mobile jaws able to chew plants
- Stiff tails

When
Iguanodontians appeared 156 million years ago, in the Late Jurassic Period. They died out at the end of the Cretaceous Period, 65 million years ago.

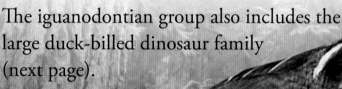

Iguanodon

ig-GWAH-no-don

- **When** 135–125 million years ago (Early Cretaceous)
- **Fossil location** Belgium, Germany, France, Spain, England
- **Habitat** Woodlands
- **Length** 30 ft (9 m)
- **Diet** Plants

Discovered in the 1820s, *Iguanodon* was the second prehistoric animal to be identified as a dinosaur. Its name means "iguana teeth" as its teeth looked like those of an iguana but were 20 times bigger. *Iguanodon* was as big as an elephant and walked mainly on all fours, feeding on low-growing plants. Its hind legs were larger and more powerful than its front legs, allowing it to stand and perhaps run on two feet.

Little finger

Thumb spike

▶ HANDY
The three middle fingers of Iguanodon's hands were joined to form a hoof. It could fold its little finger across its palm to grasp objects, and its thumb had a vicious spike, perhaps for self-defense.

Dryosaurus
DRY-oh-SORE-us

- **When** 155–145 million years ago (Late Jurassic)
- **Fossil location** USA
- **Habitat** Woodlands
- **Length** 10 ft (3 m)
- **Diet** Leaves and shoots

This small and lightly built herbivore had long and powerful legs—a sign that it was a fast runner. It had a stiff tail to help balance its body while running and may have flicked the tail sideways to make sharp turns to dodge obstacles or outwit pursuers.

Short arms may have meant it couldn't go down on all fours.

Long, horselike face

Camptosaurus
CAMP-toe-SORE-us

- **When** 155–145 million years ago (Late Jurassic)
- **Fossil location** USA
- **Habitat** Open woodlands
- **Length** 16 ft (5 m)
- **Diet** Low-growing herbs and shrubs

Camptosaurus was one of the most common iguanodontians and looked like a small version of *Iguanodon*, with a similar long, horselike face tipped by a beak. Its hands, like those of *Iguanodon*, had hooflike middle fingers and a thumb spike.

Muttaburrasaurus
MOO-tah-BUH-ruh-SORE-us

- **When** 100–98 million years ago (Early Cretaceous)
- **Fossil location** Australia
- **Habitat** Woodlands
- **Length** 23 ft (7 m)
- **Diet** Plants

The bone forming the top of *Muttaburrasaurus*'s snout bulged upward, giving this dinosaur an arched nose. It may have used its large nasal chambers to create honking sounds or to warm cold air as it breathed in. The size and shape of its snout differed between individuals and probably varied with sex and age.

Tenontosaurus
ten-NON-toe-SORE-us

- **When** 115–108 million years ago (Early Cretaceous)
- **Fossil location** USA
- **Habitat** Woodlands
- **Length** 23 ft (7 m)
- **Diet** Plants

Some dinosaurs are famous for having served as lunch for others. *Tenontosaurus* was one such unfortunate creature. Remains of this herbivore are often found with teeth of the small but ferocious carnivore *Deinonychus*, which may have brought down the bigger dinosaur by hunting in packs. Bones of both have also been found together, suggesting that *Deinonychus* didn't always survive the battles.

Hadrosaurids

Also known as "duck-billed" dinosaurs, the hadrosaurids were large plant-eaters with distinctive, ducklike bills that they used to clip leaves from plants. Hadrosaurids may have lived in large herds, and some types seem to have formed nesting colonies in which parents nursed their young after hatching.

Maiasaura
MY-a-SORE-a

- **When** 80–74 million years ago (Late Cretaceous)
- **Fossil location** USA
- **Habitat** Coastal plains
- **Length** 30 ft (9 m)
- **Diet** Leaves

The name *Maiasaura* means "good mother lizard." In Montana, scientists found numerous bowl-shaped *Maiasaura* nests close together. The site may have been a nesting colony where parents raised their young, like nesting colonies of modern seabirds.

▲ FAMILY LIFE *Fossilized eggshell pieces and young* Maiasaura *were discovered in nests in Montana. The presence of young animals suggests that hatchlings stayed in the nest while being looked after, just as many baby birds do, rather than leaving immediately as newly hatched turtles and crocodiles do.*

FAMILY FACT FILE

Key features
- Ducklike bills
- Rear of mouth was packed with thousands of teeth for grinding leaves
- Forelimbs were half as long as hindlimbs
- Many hadrosaurids had strangely shaped crests on their heads

When
Hadrosaurids lived in the Cretaceous Period, between 100 and 65 million years ago.

Hadrosaurus

HAD-roh-SORE-uss

- **When** 80–74 million years ago (Late Cretaceous)
- **Fossil location** N. America
- **Habitat** Woodlands
- **Length** 30 ft (9 m)
- **Diet** Leaves and twigs

This was one of the first dinosaurs discovered in North America. *Hadrosaurus* used a toothless beak to tear twigs and leaves from plants before grinding them to a pulp with hundreds of tiny teeth located in the back of its mouth.

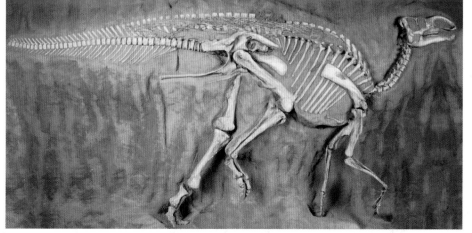

Brachylophosaurus

BRACK-ee-LOAF-oh-SORE-uss

- **When** 75–65 million years ago (Late Cretaceous)
- **Fossil location** N. America
- **Habitat** Woodlands
- **Length** 30 ft (9 m)
- **Diet** Ferns, magnolias, and conifers

Brachylophosaurus had a deep snout and a rectangular skull with a flat, paddle-shaped crest on its head. Males had wider crests and were more heavily built than females. In 2000, a near-perfect fossil skeleton was found in Montana. Large areas of its body were covered with an impression of its scaly skin.

Deep snout

Wide tip of jaw

Parasaurolophus

PA-ra-SORE-oh-LOAF-uss

- **When** 76–74 million years ago (Late Cretaceous)
- **Fossil location** N. America
- **Habitat** Woodlands
- **Length** 30 ft (9 m)
- **Diet** Leaves, seeds, and pine needles

This creature's head had a long, tubelike crest containing hollow tubes. Perhaps *Parasaurolophus* tooted air out of the crest to make trumpetlike sounds to communicate with herd members. Its heavy, muscular build and wide shoulders may have helped it push through dense under-growth in woodlands.

Lambeosaurus

LAMB-ee-oh-SORE-uss

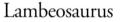

- **When** 76–74 million years ago (Late Cretaceous)
- **Fossil location** Canada
- **Habitat** Woodlands
- **Length** 30 ft (9 m)
- **Diet** Low-growing leaves, fruits, and seeds

Lambeosaurus's hollow crest was shaped like a hatchet. Perhaps the distinctive shape enabled this dinosaur to recognize others of its species quickly. The crest's shape varied between the sexes, suggesting that males used theirs to impress females.

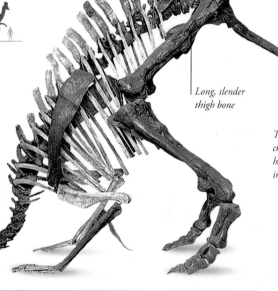

Long, slender thigh bone

▲ STIFF TAIL
All hadrosaurids had stiff, horizontal tails, the tail bones interlocking to prevent sagging.

The crest's shape changed as the hadrosaurid grew into an adult.

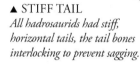

Gryposaurus

GRIP-o-SAWR-us

- **When** 65–85 million years ago (Late Cretaceous)
- **Fossil location** N. America
- **Habitat** Woodlands
- **Length** 30 ft (9 m)
- **Diet** Vegetation

Gryposaurus's large, hooked nose looked like a rounded beak. Rivals may have settled contests by butting noses and shoving each other. *Gryposaurus* also had very long arms for a hadrosaurid—perhaps they helped it reach higher leaves. Skin impressions suggest the animal had pyramid-shaped scales on its back.

131

Dinosaur droppings

Perhaps the most surprising of all dinosaur fossils are coprolites—fossilized poop. Coprolites have been found all over the world, since they were first recognized for what they were in the 1830s. They can tell us a lot about dinosaurs, most importantly, what they ate.

AN UNUSUAL COLLECTION

Karen Chin is a world expert on fossilized dinosaur dung and has a huge collection of coprolites. She cuts slices to look at under a microscope and discover what is inside—whether it be small bones or leaves or seeds.

Let's use it!

In the nineteenth century, coprolites were actually mined in parts of England and turned into fertilizer. They were rich in a substance called phosphate that was needed to help crops grow to feed a quickly expanding population.

Karen Chin found small, fossilized burrows in the coprolites of plant-eating dinosaurs. With this evidence, she discovered that dung beetles were clearing dung in the age of the dinosaurs, just as they do today.

▲ DUNG BEETLE *with dung ball.*

DINOSAURS AND BIRDS

One of the biggest

The huge coprolite below was found to contain chewed bits of bone from a cow-sized meat-eating dinosaur. It's thought to have been a *Tyrannosaurus's* dropping and measures 15 inches (38 cm) in length, although fragments found nearby suggest it was originally larger. Few dinosaur coprolites are preserved exactly as they were formed, and it's tricky to link them to a particular dinosaur.

▲ FRAGMENTS *of bone found in this* Tyrannosaurus *coprolite show that the predator swallowed bones as well as flesh.*

It's a dropping!

The fossil hunter Mary Anning (see pages 110–111) found stones in the belly region of the fossils she uncovered and described them as containing fossilized fish bones. Based on her finds, scientist William Buckland gave them the Greek name *coprolites*, meaning "dung stones."

Corythosaurus

Several complete skeletons of *Corythosaurus* were found in North America, making it one of the best-known members of the hadrosaurid family. This crested, duck-billed dinosaur wandered through the swamps and woodlands of the region 75 million years ago, perhaps in herds. Its crest may have been used as a trumpet to keep in touch with the herd.

WOODLAND HABITAT
Like most hadrosaurids, *Corythosaurus* lived in woodlands covering warm plains near the Rocky Mountains in North America. Its snout was smaller and more delicate than those of other hadrosaurids, suggesting a diet of tender leaves and juicy fruits.

Headdress

Corythosaurus means "helmet lizard." Scientists named it so because of the crest on its head, which reminded them of helmets worn by the soldiers of ancient Greece.

- **When** 76–74 million years ago (Late Cretaceous)
- **Fossil location** Canada, N. America
- **Habitat** Forests and swampy areas
- **Length** 30 ft (9 m)
- **Diet** Leaves, seeds, and pine needles

Corythosaurus was one of the larger hadrosaurids. Tall, bony spines on its back were covered with a frill of skin that formed a ridge running along its back. This frill was very prominent at the back of the head crest, where it was attached.

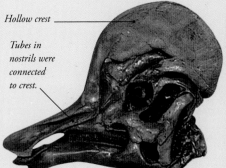

Hollow crest

Tubes in nostrils were connected to crest.

▲ SKULL

Corythosaurus's crest may have worked like a trombone, amplifying sound to make loud, booming calls that carried a long way. Perhaps these served as warning signals to alert other herd members of predators lurking nearby.

▲ FOSSILIZED SKIN

Of the skeletons discovered, some had well-preserved impressions of skin. A few of these showed that Corythosaurus's belly had strange, wartlike lumps.

DINOSAURS AND BIRDS

251 million years ago	200		145		65
	Triassic	Jurassic		Cretaceous	

Edmontosaurus

Twice as big as a fire truck, *Edmontosaurus* was one of the largest duck-billed dinosaurs (hadrosaurids) and lived alongside other giant dinosaurs such as *Triceratops* and *Tyrannosaurus*, about 66 million years ago. Like other hadrosaurids, *Edmontosaurus* had a ducklike bill for cropping leaves, but its head had no crest.

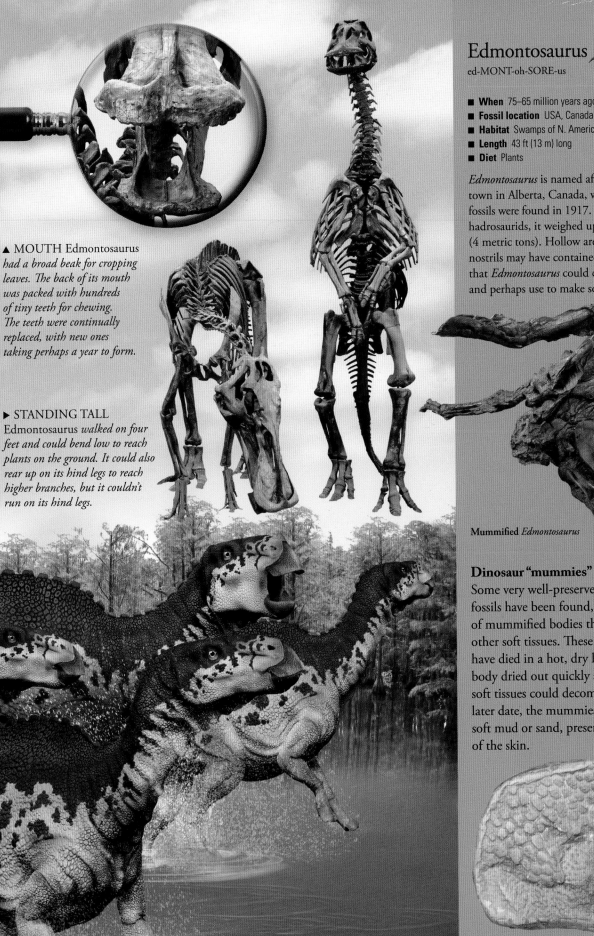

Edmontosaurus
ed-MONT-oh-SORE-us

- **When** 75–65 million years ago (Late Cretaceous)
- **Fossil location** USA, Canada
- **Habitat** Swamps of N. America
- **Length** 43 ft (13 m) long
- **Diet** Plants

Edmontosaurus is named after Edmonton town in Alberta, Canada, where the first fossils were found in 1917. One of the largest hadrosaurids, it weighed up to 4½ tons (4 metric tons). Hollow areas around its nostrils may have contained inflatable sacs that *Edmontosaurus* could expand like balloons and perhaps use to make sounds.

▲ MOUTH Edmontosaurus *had a broad beak for cropping leaves. The back of its mouth was packed with hundreds of tiny teeth for chewing. The teeth were continually replaced, with new ones taking perhaps a year to form.*

▶ STANDING TALL
Edmontosaurus *walked on four feet and could bend low to reach plants on the ground. It could also rear up on its hind legs to reach higher branches, but it couldn't run on its hind legs.*

Mummified *Edmontosaurus* — Preserved skin

Dinosaur "mummies"
Some very well-preserved *Edmontosaurus* fossils have been found, including fossils of mummified bodies that show skin and other soft tissues. These animals seem to have died in a hot, dry location where the body dried out quickly after death, before soft tissues could decompose. At some later date, the mummies were buried in soft mud or sand, preserving an imprint of the skin.

▲ SKIN IMPRESSION *Fossilized skin impressions reveal that* Edmontosaurus *had scaly skin with large bumps.*

251 million years ago	200	145	65
Triassic	Jurassic	Cretaceous	

Scelidosaurus

The most striking thing about *Scelidosaurus* was its armor. Rows of bony studs and spikes, some as big as a fist, ran from the head to the tail of this plant eater from the Early Jurassic. The armor probably made *Scelidosaurus* a slow mover and forced it to walk on four legs rather than two, but speed wasn't its main defense.

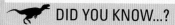
Scelidosaurus was discovered in 1858 by James Harrison, an English quarry worker, and was one of the first dinosaur skeletons found. Encased in hard limestone that was difficult to remove, the bones were largely hidden from view for more than 100 years. In the 1960s, scientists figured out how to dissolve the limestone with acid, and the whole skeleton has now been uncovered.

DINOSAURS AND BIRDS

251 million years ago	200	145	65
Triassic	Jurassic	Cretaceous	

Scelidosaurus

SKELL-ih-doe-SORE-uss

- **When** 208–195 million years ago (Early Jurassic)
- **Fossil location** England, USA
- **Habitat** Woodlands of western Europe and N. America
- **Length** 12 ft (4 m)
- **Diet** Plants

All *Scelidosaurus* fossils have been found in
rocks that formed on the seafloor, but this
animal wasn't a sea creature. Perhaps it lived near
the coast or perhaps a flood farther inland killed
a great number of the dinosaurs and washed
them out to sea. A plant-eater, *Scelidosaurus*
probably chomped on low-growing vegetation,
shredding leaves with its pointed teeth. It lived
in the Early Jurassic and was an early member of
a family of dinosaurs known as thyreophorans
("shield bearers," named for their armor).

Stegosaurs

The woodlands of the Jurassic Period teemed with massive, four-legged plant-eaters called stegosaurs. Members of the stegosaur family often had defensive spikes on their tails and shoulders, and rows of bony plates ran along their backs. The purpose of the plates is a mystery, but they may have been used for display or temperature control.

▼ SPIKES
Each shoulder had a large spike. Pairs of smaller spikes lined the tail. The spikes probably helped ward off attackers.

 FAMILY FACT FILE

Key features
- Double row of plates or spikes along the neck, back, and tail
- Narrow head
- Beaklike tip of mouth
- Hooflike toes
- Walked on all fours

When
Stegosaurs lived from 176 million years ago (Middle Jurassic) to 100 million years ago (Early Cretaceous).

Stegosaurus
STEG-oh-SORE-uss

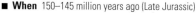

- **When** 150–145 million years ago (Late Jurassic)
- **Fossil location** USA, Portugal
- **Habitat** Woodland
- **Length** 30 ft (9 m)
- **Diet** Plants

Large, diamond-shaped plates ran along the back of this famous dinosaur. Although the plates would have made *Stegosaurus* look bigger and more fearsome, they were no good as armor. It's more likely they evolved for use in social or courtship displays. *Stegosaurus* had a toothless beak made of a hornlike substance. At the back of its mouth were rows of teeth that it used to crush leaves, chewing them to a pulp with simple up-and-down movements.

Each plate was covered with a tough, hornlike layer or skin.

The hindlimb was twice as long as the forelimb.

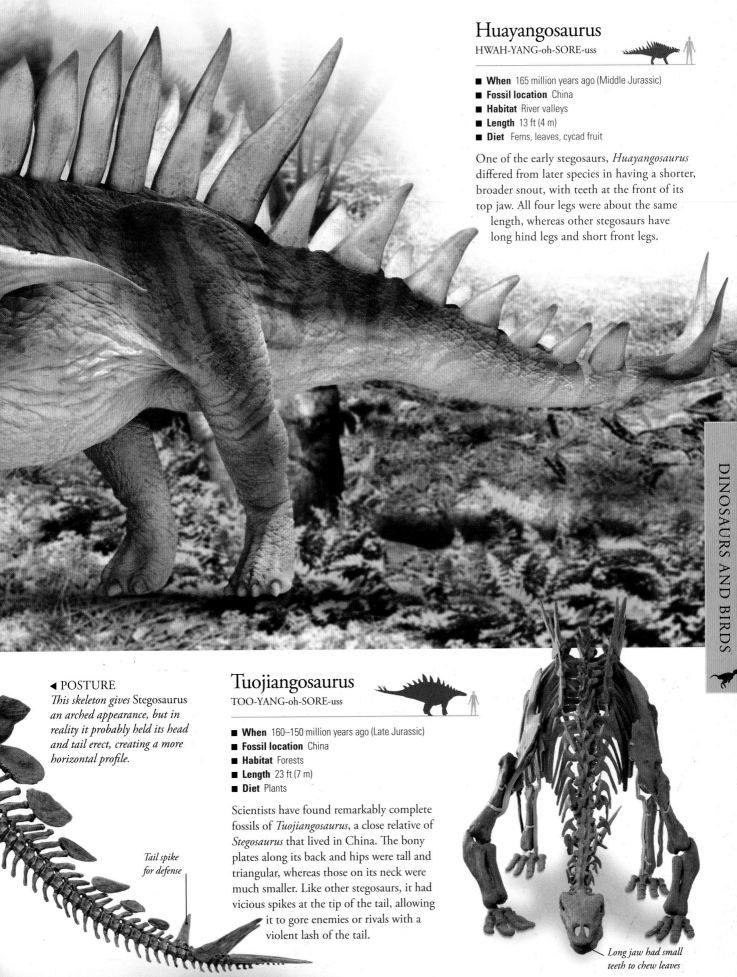

Huayangosaurus
HWAH-YANG-oh-SORE-uss

- ■ **When** 165 million years ago (Middle Jurassic)
- ■ **Fossil location** China
- ■ **Habitat** River valleys
- ■ **Length** 13 ft (4 m)
- ■ **Diet** Ferns, leaves, cycad fruit

One of the early stegosaurs, *Huayangosaurus* differed from later species in having a shorter, broader snout, with teeth at the front of its top jaw. All four legs were about the same length, whereas other stegosaurs have long hind legs and short front legs.

◄ POSTURE

This skeleton gives Stegosaurus an arched appearance, but in reality it probably held its head and tail erect, creating a more horizontal profile.

Tail spike for defense

Tuojiangosaurus
TOO-YANG-oh-SORE-uss

- ■ **When** 160–150 million years ago (Late Jurassic)
- ■ **Fossil location** China
- ■ **Habitat** Forests
- ■ **Length** 23 ft (7 m)
- ■ **Diet** Plants

Scientists have found remarkably complete fossils of *Tuojiangosaurus*, a close relative of *Stegosaurus* that lived in China. The bony plates along its back and hips were tall and triangular, whereas those on its neck were much smaller. Like other stegosaurs, it had vicious spikes at the tip of the tail, allowing it to gore enemies or rivals with a violent lash of the tail.

Long jaw had small teeth to chew leaves

141

Kentrosaurus

Kentrosaurus was a member of the stegosaur family, which lived in what is now central Africa. Its name means "sharp-point lizard"—its shoulders, back, and tail bore fearsome spikes that must have made it difficult for carnivores to attack.

Out of Africa

Tendaguru, in the dry woodlands of Tanzania, Africa, is a site famous for fossils of dinosaurs. Two complete skeletons of *Kentrosaurus* have been assembled from the 900 or so bones found there.

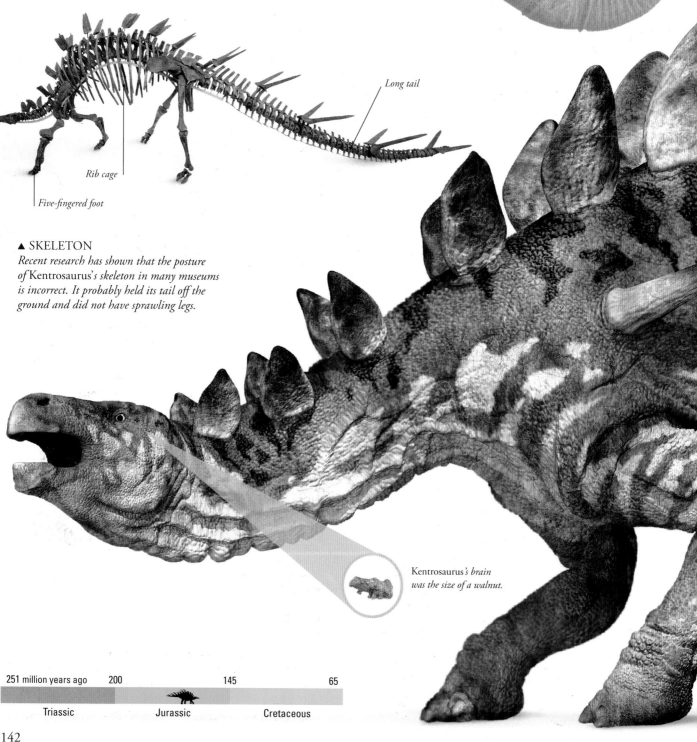

Long tail

Rib cage

Five-fingered foot

▲ SKELETON
Recent research has shown that the posture of Kentrosaurus's *skeleton in many museums is incorrect. It probably held its tail off the ground and did not have sprawling legs.*

Kentrosaurus's brain was the size of a walnut.

251 million years ago	200	145	65
Triassic	Jurassic	Cretaceous	

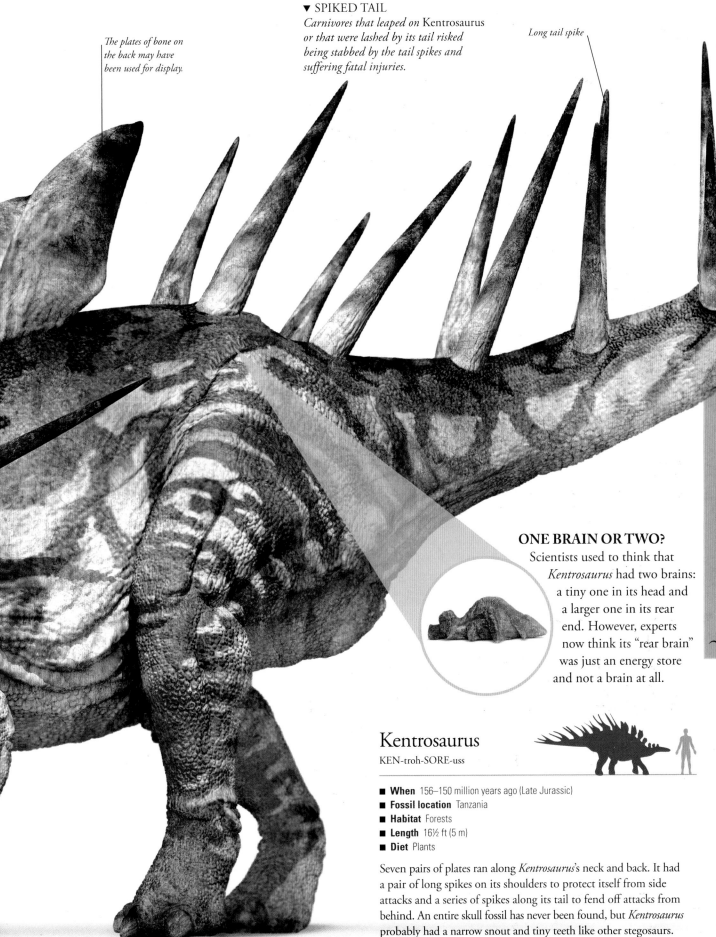

The plates of bone on the back may have been used for display.

▼ SPIKED TAIL
Carnivores that leaped on Kentrosaurus or that were lashed by its tail risked being stabbed by the tail spikes and suffering fatal injuries.

Long tail spike

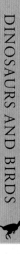

ONE BRAIN OR TWO?

Scientists used to think that *Kentrosaurus* had two brains: a tiny one in its head and a larger one in its rear end. However, experts now think its "rear brain" was just an energy store and not a brain at all.

Kentrosaurus

KEN-troh-SORE-uss

- ■ **When** 156–150 million years ago (Late Jurassic)
- ■ **Fossil location** Tanzania
- ■ **Habitat** Forests
- ■ **Length** 16½ ft (5 m)
- ■ **Diet** Plants

Seven pairs of plates ran along *Kentrosaurus*'s neck and back. It had a pair of long spikes on its shoulders to protect itself from side attacks and a series of spikes along its tail to fend off attacks from behind. An entire skull fossil has never been found, but *Kentrosaurus* probably had a narrow snout and tiny teeth like other stegosaurs.

143

Ankylosaurs

Also known as the "armored dinosaurs" or "tank dinosaurs," the members of this family were built like tanks. Their squat bodies were covered with defensive armor plates and spikes formed from bony growths that developed in the skin. Without this protection, these plant-eaters would have been at the mercy of much swifter and sometimes bigger carnivores.

Edmontonia

ED-mon-TOE-nee-a

- **When** 75–65 million years ago (Late Cretaceous)
- **Fossil location** N. America
- **Habitat** Woodlands
- **Length** 23 ft (7 m)
- **Diet** Low-growing plants

Edmontonia was twice the weight of a rhino and armed with huge spikes jutting out of its shoulders. Perhaps it drove off attackers by charging and lunging into them, using the spikes as spears. Some scientists think it used its lethal shoulder spikes to fight others of its own kind in battles over territory or mates.

Shoulder spike

Ankylosaurus

ANK-ill-oh-SORE-us

- **When** 70–65 million years ago (Late Cretaceous)
- **Fossil location** N. America
- **Habitat** Woodlands
- **Length** 20 ft (6 m)
- **Diet** Low-growing plants

Ankylosaurus was the largest ankylosaur ever. Hundreds of armor plates studded its thick skin, and small armor plates even covered its eyelids. The armor formed from bony plates called osteoderms that grew within the skin, much like the armor plating of a crocodile's skin. *Ankylosaurus* was also equipped with a huge tail club that it could swing at attackers with bone-shattering force.

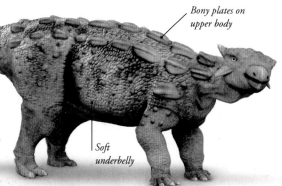

Bony plates on upper body

Long tail tipped with bony club

Soft underbelly

Minmi

MIN-mee

- **When** 120–115 million years ago (Early Cretaceous)
- **Fossil location** Australia
- **Habitat** Scrubby and wooded plains
- **Length** 10 ft (3 m)
- **Diet** Leaves, seeds, small fruit

Minmi was one of the smallest of the ankylosaurs. Small, rounded armor plates covered its body, including its belly. Extra bones along its back may have supported its back muscles. Its beak was sharp, and it had small, leaf-shaped teeth with sawtooth edges. Fossilized food remains in the belly of *Minmi* reveal that it ate leaves, seeds, and small fruits.

Tail bones

Ribs

Short, sturdy legs

Gastonia

gas-TOE-nee-ah

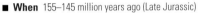

- **When** 125 million years ago (Early Cretaceous)
- **Fossil location** USA
- **Habitat** Woodlands
- **Length** 13 ft (4 m)
- **Diet** Plants

Only the bravest or most desperate predator would risk attacking *Gastonia*. A walking fortress, it was covered from head to tail with rows of huge, bladelike spikes of bone. It had no tail club, but its spiked tail could swing from side to side to inflict savage injuries. The bone forming the top of its skull was dome-shaped and extra thick—perhaps males had head-butting contests over territories or mates.

Gargoyleosaurus

GAR-goil-oh-SORE-us

- **When** 155–145 million years ago (Late Jurassic)
- **Fossil location** USA
- **Habitat** Woodlands
- **Length** 13 ft (4 m)
- **Diet** Low-lying vegetation

Gargoyleosaurus had many unusual features for an ankylosaur. Unlike other members of the family, it had teeth at the front of the upper jaw, and its armor plates were hollow. It also had straight nostrils instead of the odd, looping ones seen in other ankylosaurs.

Spikes on the sides of the body

Sauropelta

SORE-oh-PELT-ah

- **When** 120–110 million years ago (Early Cretaceous)
- **Fossil location** USA
- **Habitat** Woodlands
- **Length** 16 ft (5 m)
- **Diet** Plants

Predators risked deadly injury if they tried to bite this dinosaur's neck, which bristled with vicious, hornlike spikes. A thick shield of armor plates covered its back and tail, giving *Sauropelta* its name ("shield lizard"). The shield was a jigsaw of small plates of bone that fitted together like tiles.

Armored shield covering back and tail

Neck spikes

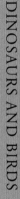

Euoplocephalus

One of the largest of the armored dinosaurs (ankylosaurs), *Euoplocephalus* was twice the size of a rhinoceros and covered in heavy armor. Despite its stocky build and weight, it had powerful legs and may have been quite nimble on its feet. A deadly tail club provided another form of defense for times when its legs or its armor were not enough to save it.

Euoplocephalus

YOU-owe-plo-SEFF-ah-luss

- **When** 70–65 million years ago (Late Cretaceous)
- **Fossil location** N. America
- **Habitat** Woodlands of N. America
- **Length** 20 ft (6 m)

▲ A TAIL OF DEFENSE
Euoplocephalus *had a heavy tail club that it could swing at attackers with bone-crushing force. But it also had a weak spot: a soft belly, which had no armor.*

Since its discovery in Canada in 1902, over 40 fossils of *Euoplocephalus* have been found. Some of the skeletons are almost complete, making it the most well-known member of the ankylosaur (armored dinosaur) family. Its armor consisted of plates of bone that mostly grew directly from the skin. In life, the bony plates were covered by a hornlike substance. Some of the plates had a central ridge, giving them a spiked appearance.

Armor plates on skull

◀ CRAZY PAVING
Euoplocephalus's *skull was covered with armor plates arranged like paving stones. There were even armored shutters on the eyelids that slid down to protect the eyes.*

Armored eyelid

▼ EUOPLOCEPHALUS
was the dinosaur equivalent of a Batmobile, with a powerful body, low profile, and heavy-duty armor plating.

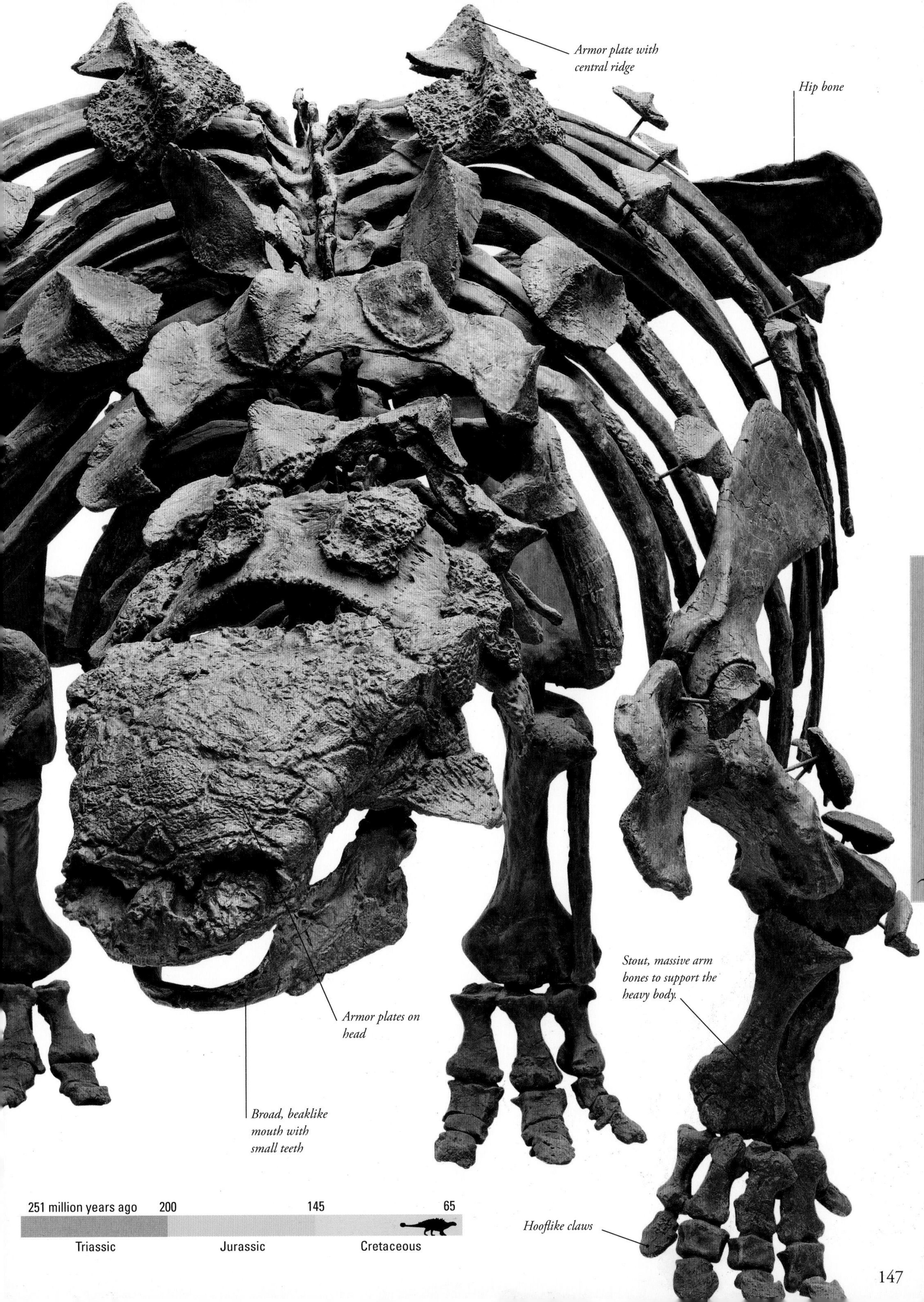

Armor plate with
central ridge

Hip bone

Stout, massive arm
bones to support the
heavy body.

Armor plates on
head

Broad, beaklike
mouth with
small teeth

251 million years ago	200	145	65

Triassic   Jurassic   Cretaceous

Hooflike claws

Prosauropods

At the start of the Triassic Period, all dinosaurs were small and stood low on the ground. Over time, a group of mainly plant-eating dinosaurs called the prosauropods grew taller and heavier than their competitors. They evolved long necks and tails and strong back legs that allowed them to stand up and reach high tree branches.

▲ SCISSOR JAWS
Sharp teeth could slice through tough leaf stems.

Plateosaurus
PLATE-ee-oh-SORE-us

- **When** 220–210 million years ago (Late Triassic)
- **Fossil location** Germany, Switzerland, Norway, Greenland
- **Habitat** Plains of western Europe
- **Length** 25 ft (8 m)
- **Diet** Plants

Plateosaurus was one of the largest of the prosauropods. It walked on its hind legs, mainly feeding on plants at ground level. It could also stand like a kangaroo, rearing up on its hindlimbs and stretching its long neck to eat leaves from trees. More than 50 complete skeletons of *Plateosaurus* have been found.

FAMILY FACT FILE

Key features
- Small heads
- Long, flexible necks
- Very long thumb claws
- Hindlimbs longer than forelimbs

When
Prosauropods first appeared in the Late Triassic, 217 million years ago. They died out in the Middle Jurassic, 184 million years ago.

Long, curved thumb claw was used for defense and for grasping tree branches.

Massospondylus

MASS-oh-SPON-dill-us

- **When** 200–183 million years ago (Early Jurassic)
- **Fossil location** S. Africa
- **Habitat** Woodlands of S. Africa
- **Length** 13–20 ft (4–6 m)
- **Diet** Plants

Massospondylus had five-fingered hands, which it used to grasp and pull down branches. It may also have used its long thumb claws to tear off pieces of plant material. Small, coarse teeth suggest that it could chew both meat and plants. It may also have swallowed small stones to help digest its food, as many "stomach stones" have been found among its bones. Several complete skeletons and skulls of *Massospondylus* have been discovered in South Africa. Some eggs containing embryos have also been found.

Long tail held out for balance

◀ STRONG BODY
Muscled hindlimbs helped
Massospondylus *rear up to feed from trees.*

Thecodontosaurus

THEE-co-DON-toe-SORE-us

- **When** 225–208 million years ago (Late Triassic)
- **Fossil location** British Isles
- **Habitat** Wooded offshore islands of western Europe
- **Length** 7 ft (2 m)
- **Diet** Plants

Widely spaced teeth could rake leaves off branches.

Thecodontosaurus was the first prosauropod to be discovered, and was named "socket-toothed" after its unusual leaf-shaped, sawlike teeth. Unlike lizards today, whose teeth are fused to their jaw bones, this prosauropod's teeth were rooted in separate sockets in its jaw bones. As it is smaller than its relatives, scientists think it may have lived on islands, since animals that live on islands are often small in size. Many fossils of *Thecodontosaurus* have been found in caves, and may have been washed there by rising sea levels.

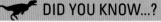 **DID YOU KNOW...?**

During World War II, a bomb set fire to the Bristol City Museum in Britain, destroying a precious fossil kept in it. This fossil was of *Thecodontosaurus*—the oldest dinosaur ever found in Britain. Luckily, some bones were saved and can still be seen in the museum.

Lufengosaurus

loo-FENG-oh-SORE-us

- **When** 200–180 million years ago (Early Jurassic)
- **Fossil location** China
- **Habitat** Woodlands of Asia
- **Length** 20 ft (6 m)
- **Diet** Plants, including cycad and conifer leaves

Lufengosaurus was a heavy, stout-limbed dinosaur. Its head was deep and narrow, with bony lumps around its snout and jaws. It used its widely spaced, bladelike teeth to eat tough plants or to nibble on leaves from trees. It may have also eaten small animals. *Lufengosaurus* probably moved around on two legs most of the time and could rear up to reach higher branches. Its broad hands had long fingers, and each of its thumbs had a massive claw.

Sauropods and relatives

These lumbering giants were the largest creatures ever to walk the Earth. Amazingly long necks let them reach far higher than other plant eaters could, making it possible to feed on treetops as giraffes do today. But they needed pillarlike limbs to support their immense weight, and, unlike most dinosaurs, they usually had to walk on all fours.

▲ **BRACHIOSAURUS** *used its spoon-shaped teeth to snip leaves from the tops of conifers, tree ferns, and other trees. It ate about 440 lb (200 kg) of leaves and twigs a day.*

Brachiosaurus

brackee-oh-SORE-uss

- **When** 150–145 million years ago (Late Jurassic)
- **Fossil location** USA
- **Habitat** Plains
- **Length** 75 ft (23 m)
- **Diet** Treetop leaves and twigs of conifers

One of the largest sauropods, *Brachiosaurus* weighed an incredible 33–55 tons (30–50 metric tons)—nearly 12 times more than an African elephant. *Brachiosaurus's* long neck helped it to feed at heights of more than 50 ft (15 m), which is twice as high as any giraffe can reach.

FAMILY FACT FILE

Key features
- Small heads and large bodies
- Long, flexible necks
- Long, whiplike tails

When
Sauropods first appeared in the Late Triassic, almost 227 million years ago, and died out at the end of the Cretaceous, 65 million years ago.

Barapasaurus

buh-RAH-pah-SORE-uss

- **When** 189–176 million years ago (Early Jurassic)
- **Fossil location** India
- **Habitat** Open woodland
- **Length** 59 ft (18 m)
- **Diet** Vegetation

Barapasaurus probably had a short head. Its neck was supported by a series of long bones and its limbs were slender. Fossils of its teeth show that unlike other sauropods, this creature had sharp teeth with sawlike edges.

Strong neck

Huge belly for digesting swallowed leaves

Camarasaurus

KAM-a-ra-SORE-uss

- **When** 150–140 million years ago (Late Jurassic)
- **Fossil location** USA
- **Habitat** Open woodland
- **Length** 59 ft (18 m)
- **Diet** Tough tree leaves

Numerous *Camarasaurus* fossils have been found in the United States, making it the best-known sauropod. Its broad and sturdy neck helped it feed on vegetation much lower than that eaten by the larger sauropods. Some of its hollow bones had large air chambers connected to its lungs. These chambers helped reduce body weight and also gave *Camarasaurus* its name, which means "chambered lizard."

▲ LARGE HEAD
Camarasaurus *had a box-shaped head with a blunt snout and huge nostrils.*

Mamenchisaurus

ma-MEN-chee-SORE-uss

- **When** 155–145 million years ago (Middle to Late Jurassic)
- **Fossil location** China
- **Habitat** Deltas and forested plains
- **Length** 85 ft (26 m)
- **Diet** Vegetation

Mamenchisaurus was named after the Chinese village where its fossils were found. It had one of the longest necks of any known animal. Its skull was less pointed than that of *Brachiosaurus*, and its shoulders were lower and smaller.

▲ LONG NECK
Nineteen long bones supported Mamenchisaurus's neck, which could move freely from side to side. This made it easier for the creature to reach around.

Vulcanodon

vul-KAN-o-don

- **When** Early Jurassic
- **Fossil location** Zimbabwe
- **Habitat** Forested plains
- **Length** 23 ft (7 m)
- **Diet** Vegetation

Vulcanodon was so named because its first fossils were found in rocks near volcanoes. Like other sauropods, *Vulcanodon* moved slowly on land. Its stubby, pillarlike limbs were useful in supporting its heavy body, but were not meant for running.

Elephantlike feet

Anchisaurus

ankee-SORE-uss

- **When** 190 million years ago (Early Jurassic)
- **Fossil location** USA
- **Habitat** Woodland
- **Length** 6½ ft (2 m)
- **Diet** Leaves

Anchisaurus was a distant cousin of the sauropods. Like most dinosaurs, it walked only on its hindlimbs. It had a narrow snout and fed mainly on plants but may sometimes have eaten small animals too.

151

Inside a dinosaur

What was a dinosaur's anatomy (its insides) like? Was there a difference in the digestive systems of meat-eaters and plant-eaters? Remarkably, thanks to fossil evidence, we have an idea of what the insides of various dinosaurs would have looked like, as these models show.

PLANT-EATER!

Euoplocephalus lived on tough plants and needed a digestive system that could help break these plants down. This dinosaur could not chew, so instead it mashed its food using small, leaf-shaped cheek teeth, before swallowing. The plant matter went into a gizzard, a churning, muscular stomach, where the plant fibers were broken down. Many modern-day birds and reptiles have a gizzard.

Small intestine

Lung

Shoulder joint

Short neck

Elbow joint

Wrist joint

Heart

Gizzard

Liver

▲ EUOPLOCEPHALUS *was an armored dinosaur (an ankylosaur). These dinosaurs were heavily defended with tough, leathery skin and bony plates (see pages 144–147).*

152

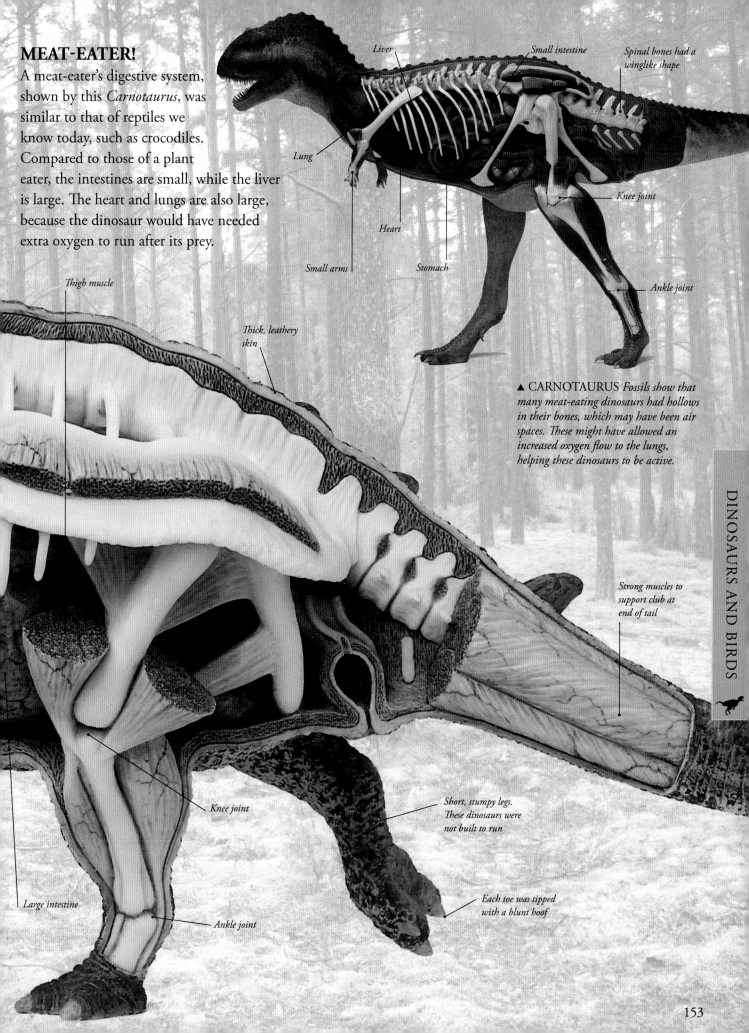

MEAT-EATER!

A meat-eater's digestive system, shown by this *Carnotaurus*, was similar to that of reptiles we know today, such as crocodiles. Compared to those of a plant eater, the intestines are small, while the liver is large. The heart and lungs are also large, because the dinosaur would have needed extra oxygen to run after its prey.

Liver

Small intestine

Spinal bones had a winglike shape

Lung

Knee joint

Heart

Small arms

Stomach

Ankle joint

▲ CARNOTAURUS *Fossils show that many meat-eating dinosaurs had hollows in their bones, which may have been air spaces. These might have allowed an increased oxygen flow to the lungs, helping these dinosaurs to be active.*

Thigh muscle

Thick, leathery skin

Strong muscles to support club at end of tail

Knee joint

Short, stumpy legs. These dinosaurs were not built to run

Large intestine

Ankle joint

Each toe was tipped with a blunt hoof

251 million years ago	200		145	65
	Triassic	Jurassic	Cretaceous	

Isanosaurus

The sauropods were the largest dinosaurs ever to walk on Earth. Some were longer than a blue whale, and the heaviest weighed as much as 12 elephants. *Isanosaurus* was one of the smaller members of the sauropod family. Like other sauropods, whose fossilized tracks show groups walking together, it might have lived in family groups or herds for safety. It lived during the late Triassic Period, making it one of the earliest known sauropods.

Isanosaurus

ee-sahn-oh-SAW-rus

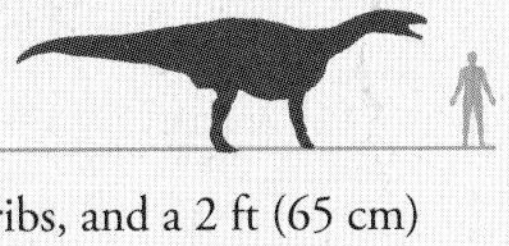

- **When** 216–199 million years ago (Late Triassic)
- **Fossil location** Thailand
- **Habitat** Forests and swamps
- **Length** 40 ft (12 m)
- **Diet** Plants

Isanosaurus was discovered in the Isan region of Thailand. Unfortunately, the remains are incomplete, including only a few back bones, ribs, and a 2 ft (65 cm) long thigh bone. Even so, scientists can tell a lot about *Isanosaurus* by comparing it to close relatives. It walked on all fours to carry its great weight but it could probably rear up on its back legs to reach high branches. It likely had a small head and spoon-shaped teeth for cropping leaves.

Diplodocoids

The diplodocoids were a group of giant plant-eating dinosaurs that walked on all fours. They had incredibly long necks, balanced by even longer whiplike tails, which they used to lash out at enemies. Their legs were longer at the back than the front, which may have helped them to stand up, using the tail as a prop. One of the largest diplodocoids was *Amphicoelias*—a dinosaur as long as a football field and as heavy as a blue whale.

FAMILY FACT FILE

Key features
- Long, flexible necks
- Long, slender tails
- Small heads and large bodies

When
Diplodocoids first appeared in the Middle Jurassic, 170 million years ago. They died out at the start of the Late Cretaceous, 99 million years ago.

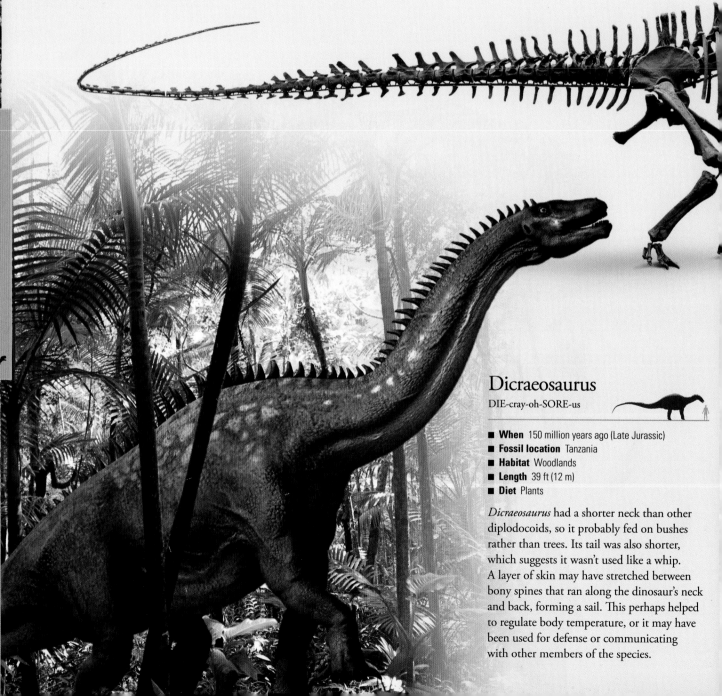

Dicraeosaurus
DIE-cray-oh-SORE-us

- **When** 150 million years ago (Late Jurassic)
- **Fossil location** Tanzania
- **Habitat** Woodlands
- **Length** 39 ft (12 m)
- **Diet** Plants

Dicraeosaurus had a shorter neck than other diplodocoids, so it probably fed on bushes rather than trees. Its tail was also shorter, which suggests it wasn't used like a whip. A layer of skin may have stretched between bony spines that ran along the dinosaur's neck and back, forming a sail. This perhaps helped to regulate body temperature, or it may have been used for defense or communicating with other members of the species.

Diplodocus

dip-LOD-oh-kuss

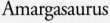

- **When** 150–145 million years ago (Late Jurassic)
- **Fossil location** USA
- **Habitat** Plains
- **Length** 82 ft (25 m)
- **Diet** Leaves

Diplodocus is the longest dinosaur known from a complete skeleton. It is likely that it had spines running along its neck, back, and tail. It had an incredibly long tail—as long as the rest of its body—which it could move at an amazing speed, creating a whiplike crack. *Diplodocus's* neck was almost three times the length of a giraffe's neck and was probably held up at a high angle. Its backbone was strong enough to support its enormous weight, but the bones were hollow. Some scientists think it was a tree-browser, using the peglike teeth at the front of its jaws to strip leaves off branches. Others think it couldn't lift its head high enough and probably swung it from side to side to browse on low shrubs. *Diplodocus* may have grown at a very fast rate, taking around 10 years to become full-sized adult.

▲ BONY BRIDGE *To support its long neck and tail, Diplodocus's backbone acted like the cables in a suspension bridge. The cables take the weight of the road (the neck and tail) and pass it down through the piers (the legs), which anchor it to the ground.*

Amargasaurus

ah-MAR-gah-SORE-us

- **When** 130 million years ago (Early Cretaceous)
- **Fossil location** Argentina
- **Habitat** Woodlands
- **Length** 36 ft (11 m)
- **Diet** Plants

This relatively small and short-necked diplodocoid was unusual because it had a double row of spines running along its neck and back that became a single line down its tail. There may have been a web of skin running between the spines, forming a double sail. Why it had a sail on its back is a mystery, but perhaps *Amargasaurus* used it for display. Some scientists think it didn't have a sail and simply rattled the spines to make a noise.

▼ GIANT FOOTPRINTS
The Morrison Formation in the US has revealed many bones and footprints of giant diplodocoids such as Apatosaurus and Diplodocus, along with fossils of the trees and plants they ate.

Apatosaurus

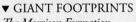

a-PAT-oh-SORE-us

- **When** 150 million years ago (Late Jurassic)
- **Fossil location** USA
- **Habitat** Woodlands
- **Length** 75 ft (23 m)
- **Diet** Plants

Weighing as much as four elephants, *Apatosaurus* (or *Brontosaurus*, as it is popularly known) was shorter and heavier than its relatives, with thicker legs. Some scientists think that instead of rearing up to feed from trees, *Apatosaurus* may have used its strong limbs and massive weight to knock trees down, as elephants do today. Pencil-like teeth lined the front of its broad muzzle.

Barosaurus

BAH-roe-SORE-us

- **When** 155–145 million years ago (Late Jurassic)
- **Fossil location** USA
- **Habitat** Plains of N. America
- **Length** 92 ft (28 m)
- **Diet** Plants

The first *Barosaurus* remains were found during the "Bone Wars" of the late 1800s, when a number of fossil hunters raced to out-do each other with new dinosaur fossil discoveries. In 1922, three *Barosaurus* skeletons were found at Carnegie Quarry in Utah, suggesting that *Barosaurus* may have roamed in herds.

Feeding on stones

Barosaurus's large peglike teeth were perfect for pulling leaves off trees, but not for chewing them. Some scientists thought it swallowed stones to help grind food in its stomach, but recent research has shown that it used bacteria in its gut to digest food.

Sticking its neck out?

In 1993, a model *Barosaurus* was mounted rearing on its hind legs. Some scientists think this position is incorrect—the heart could not have been strong enough to pump blood vertically upward to the brain. New research suggests that with the right-sized heart, this is indeed possible.

Spiny back

No one is sure why *Barosaurus* had spines running along its back—they may have been used for defense, or may simply have been a decorative feature. These spines were bony plates fixed in the skin and were not attached to the skeleton. *Barosaurus*'s rough, scaly skin gave it much needed protection against scratches and bite wounds. It also helped reduce moisture loss from its body when the climate turned dry.

Barosaurus

Barosaurus must have made an impressive sight as it browsed its way through the Jurassic forests. This dinosaur had all the usual sauropod features—a bulky body, tiny head, and relatively short legs. It was heavier than three elephants and longer than a tennis court. But what really gave it an advantage over other plant eaters was its 30 ft (9.5 m) neck, which allowed it to reach leaves right at the tops of the trees.

251 million years ago	200		145		65
	Triassic		Jurassic		Cretaceous

Building a dinosaur

At the American Museum of Natural History in New York City, a *Barosaurus* mother rears up on her hind legs to drive a predatory *Allosaurus* away from her calf. These fossils may look real, but, in fact, they are lightweight replicas. Reconstructing dinosaur fossils for display in museums is a complicated but fascinating task requiring many different skills and a lot of careful preparation.

PUTTING TOGETHER A DINOSAUR

▲ *Careful planning is essential before the skeleton is constructed. Every bone is labeled and marked on a plan to show where it belongs.*

▲ *Here the ribs of the* Barosaurus *are joined to part of its backbone. The backbone is supported by a metal frame.*

▲ *The hind legs and pelvis (hip bones) are lowered into position in the museum by a small crane.*

▲ *The skeleton of the attacking Allosaurus is also assembled. It will face* Barosaurus *in the display.*

MAKING A REPLICA OF A DINOSAUR

There are different methods of making a replica of a dinosaur's fossilized skeleton. One way is to make a mold of each fossilized bone and use these molds to make a cast.

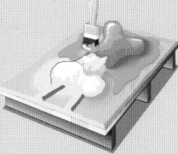

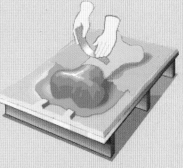

▲ STEP 1 *The fossil is first pressed halfway into a clay base, and liquid rubber (shown in blue) is painted over both the fossil and the base. This will set to form a flexible coat.*

▲ STEP 2 *Once dry, the rubber is covered with fiberglass sheets. The sheets make the rubber mold rigid enough to keep its shape when it is removed.*

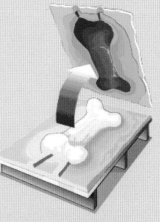

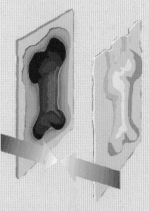

▲ STEP 3 *Once set, the outer mold is removed. Now a second mold is made in the same way of the other side of the fossil.*

▲ STEP 4 *The two molds are joined and held together.*

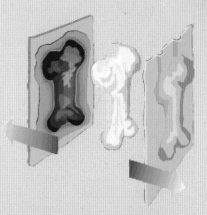

▲ STEP 5 *The complete mold is filled with liquid polyester or some other lightweight material. This will form a cast.*

▲ STEP 6 *Finally, the mold can be opened gently. If the technicians have been careful, a perfect cast is revealed.*

▲ *A welder joins every part of the Barosaurus to the metal frame inserted in its skeleton.*

▲ *The final stage is to join Barosaurus's upper neck and head to its lower neck.*

Titanosaurs

Named after the Titans, a race of giants in Greek mythology, titanosaurs were among the heaviest animals ever to walk on Earth. They were also among the last of the dinosaurs. Titanosaurs were plant eaters and probably lived in herds to protect themselves against predators. The discovery of thousands of eggs scattered across a vast area in Argentina suggests that they also nested together.

 FAMILY FACT FILE

Key features
- Small, wide heads and flexible necks
- Small teeth
- Long tails, but shorter than diplodocoids
- Walked on all four legs
- Many had tough armor plates of bone covering their bodies

When
Titanosaurs first appeared in the Middle Jurassic, 168 million years ago. They died out in the Late Cretaceous, 65 million years ago. They were first thought to be restricted to the southern hemisphere, but are now known to have been more widespread.

Nemegtosaurus
nem-EGG-toe-SORE-us

- **When** 80–65 million years ago (Late Cretaceous)
- **Fossil location** Mongolia
- **Habitat** Woodlands
- **Length** 50 ft (15 m)
- **Diet** Plants

Nemegtosaurus was named after the Nemegt Basin—in the Gobi Desert of Mongolia—where it was first discovered. Only its skull was found, which shows that it may have had a sloping head and small, peg-shaped teeth at the front of its jaws. Like most other titanosaurs, its neck was probably long and flexible, allowing it to feed on high tree branches.

Argentinosaurus

ARE-jen-teen-oh-SORE-us

- **When** 112–95 million years ago (Late Cretaceous)
- **Fossil location** Argentina
- **Habitat** Forested areas
- **Length** 100 ft (30 m)
- **Diet** Conifers

Argentinosaurus was one of the largest and heaviest land animals ever. Only a few bones have been found, including some enormous, 6 ft (1.8 m) tall spine bones. By comparing these to other sauropods, scientists have calculated that *Argentinosaurus* was longer than a tennis court and nearly 20 times heavier than an elephant. Its eggs were the size of footballs, so it probably took around 40 years to reach adult size. Despite its massive size, it was hunted by *Mapusaurus*, a giant flesh-eating dinosaur.

Thick limbs with clawed toes

Titanosaurus

tie-TAN-oh-SORE-us

- **When** 80–65 million years ago (Late Cretaceous)
- **Fossil location** Asia, Europe, Africa
- **Habitat** Woodlands
- **Diet** Plants

Titanosaurus is something of a mystery. Even though discovery of its tail bones led to a whole family of dinosaurs being named after it, it is probably a case of mistaken identity. The features that once marked it out as a unique species have since been found in other titanosaurs. Without a full skull and skeleton to examine, it is hard to say whether the species actually existed.

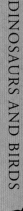

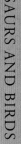

Saltasaurus

SALT-ah-SORE-us

- **When** 80–65 million years ago (Late Cretaceous)
- **Fossil location** Argentina
- **Habitat** Woodlands
- **Length** 40 ft (12 m)
- **Diet** Plants

This relatively small titanosaur was well protected against attack. Large predators couldn't rip open its thick armored hide, which had plates and studs made of bone. Its strong hips and wide upper-tail bones suggest that it may have been able to stand on its hind legs, using its tail to prop itself up. However, *Saltasaurus* had no toes or claws on its front feet.

Isisaurus

ISS-ee-SORE-us

- **When** 70–65 million years ago (Late Cretaceous)
- **Fossil location** Asia
- **Habitat** Woodlands
- **Length** 60 ft (18 m)
- **Diet** Plants

With its long front legs and shorter neck, *Isisaurus* differed from other titanosaurs by standing more like a hyena. Its fossilized dung contained fungi found on many types of leaf. This suggests that it sampled leaves from different trees.

Dinosaur tracks

About 190 million years ago, a large predatory dinosaur was walking along the shore of a river when it suddenly stopped in its tracks. It turned, and then broke into a run, perhaps in a dash for prey. How do we know this? Because its footprints became fossilized. Dinosaur tracks can give us an amazing glimpse into the behavior of the animals that left them.

▲ THIS PRINT *is one of about 2,000 that were found at Dinosaur State Park in Connecticut. No remains of the dinosaurs were found, but scientists think they may have been* Dilophosaurus *or something similar. The animals seem to have been crossing an ancient mudflat.*

This set of tracks was found in Spain. The prints are nearly 3 ft (1 m) apart, suggesting a big animal made them. The shape of the foot indicates it was a theropod (a meat-eater).

POSITIVE OR NEGATIVE?

Fossil footprints can be positive or negative. Positive prints are simply impressions in rock and look like ordinary footprints. Negative prints look like the underside of a dinosaur foot, as though viewed from below. They form when a footprint fills with sand to form a natural cast. Millions of years later, the sandstone cast is all that is left behind.

◀ POSITIVE
These tracks look like ordinary footprints.

▶ NEGATIVE
These tracks look like the bottom of a dinosaur's foot.

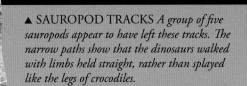

▲ SAUROPOD TRACKS *A group of five sauropods appear to have left these tracks. The narrow paths show that the dinosaurs walked with limbs held straight, rather than splayed like the legs of crocodiles.*

TRACKING DINOSAURS

Dinosaur footprints that form a long trail are rare but give us fascinating clues about the way dinosaurs lived. Most tracks do not show drag marks left by the tail, telling us that dinosaurs held their tails up. Parallel tracks (tracks that run side by side) show that some species traveled in herds.

◀ A LONG TRACKWAY
The world's longest dinosaur trackway is found on a cliff face in Bolivia, South America. The tracks are those of a titanosaur.

Why are they on a cliff face?
The dinosaurs that left these tracks were walking along a sandy shore or a mudflat. Later, the prints became buried and the mud or sand turned to rock. Movements in Earth's crust have since tilted the layer of rock, so the prints now run vertically.

Theropods

Theropods were the world's top predators throughout much of the dinosaurs' reign. This branch of the dinosaur family tree gave rise to some truly gigantic carnivores (although not all were meat-eaters). A selection of these immense animals is shown here. Interestingly, one group of theropods would evolve into the birds that share our world today.

FAMILY FACT FILE

Key features
- Long skulls with large eye sockets, and often horns or crests on top
- Air-filled bones
- Many had a furcula, or wishbone. Birds today have this feature.
- Immense jaws with curved teeth
- Strong arms with three-fingered hands
- Three-toed feet

When
Theropods flourished from the Late Triassic to the Late Cretaceous (230–65 million years ago).

▲ THEROPODS *walked on immense hind legs, using a stiff, muscular tail to balance the great weight of a massive head and fang-lined jaws.*

Giganotosaurus

gig-AN-oh-toe-SORE-rus

- **When** Late Cretaceous
- **Fossil location** Argentina
- **Habitat** Woodlands
- **Size** 39 ft (12 m) long

Giganotosaurus was a formidable predator—it was as heavy as 125 people. It was more than capable of preying on the giant sauropods that roamed South America in the late Cretaceous.

Monolophosaurus

MON-oh-LOAF-oh-SORE-rus

- **When** Middle Jurassic
- **Fossil location** China
- **Habitat** Woodlands
- **Size** 20 ft (6 m) long

Monolophosaurus had a thick and bumpy head crest. This was hollow and may have acted as a means for the dinosaur to produce loud noises, possibly to attract a mate or to warn off a rival. It had a particularly slender lower jaw, but enormous nostril openings.

▶ THIS *dinosaur was probably reasonably agile.*

Sinraptor

SIN-rap-tor

- **When** Late Jurassic
- **Fossil location** China
- **Habitat** Woodlands
- **Size** 25 ft (7.5 m) long

"*Sinraptor*" means "Chinese hunter." Scientists have found tooth marks on a *Sinraptor's* skull that seem to have been made by another *Sinraptor*, which suggests that these dinosaurs may have engaged in vicious fights.

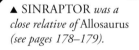

▲ SINRAPTOR *was a close relative of* Allosaurus *(see pages 178–179).*

Carcharodontosaurus

CAR-ka-roe-DON-toe-sore-us

- **When** Late Cretaceous
- **Fossil location** North Africa
- **Habitat** Floodplains and mangroves
- **Size** 39–43 ft (12–13 m) long

Carcharodontosaurus was one of the biggest carnivorous dinosaurs ever. This monster was twice the weight of an elephant and had massive jaws equipped with teeth 8 in (20 cm) long. Its name means "shark-toothed lizard"—it was named for the rough similarity once observed between its teeth and those of *Carcharodon*, the great white shark.

Gasosaurus

GASS-oh-sore-us

- **When** Middle Jurassic
- **Fossil location** China
- **Habitat** Woodlands
- **Size** 11½ ft (3.5 m) long

Just a few of this dinosaur's bones were discovered accidentally in 1985 when a Chinese gas-mining company was using dynamite to clear rocks. This unusual means of its discovery is reflected in its name, which means "gas lizard." No skull has ever been found, so its proposed shape is based on other similar dinosaurs.

Eoraptor

Eoraptor was one of the earliest dinosaurs. Its name means "dawn thief" in recognition of its place at the dawn of the dinosaur era. About the size of a fox, *Eoraptor* stood and ran quickly on its two hind legs. It killed prey by using its claws and teeth to tear the victim apart.

Moon reptile

The first *Eoraptor* fossils were discovered in 1991 in the Valley of the Moon, a region in northwestern Argentina. It is a barren landscape of bare rock, and looks like the surface of the Moon. When *Eoraptor* lived there in the Late Triassic the area was a lush river valley.

Eoraptor

EE-oh-rap-tor

- **When** 230–225 million years ago (Middle Triassic)
- **Fossil location** Argentina
- **Habitat** River valleys
- **Length** 3 ft (1 m)
- **Diet** Lizards, small reptiles, sometimes plants

Only one complete fossil skeleton of *Eoraptor* has been found so far, but it reveals much about early dinosaurs. *Eoraptor* had primitive features, including five fingers on its front limbs, weak claws, and lizardlike hips. Scientists are not sure whether it had scales or feathers. Eoraptor is thought to have been a fierce and quick-witted hunter.

Strong thigh bones and muscles helped Eoraptor *to stand upright.*

▶ BECAUSE Eoraptor's *eyes were set on the side of its head, it couldn't see straight ahead well, but it did have a good all-around view.*

The mouth was full of sawlike teeth, ideal for slicing through flesh. Some scientists think Eoraptor *may have eaten plants too.*

Eoraptor *had a shorter neck than the later carnivorous dinosaurs, but its neck was flexible enough for snatching prey from the ground.*

Eoraptor *only had claws on the three longest fingers of its hands. The other two fingers were shorter but probably helped when searching through vegetation for prey.*

▲ JAWS Eoraptor *had the bladelike teeth of a carnivore—suitable for slicing through meat. It mainly hunted small animals, but may have taken on bigger prey by tearing out lumps of flesh and waiting for its victim to weaken.*

251 million years ago	200	145	65
Triassic		Jurassic	Cretaceous

Coelophysis

One of the earliest theropods, *Coelophysis* was a small and nimble, birdlike carnivore that darted after prey in the riverside forests of the Triassic Period, snapping up small lizards. It was built for speed, with lightweight, hollow bones and a slender frame. In 1998 a *Coelophysis* skull was taken on board space shuttle *Endeavour*, making it the second dinosaur (after *Maiasaura*) to visit space.

Coelophysis
SEE-low-FYE-sis

- **When** 215 million years ago (Late Triassic)
- **Fossil location** N. America, southern Africa, China
- **Habitat** Desert plains
- **Length** 10 ft (3 m)
- **Diet** Lizards and fish

Coelophysis was as long as a small car but as light as an 8-year-old child. With a long, curved neck and slender legs, it resembled a long-legged bird. In 1947 scientists made an amazing discovery of 500 *Coelophysis* skeletons piled together at Ghost Ranch in New Mexico—a *Coelophysis* "graveyard." They seem to have died together, perhaps victims of a sudden flood. The find inspired stories of *Coelophysis* hunting in huge packs to overpower large prey, but there is no evidence this happened.

Coelophysis *had hundreds of small, sharp teeth. They had sawtooth edges—a sign that it ate flesh.*

Coelophysis *had a long, flexible neck that formed an S-shape when relaxed, like the neck of a heron. By straightening its neck quickly, it could dart for fast-moving prey on the ground.*

▼ CANNIBALISM *Tiny bones in the stomach of this fossilized* Coelophysis *were once thought to be those of a baby* Coelophysis *and a sign of cannibalism. However, some experts now think the bones were those of other reptiles that* Coelophysis *hunted.*

The tail was long and stiff. It acted like a rudder, helping Coelophysis *balance when running after prey or fleeing from bigger carnivores.*

251 million years ago	200		145	65
	Triassic	Jurassic	Cretaceous	

Dubreuillosaurus

Prowling through the coastal swamps of the Jurassic Period was the carnivorous predator *Dubreuillosaurus*. Like its relative *Spinosaurus*, it may have been a fish hunter that specialized in snatching slippery prey from shallow waters with its pointed, fang-filled snout.

Dubreuillosaurus

doo-BRAY-oh-sore-us

- **When** 170 million years ago (Middle Jurassic)
- **Fossil location** France
- **Habitat** Mangrove swamps
- **Length** 20 ft (6 m)
- **Diet** Fish and other marine animals

Little is known about *Dubreuillosaurus*, since only a single partial skeleton has been found. It had an unusually long and shallow skull, which was three times as long as it was deep. The skull did not have any distinct crests or horns, like those seen on other dinosaur skulls, but since the only known specimen is a young *Dubreuillosaurus*, these structures may have developed in adults.

Mistaken identity

Dubreuillosaurus was named in 2002 and was originally thought to be a new species of *Poekilopleuron*, a large allosaur-like theropod. Later study of its hollow skull showed *Dubreuillosaurus* was more closely related to the megalosaurids. Like its relatives, it probably had short, powerful arms with three-fingered hands, heavily muscled legs, and a stiff tail that it held out for balance.

251 million years ago	200		145	65
	Triassic	Jurassic		Cretaceous

Spinosaurids

Spinosaurids were huge, sail-backed dinosaurs that lived in swamps and estuaries. With their crocodile-like snouts and powerful clawed hands, they were ideally built for catching the monster fish of the time. They were also skilled at hunting on land.

Spinosaurus

SPINE-oh-SORE-us

- **When** 97 million years ago (Late Cretaceous)
- **Fossil location** Morocco, Libya, Egypt
- **Habitat** Tropical swamps
- **Length** 40–60 ft (12–18 m)
- **Diet** Fish and other animals

Even bigger than *Tyrannosaurus*, *Spinosaurus* was the largest land-dwelling predator of all time. What made it spectacular was an enormous "sail" running along its back. This was supported by spines made of bone, which were as tall as a man—giving it the name *Spinosaurus*, meaning "spine lizard." It may have hunted on land and in water, just like crocodiles today. It probably ate smaller dinosaurs, turtles, and birds, as well as fish.

Powerful hind leg

Short, raised toe at the back of the foot

▲ **LONG TEETH**
Irritator *used its long teeth to grab and hold on to fish. It may have fed on dead meat and land animals, too.*

Irritator

IH-rih-tay-tore

- **When** 110 million years ago (Early Cretaceous)
- **Fossil location** Brazil
- **Habitat** Lakesides
- **Length** 26 ft (8 m)
- **Diet** Meat and fish

In 1996 this spinosaurid's long, crocodile-like skull was discovered in Brazil by a fossil hunter. Its name is the result of a clumsy attempt to mend the snout with plaster, which irritated the scientists who tried to undo the damage. In addition to a sail along its back, it may also have had a small crest on the back of its head.

Smooth sailing

Spinosaurus's sail might have had various uses. Some scientists think it was for display or that it acted as a radiator, helping *Spinosaurus* to keep cool in the hot climate. Others think the sail was a hump that stored body fat for energy, as in modern camels.

FAMILY FACT FILE

Key features
- Crocodile-like heads and snouts
- Big conical teeth
- Large sail on back
- Stiff tails, held out for balance

When
Spinosaurids first appeared in the Late Jurassic, 155 million years ago. They died out in the Late Cretaceous, 93 million years ago, when sea levels dropped on Earth and the swamps that spinosaurids lived in dried up.

Baryonyx

bah-ree-ON-ix

- **When** 125 million years ago (Early Cretaceous)
- **Fossil location** British Isles, Spain, Portugal
- **Habitat** Riverbanks
- **Length** 30 ft (9 m)
- **Diet** Fish and meat

Remains of partly digested dinosaurs were found in *Baryonyx*'s fossilized stomach, indicating that it ate land animals as well as fish. It had a very long, low skull, and its jaws had 96 pointed teeth—twice as many as other members of its family. *Baryonyx* may have had a ridge on its back and a small crest on its snout.

▲ CURVED CLAW
Baryonyx *means "heavy claw," referring to its huge, hooklike thumb claws, which it may have used to spear fish, as grizzly bears do today.*

Nostrils set back from the tip of the snout enabled spinosaurids to breathe while fishing.

Suchomimus

One of the spinosaurids that stalked the lush Cretaceous swamps was *Suchomimus*. It was as big as *Tyrannosaurus* but hunted fish. *Suchomimus* probably stood in water watching for passing fish, which it then snapped up in its huge mouth or speared with its thumb claws. With its long jaws and sharp teeth, it was the perfect swamp predator.

Suchomimus

soo-ko-MIME-us

- **When** 112 million years ago (Early Cretaceous)
- **Fossil location** Africa
- **Habitat** Mangrove swamps
- **Length** 30 ft (9 m)
- **Diet** Fish, possibly meat

Suchomimus, meaning "crocodile mimic," got its name from its crocodile-like snout and sharp teeth, which it used to catch fish and other slippery prey. Compared to other meat eaters, it had long and powerful arms—perhaps it used them to reach into the water to grasp prey. A bladelike sail ran along its back and perhaps its tail.

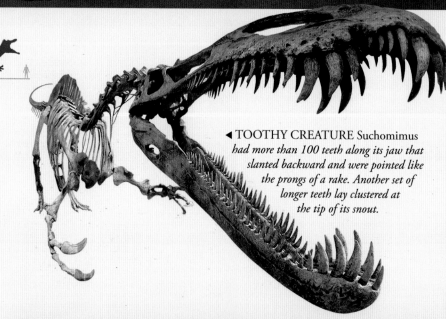

◀ TOOTHY CREATURE Suchomimus *had more than 100 teeth along its jaw that slanted backward and were pointed like the prongs of a rake. Another set of longer teeth lay clustered at the tip of its snout.*

Breathing easy

Suchomimus's nostrils were set a long way back from the tip of its snout. This allowed it to breathe while feeding in water or when scavenging inside the body of a dead dinosaur.

251 million years ago	200		145	65
Triassic		Jurassic		Cretaceous

DINOSAURS AND BIRDS

Desert find

In 1997, scientists found a nearly complete *Suchomimus* skeleton in the Sahara Desert. The bones had been partly exposed by wind, but removing them meant shifting 16½ tons (15 metric tons) of rock and sand. One of the first things they saw was a huge, sickle-shaped claw.

Suchomimus's discoverers Rod Sadleir and Paul Sereno in the Sahara.

Sereno excavates a bone.

Suchomimus's thumb claw is longer than a human hand.

177

251 million years ago	200	145	65
Triassic		Jurassic	Cretaceous

Allosaurus

One of the best-known of the giant flesh-eating dinosaurs of the Jurassic Period was *Allosaurus*. This animal resembled *Tyrannosaurus*, the monster dinosaur that would appear 70 million years later. Since fossil footprints of several *Allosaurus* have been found together, some scientists believe these animals may have hunted in packs to bring down much bigger game. Others think that large allosaurs may have killed and eaten smaller individuals that tried to muscle in on their dinner.

KILLER TEETH

Although *Allosaurus* was a fierce predator, scientists think it had a rather weak jaw that prevented it from crunching bones. Its teeth were like saw blades and could slice through skin and muscle to tear out great ribbons of flesh. Victims that managed to escape after being attacked would probably have bled to death.

Allosaurus

al-oh-SORE-us

- **When** 150 million years ago (Late Jurassic)
- **Fossil location** USA, Portugal
- **Habitat** Plains
- **Length** 39 ft (12 m)
- **Diet** Meat

When young, *Allosaurus* was a fast runner and probably actively chased after prey, sprinting on its long and powerful hindlimbs. Older individuals were heavier and probably relied more on ambushing victims than running them down. The long, curved claws on the hands were used like meat hooks to capture prey. As well as hunting, *Allosaurus* may have also scavenged on dead animals.

Tail held outstretched for balance

▼ HOLEY SKULL *The massive skull had large openings that made it lightweight, yet strong. The bone was also riddled with smaller holes that may have contained air sacs linked to the lungs.*

Triangular horns in front of each eye, perhaps for display

Deep and narrow jaw

Teeth had serrated edges like a saw

Tyrannosauroids

Among the largest and most terrifying predators of all time were the tyrannosauroids ("tyrant lizards"). The first tyrannosauroids were small, possibly feathered dinosaurs, but over millions of years they evolved into giants, the biggest being *Tyrannosaurus* (next page). The giant tyrannosauroids had immensely powerful jaws lined with bone-crunching fangs, equipping them to butcher and consume almost any animal they came across.

FAMILY FACT FILE

Key features
- Large skull and jaws relative to body size
- Small but powerful arms with only two or three fingers on each hand
- Long back legs built for running

When
Tyrannosauroids appeared in the Jurassic Period, 200 million years ago and died out at the end of the Cretaceous Period, 65 million years ago.

Tarbosaurus

TAR-bow-SORE-us

- **When** 70–65 million years ago (Late Cretaceous)
- **Fossil location** Mongolia, China
- **Habitat** Floodplains
- **Length** 39 ft (12 m)
- **Diet** Flesh

While *Tyrannosaurus* was terrorizing the wildlife of North America, its close relative *Tarbosaurus* was doing the same in China. *Tarbosaurus* was almost as big as its cousin but had a more slender skull and even tinier arms. It probably used the same feeding technique, crushing victims in its jaws and then tearing off chunks of flesh while holding the carcass down with its feet.

Proceratosaurus

PRO-seh-RAT-oh-SORE-us

- **When** 175 million years ago (Middle Jurassic)
- **Fossil location** British Isles
- **Habitat** Open woodland
- **Length** 6 ft (2 m)
- **Diet** Flesh

The only fossil of *Proceratosaurus* is a remarkably well-preserved skull found in England in 1910. The dinosaur is thought to be a small, early tyrannosauroid and a close relative of *Guanlong* (below). Its most distinctive feature is a strange crest perched on the tip of its snout. Because the top of the skull is missing, scientists don't know if the small nose crest was actually part of a much longer crest like that of *Guanlong*.

Albertosaurus

al-BERT-oh-SORE-us

- **When** 75 million years ago (Late Cretaceous)
- **Fossil location** Canada
- **Habitat** Forests
- **Length** 30 ft (9 m)
- **Diet** Flesh

Albertosaurus was more lightly built than the largest tyrannosauroids, suggesting it was a swift runner. Its head was huge, with triangular horns in front of the eyes, and its jaws were lined with 60 banana-shaped teeth. More than 30 specimens of *Albertosaurus* have been found, including 22 at a single site that contained a mix of old and young individuals. Some experts think the mass grave is evidence that *Albertosaurus* lived and hunted in packs. The species was named after Alberta in Canada, where it was first discovered.

Guanlong

GWON-long

- **When** 160 million years ago (Late Jurassic)
- **Fossil location** China
- **Habitat** Woodlands
- **Length** 8 ft (2.5 m)
- **Diet** Flesh

Guanlong was discovered in China in 1996. Its name means "crowned dragon" in Chinese and refers to a hollow crest on the skull, running from the nose to the back of its head. The crest was probably used in display, perhaps helping to attract mates. An early tyrannosauroid, *Guanlong* was much smaller than the later giants and had three fingers on each hand rather than two. It was a close relative of early feathered dinosaurs and may well have had a coat of fuzzy feathers itself.

Crest

▲ TARBOSAURUS *was typical of the gigantic, late tyrannosauroids, with a massive skull, powerful jaws, and huge, banana-shaped teeth. In contrast, its arms were almost ridiculously tiny and its hands had only two fingers each.*

Tyrannosaurus

Tyrannosaurus's starring role in the movie *Jurassic Park* confirmed its status as the most fearsome and famous dinosaur of all. Though not the largest carnivore ever to walk on land, it was the biggest of its time, and the strength of its bite was greater than that of any other land animal. Some experts think *Tyrannosaurus* was a scavenger as much as a killer, its huge jaws and teeth adapted to eating bones.

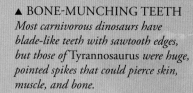

▲ BONE-MUNCHING TEETH
Most carnivorous dinosaurs have blade-like teeth with sawtooth edges, but those of Tyrannosaurus were huge, pointed spikes that could pierce skin, muscle, and bone.

▶ TINY ARMS *Tyrannosaurus had tiny arms and odd hands with just two clawed fingers each. The arms could not reach the mouth or even each other, but they were very strong. Perhaps Tyrannosaurus dug its claws into victims while holding them in its mouth to stop them from struggling free.*

▲ SKELETON *About 30* Tyrannosaurus *fossils have been found, including several skeletons, though none is complete. Skin impressions show adults had scaly skin, but babies are likely to have had fluffy feathers like those of smaller tyrannosauroids.*

Tyrannosaurus

TIE-ran-oh-SORE-us

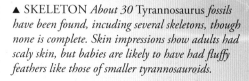

- **When** 70–65 million years ago (Late Cretaceous)
- **Fossil location** N. America
- **Habitat** Forests and swamps
- **Length** 39 ft (12 m)
- **Diet** Flesh

As long as a bus and twice the weight of an elephant, *Tyrannosaurus* was undoubtedly the top predator in its environment. Deep holes in the bones of prey such as *Triceratops* and *Edmontosaurus* show that *Tyrannosaurus* used its immensely powerful jaws and bone-piercing teeth as its main weapons. Small victims were probably shaken apart; larger animals were crippled by horrible injuries. Holding the body down with a foot, *Tyrannosaurus* used its huge neck muscles to tear off mouthfuls of flesh and bone with its mouth, before swallowing it all.

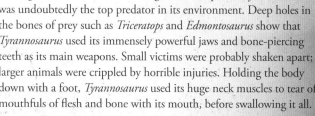

◀ LONG LEGS *The hind legs were long, with powerful thigh muscles but slender ankles and feet. Their athletic build suggests* Tyrannosaurus *could run very fast, though perhaps it did so only rarely, since a high-speed fall could have proved fatal for such a heavy animal.*

DINOSAURS AND BIRDS

Compsognathids

When most people think of a dinosaur they imagine something huge and fierce like *Tyrannosaurus*, with its teeth bared, ready to kill. But some members of the compsognathid family were no bigger than chickens. The compsognathids were nimble little predators that hunted small animals. They were related to the ancestors of birds and probably had simple, fuzzy feathers to keep their small bodies warm.

FAMILY FACT FILE

Key features
- Small, lightweight bodies with hollow bones
- Skin covered with scales or furry feathers
- Long tails used for balance

When
Compsognathids first appeared in the Late Jurassic, 151 million years ago. They died out in the Early Cretaceous, 108 million years ago.

Compsognathus

COMP-sog-NAITH-us

- **When** 150 million years ago (Late Jurassic)
- **Fossil location** Germany, France
- **Habitat** Scrubland and marshes
- **Length** 3 ft (1 m)
- **Diet** Lizards, small mammals, baby dinosaurs

With its large eyes, clawed hands, and sharp, curved teeth, *Compsognathus* was a typical carnivorous dinosaur, but it was only the size of a chicken. Like a bird, it had hollow bones that kept its body light. Running swiftly on the tips of its toes, this lightweight predator could outpace fast-moving prey such as lizards, before pouncing on its victim. Its long tail was more than half of its total body length and was used for balance, helping it make sharp turns as it dashed about. Scientists think fuzzy feathers covered most of its body, especially its back.

Compsognathus **fossil**

▼ HUNTER OR SCAVENGER?

Like any carnivore, Compsognathus *sometimes came across dead animals and would have scavenged for scraps of meat. But its agile build and sharp little teeth show it was more of a hunter than a scavenger, built to capture nervous little animals before they scampered under rocks or disappeared into the undergrowth.*

Sinosauropteryx

SIGH-no-sore-OP-ter-ix

- **When** 130–125 million years ago (Early Cretaceous)
- **Fossil location** China
- **Habitat** Woodlands
- **Length** 3 ft (1 m)
- **Diet** Small animals

In 1996 the first feathered dinosaur, *Sinosauropteryx*, was discovered in the Liaoning Quarry, China. The fossil bore clear marks of simple, fluffy feathers covering the back and sides of the body. Such feathers probably served to keep the animal warm by trapping a layer of air next to the skin.

Sinosauropteryx also had the longest tail, relative to its body size, of any flesh-eating dinosaur.

Ornithomimids

Also known as "ostrich dinosaurs," the members of the ornithomimid family were built like ostriches and were just as quick on their feet. They were the fastest dinosaurs of all, capable of reaching perhaps 50 mph (80 kph) when running. They evolved from flesh-eaters, but their birdlike beaks and lack of big teeth suggest a more varied diet.

Gallimimus

GAL-ih-MIME-us

- **When** 75–65 million years ago (Late Cretaceous)
- **Fossil location** Mongolia
- **Habitat** Desert plains
- **Length** 20 ft (6 m)
- **Diet** Leaves, seeds, insects, and small animals

One of the best known of all ornithomimids is *Gallimimus* ("chicken mimic"). It was the largest ornithomimid, three times as tall as a man and, at 1,000 lb (450 kg) in weight, a lot heavier than any chicken. *Gallimimus* was the fastest sprinter of any dinosaur and could have outrun a racehorse. It had a birdlike skull, with a brain about the size of a golf ball (only slightly larger than an ostrich's). Its long, toothless beak was used to pick up leaves, seeds, insects, and small mammals.

◀ BIRD VISION
Gallimimus had wide eye sockets with eyes facing sideways. This helped it spot enemies in almost any direction. Inside each eyeball was a supporting ring of small bony plates. Modern birds still have this feature.

LIVING RELATIVE

Ornithomimids may have run just like ostriches run today. Ostriches take great strides with their powerful, long legs, with their tails jutting out behind. The fastest bird today, an ostrich can run at about 45 miles (72 km) per hour, while an average human can reach only 6–11 mph (10–18 kph).

Struthiomimus

STROO-thee-oh-MIME-us

- **When** 75 million years ago (Late Cretaceous)
- **Fossil location** Canada
- **Habitat** Open country, riverbanks
- **Length** 15 ft (4 m)
- **Diet** Omnivorous

Struthiomimus was so similar to *Ornithomimus* that its fossil was for many years thought to be that of *Ornithomimus*. The only difference is that it had longer arms with stronger fingers. At the ends of its fingers were long, straight claws, but it probably could not use them to grasp prey, like *Ornithomimus* did. Instead, like modern sloths, *Struthiomimus* may have used its arms and hands to pull tree branches within reach of its beak. It probably ate buds and shoots from trees and other plants, but its diet may also have included small animals and insects. Like other ornithomimids, *Struthiomimus* had long, powerful legs built for speed, and a small head perched on a slender, flexible neck.

▼ FEATHERS OR SCALES?

Most models and artworks show ornithomimids with scaly skin. However, many scientists now believe they had primitive, fuzzy feathers ("protofeathers"), in common with closely related dinosaur families.

Ornithomimus

OR-nith-oh-MIME-us

- **When** 75–65 million years ago (Late Cretaceous)
- **Fossil location** USA, Canada
- **Habitat** Swamps, forests
- **Length** 10 ft (3 m)
- **Diet** Omnivorous

Ornithomimus had the typical short body and long back legs of an ornithomimid. A fast runner, it could make sudden turns even while sprinting by swinging its tail from side to side. For its size and time, it had a fairly large brain, but was far less intelligent than an ostrich.

Long, stiff tail

Animatronic dinosaurs

You've probably seen dinosaurs brought to life in movies, and you may have been lucky enough to see a moving dinosaur at a special exhibition. Some of these are animatronic dinosaurs, and they take a long time to build. They look very realistic, but they are really just mechanical puppets.

▼ LIFE-SIZED *This animatronic* Tyrannosaurus *was made for an exhibition in 2007.*

Inner robot

Animatronic dinosaurs are not completely true-to-life. This *Tyrannosaurus* is much fatter than it would have been, but a slender dinosaur body would not have hidden the robot's inner workings.

HOW IS IT DONE?

An animatronic dinosaur begins life as a sketch, and takes months to build. These pictures were taken during the building of the *Tyrannosaurus* used in *The Lost World* (1997), the second *Jurassic Park* film. Not all the dinosaurs in the *Jurassic Park* films were animatronic models. Many were "CG dinosaurs" – computer-generated 3D models.

▲ A BIG COVER UP *The dinosaur's skin is set over a plastic and steel frame, much of which has to be welded into position.*

▲ KILLER JAWS *Teeth are glued to the jaws, the mouth is lined with flesh-coloured latex, and flexible skin is wrapped around the steel skull.*

▲ PUPPET MASTER *The dinosaur's movements are controlled by a "telemetry suit" worn by an operator. This suit controls the arms.*

TAKE A LOOK

Animatronic dinosaurs are not only used for films and shows. US scientist Peter Dilworth hopes the technology will one day help people with disabilities. His 45 cm (18 in) tall robotic dinosaur is a replica of *Troodon*, a Cretaceous meat-eating dinosaur. It was nicknamed "Troody". Troody took five years to develop and can rise from a sitting position and walk on its own.

Oviraptorosaurs

The oviraptorosaurs are a family of odd-looking, feathered dinosaurs with parrotlike beaks. Although they evolved from flesh-eating dinosaurs (theropods), they were omnivores or plant-eaters. They had few or no teeth, short snouts, and often a decorative crest on the head. Fossils show they brooded their eggs as birds do. Some oviraptorosaurs were so birdlike that the scientists who discovered them thought they must be ancient flightless birds.

FAMILY FACT FILE

Key features
- Short skull, sometimes with a crest
- Parrotlike beaks with small or no teeth
- Feathers
- Plant eaters

When
Oviraptorosaurs lived in the Cretaceous Period, between 84 and 65 million years ago.

Citipati
SIH-tee-PAH-tee

- **When** 75 million years ago (Late Cretaceous)
- **Fossil location** Mongolia
- **Habitat** Plains of Central Asia
- **Length** 9 ft (3 m)

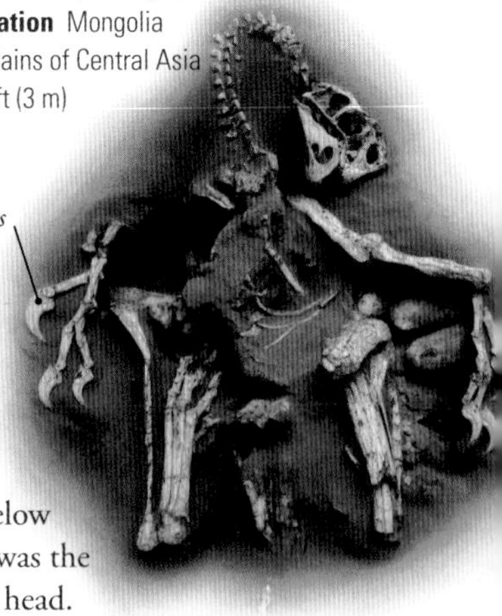

Claws at tips of long fingers

The most distinctive feature of *Citipati* (below and right) was the crest on its head. Many *Citipati* specimens have been found crouching on their eggs in nests, sheltering them with arms that were probably feathered, as modern birds do. *Citipati*'s oval eggs were huge—even bigger than a man's hand.

Ingenia

IN-jeh-NEE-ah

- **When** 70 million years ago (Late Cretaceous)
- **Fossil location** Mongolia
- **Habitat** Woodlands
- **Length** 5 ft (1.5 m)

Ingenia was a small, feathered dinosaur, barely as tall as a man. It was named after the Ingen province in Mongolia where it was first found. Very few fossils of this dinosaur have been discovered. From the existing specimens, however, scientists know it had stout hands with unusually large thumbs and thumb claws, which may have been defensive weapons. *Ingenia* may have been an omnivore, feeding on a mix of plant and animal food.

Caudipteryx

caw-DIP-ter-ix

- **When** 130–120 million years ago (Early Cretaceous)
- **Fossil location** China
- **Habitat** Lakesides and riverbeds
- **Length** 3 ft (1 m)

Fan of feathers on tail

Turkey-sized *Caudipteryx* was covered in feathers. It had large plumes on its short, winglike arms; a large tail fan; and short, downy feathers all over. The feathers were probably used to keep it warm and to attract mates rather than to fly. *Caudipteryx*'s bony tail was shorter than that of most dinosaurs, which meant it couldn't be used as a counterbalance. As a result, it most likely walked like a stocky, flightless bird. Its pointed beak might have been used to shred plants and crack seeds, but *Caudipteryx* may also have eaten meat.

DINOSAUR EGGS

In the 1920s, scientists found this amazing 75-million-year-old nest buried deep in the sands of the Gobi Desert in Mongolia. In it were a number of long, narrow eggs arranged in a circle. This was the fossilized nest of an *Oviraptor*, a type of feathered dinosaur. The scientists also found the skeleton of the mother near to the nest, but at first they mistook mother and eggs for two different species. They named the mother *Oviraptor*, meaning "egg thief," thinking she was a predator trying to steal the eggs. The name stuck, and all dinosaurs in the same family are now called oviraptorosaurs.

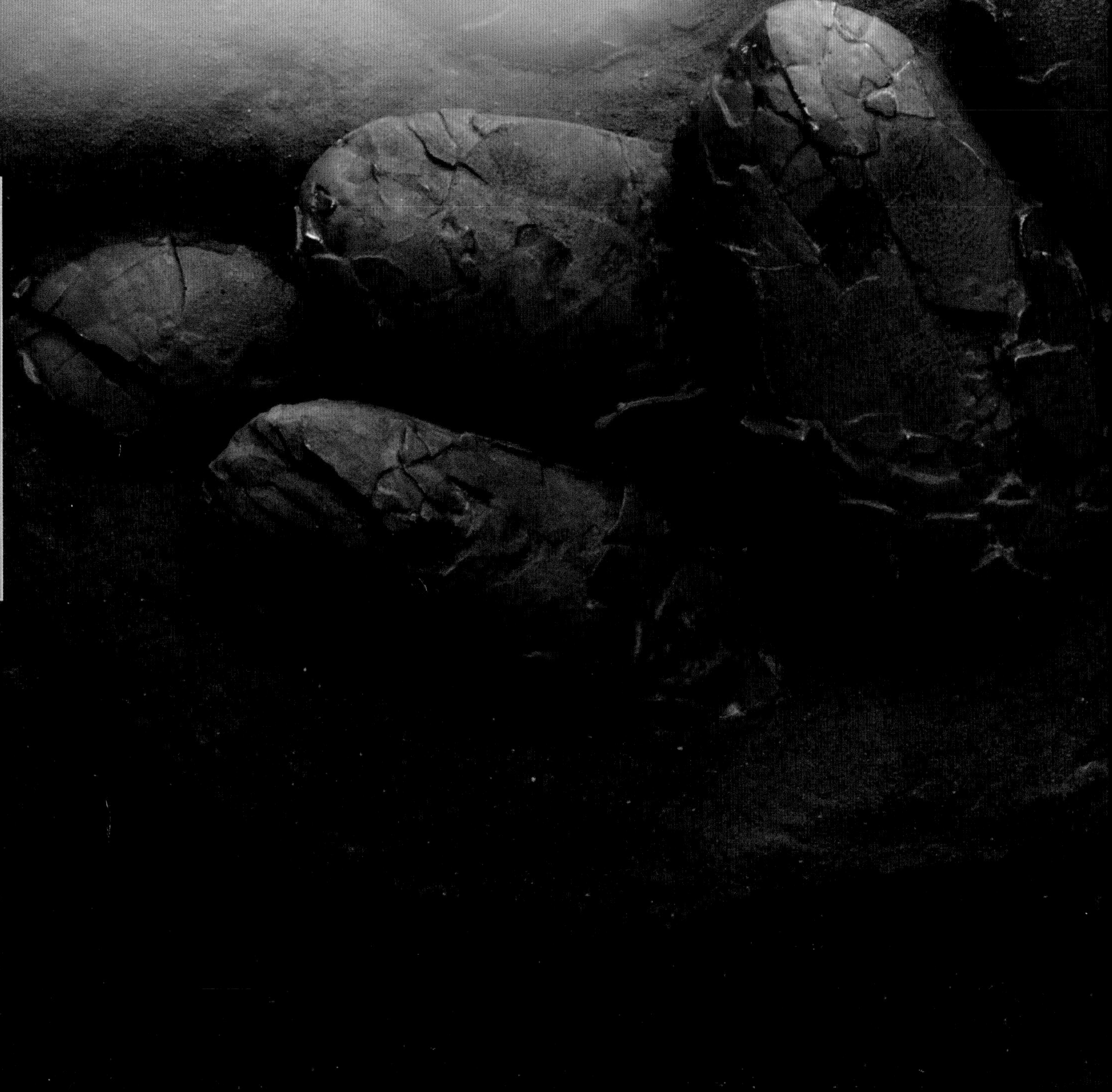

▲ INSIDE THE EGG *Scientists have found many clutches of dinosaur eggs, but not all of them contain baby dinosaurs. To find out if anything is inside, the eggs are scanned and the rock is then carefully chipped with tiny chisels or dissolved in weak acid. It can take as long as a year to reveal the tiny bones and tissues of an embryo hidden inside the egg.*

Therizinosaurs

When scientists put together bits and pieces of therizinosaur fossils, they turned out to be some of the most bizarre-looking dinosaurs ever. They were tall with small heads, stumpy feet, and pot bellies. While their bones show they were relatives of predatory dinosaurs, their teeth and digestive system seem to have evolved to eat plants instead of meat.

Therizinosaurus
THERRY-zin-oh-SORE-us

- **When** 80–70 million years ago (Late Cretaceous)
- **Fossil location** Mongolia
- **Habitat** Woodlands
- **Length** 26–36 ft (8–11 m)
- **Diet** Plants

Therizinosaurus was one of the bigger therizinosaurs. Its fossils were found in what is now the cold, barren Gobi Desert. During the Late Cretaceous, this region was warmer and wetter, with tall trees. Perhaps *Therizinosaurus*'s immense height helped it to gather leaves from tall trees, like a giraffe.

▲ SCISSOR HANDS
Therizinosaurus had astonishingly long claws on its hands, each measuring nearly 3 ft (1 m) long. These may have been defensive weapons used for slashing at tyrannosaurids, such as the Tarbosaurus shown here. They might also have been used to pull high branches down from trees.

Alxasaurus

ALK-sah-SORE-us

- **When** 130 million years ago (Early Cretaceous)
- **Fossil location** China
- **Habitat** Woodlands
- **Length** 13 ft (4 m)
- **Diet** Plants

In 1988, five specimens of a previously unknown dinosaur were found in Mongolia. This was *Alxasaurus*, a therizinosaur. Its leaf-shaped teeth were not sharp enough to tear off flesh, so it probably fed on plants. The swollen stomach of *Alxasaurus* indicates that it ate great quantities of leaves. Its big belly may have made it too clumsy to run fast. If attacked by another dinosaur, it probably lashed out with its claws rather than trying to escape.

FAMILY FACT FILE

Key features
- Long necks
- Enormous curved claws on fingers
- Short tails
- Four-toed feet
- Partly feathered

When
Therizinosaurs first appeared in the Early Cretaceous, 130 million years ago. They died out in the Late Cretaceous, 65 million years ago.

Dromaeosaurs

The dromaeosaurs were small but ferocious hunters with bladelike teeth and vicious, hooked claws on their hands and feet. They were closely related to birds and may have evolved from a flying ancestor. Their long arms folded up like wings, and their bodies were fully feathered. Dromaeosaurs are sometimes also called "raptors," a word that means "thief" or "grabber."

Dromaeosaurus
DROM-ee-oh-SORE-us

- **When** 75 million years ago (Late Cretaceous)
- **Fossil location** Canada
- **Habitat** Forests, plains
- **Length** 6½ ft (2 m)
- **Diet** Flesh

Dromaeosaurus skull

About the size of *Velociraptor*, *Dromaeosaurus* had a stockier skull and a deeper lower jaw, suggesting it had a more powerful bite. It had large eyes and hunted by vision, perhaps stalking prey quietly like a cat does before leaping for the kill. Only a partial skull and a few bones of *Dromaeosaurus* have been found. The skeleton shown below is based on these and other closely related dromaeosaurs.

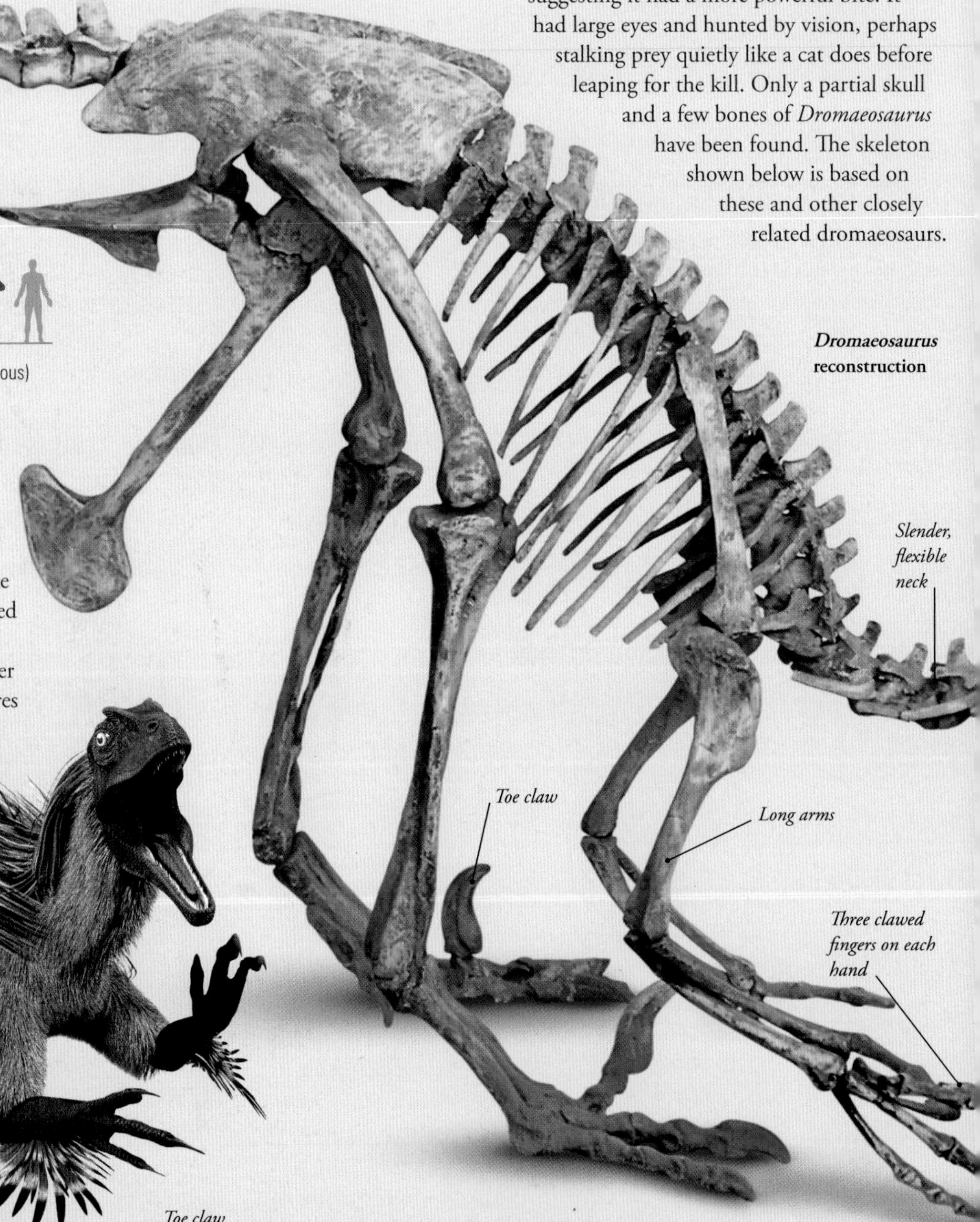

Dromaeosaurus reconstruction

Slender, flexible neck

Utahraptor
YOU-tah-RAP-tor

- **When** 130–120 million years ago (Early Cretaceous)
- **Fossil location** USA
- **Habitat** Plains
- **Length** 23 ft (7 m)
- **Diet** Flesh

Utahraptor was the largest dromaeosaur and reached about half a ton in weight, making it heavier than a grizzly bear. Like other dromaeosaurs, it had a large, hooked claw on its second toe that it might have used for slashing or stabbing a victim after leaping on it. One fossilized claw measures 9 in (24 cm) in length.

Toe claw

Long arms

Three clawed fingers on each hand

Toe claw

Deinonychus

dye-NON-ee-cuss

Stiffened tail hinged at base

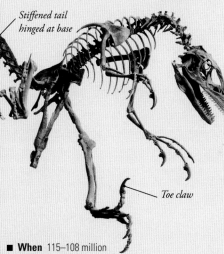

Toe claw

- **When** 115–108 million years ago (Early Cretaceous)
- **Fossil location** USA
- **Habitat** Subtropical swamps and forests
- **Length** 10 ft (3 m)
- **Diet** Flesh

Leopard-sized *Deinonychus* ("terrible claw") is famous for its large toe claws. As in other dromaeosaurs, the claws flipped up off the ground when it was walking in order to stay sharp. Some experts think *Deinonychus* used its toe claws to slash the throat or belly of prey while kicking violently. Others think the claws were climbing aids in juveniles or used for clinging to prey. A stiff tail provided balance when leaping or climbing.

Velociraptor

vel-OSS-ee-rap-tor

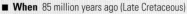

- **When** 85 million years ago (Late Cretaceous)
- **Fossil location** Mongolia
- **Habitat** Scrubland and deserts
- **Length** 6½ ft (2 m)
- **Diet** Lizards, mammals, small dinosaurs

Velociraptor played a starring role in *Jurassic Park*, where it was shown as twice its actual size. In reality it was a slender, feathered animal about the size of a wolf. The most spectacular fossil of *Velociraptor* is a complete skeleton locked in combat with a *Protoceratops* (below).

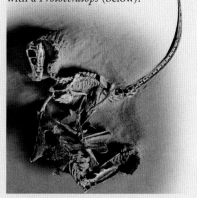

They died in midfight, perhaps buried by a sudden sandstorm. Like other dromaeosaurs, *Velociraptor* had huge, flickable toe claws and long, clawed arms that unfolded like wings to grapple prey. Although no feathered fossils of *Velociraptor* have been found, its arm bones have "quill nodes"—small bumps to which long feathers were anchored.

Unusually slender snout

Long sharp claw

Bambiraptor

BAM-bee-rap-tor

- **When** 75 million years ago (Late Cretaceous)
- **Fossil location** N. America
- **Habitat** Woodland
- **Length** 2 ft (6 m)
- **Diet** Flesh

In 1995, 14-year-old Wes Linster was hunting for fossils with his parents in the mountains of Glacier National Park in Montana. He was thrilled to find parts of a skeleton. Later excavation revealed that Wes had found a tiny but perfectly preserved dromaeosaur. Because

of its size, scientists named it after the Disney character Bambi the deer. *Bambiraptor* was birdlike and probably feathered, with long hindlimbs that suggest it was a fast runner. It probably hunted small mammals and reptiles, snatching them in its clawed hands as a cat catches a mouse. It had a very large brain relative to its body size, suggesting it was a quick-witted animal (or an infant). Some scientists think its small size allowed it to climb trees.

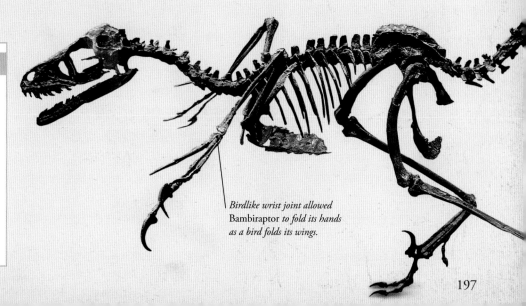

Birdlike wrist joint allowed Bambiraptor to fold its hands as a bird folds its wings.

FAMILY FACT FILE

Key features
- Long, birdlike feathers on the arms, legs, and tail; downy feathers on body
- Sickle-shaped claw on second toe
- Long arms that fold against the body like wings

When
Dromaeosaurs appeared in the Jurassic, 167 million years ago, and died out at the end of the Cretaceous, 65 million years ago.

Fight to the death

In North America, teeth of the ferocious dinosaur *Deinonychus* are often found near remains of the huge plant-eater *Tenontosaurus*. At one site, a group of five *Deinonychus* was found with a *Tenontosaurus*. The plant-eater was much too big for a *Deinonychus* to kill on its own, but could they have been hunting as a pack?

◄ SOFT TARGET?
Tenontosaurus *had no protective armor and few weapons, making it a soft target for predators. But its great size helped defend it. At about 2 tons in weight, an adult was nearly 30 times heavier than* Deinonychus.

PACK HUNTING
Pack hunters such as wolves can bring down huge prey by cooperating. There's no proof dinosaurs hunted in packs, and not all scientists think they did. In birds—the living descendants of dinosaurs—pack hunting is almost unknown.

◀ A LIGHTWEIGHT hunter such as Deinonychus would have been amazingly agile—a quality it would have needed to dodge the swinging tail and flailing limbs of heavy prey such as Tenontosaurus.

DID YOU KNOW?

Deinonychus's most famous feature, an enlarged claw on the second toe of its hind feet, provided its name, which means "terrible claw."

Curved sickle claw

▲ THE SECOND CLAW might have been used to disembowel prey, with the predator slicing open the prey's stomach area with a series of raking kicks.

◀ DEINONYCHUS'S JAWS contained about 60 curved, bladelike teeth, each with a sawtooth edge like the blade of a steak knife. Such teeth were ideal for slicing through tough skin and flesh.

Microraptor

Only slightly larger than a pigeon, *Microraptor* ("tiny thief") is one of the smallest known dinosaurs. It was completely covered with feathers and could fly (or at least glide) from tree to tree, sailing on what appear to be four wings. A member of the dromaeosaur family, *Microraptor* was a carnivore and a close relative of *Velociraptor*, but it wasn't a true bird.

Microraptor

MY-crow-rap-tor

- **When** 130–125 million years ago (Early Cretaceous)
- **Fossil location** China
- **Habitat** Woodlands
- **Length** 3 ft (1 m)
- **Diet** Probably small mammals, lizards, and insects

Scientists have found dozens of fossils of *Microraptor* in China, including more than 20 well-preserved skeletons. Unlike a bird, this creature had teeth, a bony tail, and front legs with large claws, but its fossils also show unmistakeable signs of flight feathers, proving that feathers are not a unique feature of birds but were found in other dinosaurs too. *Microraptor* didn't have the big flight muscles needed to take off by flapping, but it could have used its wings for gliding, much like a flying squirrel. Its tail had a diamond-shaped fan of feathers at the end, perhaps to steady it in midair. The long feathers on its feet would have gotten in the way when walking or running, so perhaps *Microraptor* stayed in the trees.

251 million years ago	200	145	65
Triassic		Jurassic	Cretaceous

A FOUR-WINGED DINOSAUR?

Microraptor had long, bird-style flight feathers on its arms and legs, giving it what seem to be four wings. How it used these is a mystery. Some scientists suggest it could spread out its hind legs when gliding, but its hip joints may not have had enough flexibility to do this.

◄ FEATHERED FOSSIL
This well-preserved fossil shows impressions of long feathers on the arms and legs. A stiff tail, typical of a dromaeosaur, is also visible.

Sinornithosaurus

Sinornithosaurus was an early member of the dromaeosaur family. As this beautiful fossil shows, its entire body was covered from head to tail with feathers. *Sinornithosaurus* means "Chinese bird lizard," but this species wasn't a true bird, since it was probably too heavy to fly, although like other dromaeosaurs it may have evolved from a flying ancestor.

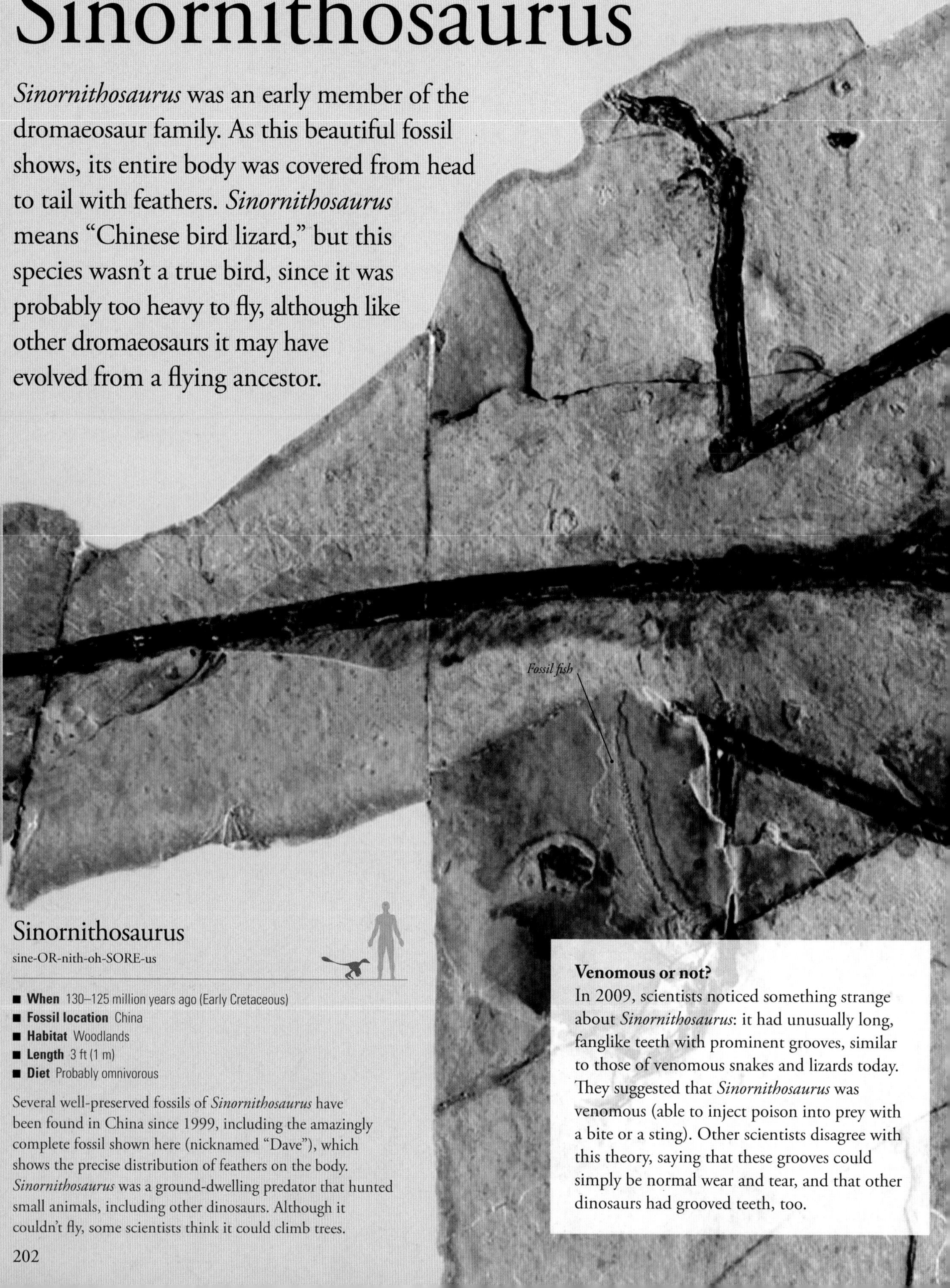

Fossil fish

Sinornithosaurus

sine-OR-nith-oh-SORE-us

- **When** 130–125 million years ago (Early Cretaceous)
- **Fossil location** China
- **Habitat** Woodlands
- **Length** 3 ft (1 m)
- **Diet** Probably omnivorous

Several well-preserved fossils of *Sinornithosaurus* have been found in China since 1999, including the amazingly complete fossil shown here (nicknamed "Dave"), which shows the precise distribution of feathers on the body. *Sinornithosaurus* was a ground-dwelling predator that hunted small animals, including other dinosaurs. Although it couldn't fly, some scientists think it could climb trees.

Venomous or not?

In 2009, scientists noticed something strange about *Sinornithosaurus*: it had unusually long, fanglike teeth with prominent grooves, similar to those of venomous snakes and lizards today. They suggested that *Sinornithosaurus* was venomous (able to inject poison into prey with a bite or a sting). Other scientists disagree with this theory, saying that these grooves could simply be normal wear and tear, and that other dinosaurs had grooved teeth, too.

Triassic   Jurassic   Cretaceous

Feathers

Claw

Feathers on head

DINOSAURS AND BIRDS

▲ FUZZY FEATHERS Sinornithosaurus *probably had feathers in various colors and sizes. Fluffy ones on its body may have helped in trapping heat. Long feathers on its arms were perhaps used for show or for protecting its young.*

Troodon

Troodon was a small but agile dinosaur, built like a bird and covered with feathers. About the weight of a child, it wasn't powerful enough to tackle large dinosaurs, but it was swift on its feet and adept at catching small animals in the undergrowth of woodlands. With an unusually large brain for a dinosaur and sharp eyes, *Troodon* seems to have been a quick-witted hunter with the lightning reactions and killer instinct of a cat.

ON THE CHASE
Long, slender legs and an athletic build made *Troodon* a fast sprinter, able to outrun small animals such as lizards and baby dinosaurs. The second toe on each foot had a large, sickle-shaped claw that *Troodon* may have used to pin down prey. The claw could swivel upward to stay off the ground while *Troodon* was running.

Troodon
TROH-o-don

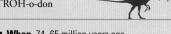

- **When** 74–65 million years ago (Late Cretaceous)
- **Fossil location** N. America
- **Habitat** Wooded plains
- **Length** 10 ft (3 m)
- **Diet** Small animals and possibly plants

Troodon had unusual teeth with very jagged edges. Although small animals probably made up most of its diet, the teeth might also have been used for shredding leaves. The name *Troodon* means "wounding tooth."

Seen by both eyes, giving 3-D vision

Seen by right eye

Seen by left eye

▶ 3-D VISION
Troodon's eyes, unlike those of most dinosaurs, faced forward rather than sideways. This gave it 3-D vision in the area seen by both eyes (as in humans). This special ability enabled Troodon *to judge the distance to its prey before pouncing for the kill.*

251 million years ago	200		145	65
	Triassic	Jurassic	Cretaceous	

The legs were tightly folded inside the egg.

▲ TROODON EGGS *were found at Egg Mountain in Montana. Scientists used the tiny bones in a fossil egg to recreate this lifelike model of a baby* Troodon *about to hatch. Both parents sat in egg-filled nests, using their feathered arms to protect the eggs.*

BIRDBRAINED

Troodon had perhaps the largest brain relative to its body weight of any dinosaur. But while it may have been a quick thinker by dinosaur standards, its brain was only as big as that of a flightless bird such as a cassowary and much smaller than the average mammal's brain.

Cassowary

205

Death of the dinosaurs

Just before the dinosaurs first emerged, Earth suffered a mass extinction that wiped out nearly 90 percent of all species. The planet took millions of years to recover. Then, 65 million years ago, virtually all dinosaurs were wiped out in another sudden mass death. What caused their mysterious disappearance?

ATTACK FROM ABOVE

In 1980, an American scientist named Luis Alvarez made an amazing discovery. Studying rocks that formed at around the time the dinosaurs disappeared, he found that the level of iridium (a metal that's rare on Earth but common in meteorites) was 100 times higher than normal. He found the same high level all over the world and concluded that a massive meteorite or asteroid must have slammed into Earth. Such a huge impact could have wrecked Earth's climate and killed off the dinosaurs.

Coal

Iridium layer

Clay

 DID YOU KNOW?

Not all animals perished. Those that survived included:

- Sharks and other fish
- Jellyfish
- Scorpions
- Birds
- Insects
- Mammals
- Snakes
- Turtles
- Crocodiles

The Chicxulub crater was about 112 miles (180 km) wide.

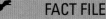
FACT FILE

There are been five major extinctions in the past 550 million years. A mass extinction means that more than 50 percent of animal species die at one time. The mass extinction that ended the Mesozoic Era (the time of the dinosaurs) was the most recent, and more than 80 theories have been put forward to account for what happened.

Hidden crater

A meteorite produces a crater, and a meteorite big enough to change the world's climate would produce a giant crater, so where is it? The answer came in the 1970s when scientists searching for oil found a vast crater buried more than half a mile (1 km) underground on the coast of Mexico. The space rock that left this scar was an estimated 6 miles (10 km) wide and would have hit the Earth with tremendous force, sending shockwaves all over the world.

The sea would have filled the Chicxulub crater with water soon after the impact.

No land **animal** larger than a **dog survived** the mass extinction that killed the dinosaurs.

Double trouble

The meteorite impact almost certainly contributed to the death of the dinosaurs, but other catastrophic events were going on at the same time, and some scientists believe that it was a chain of events rather than simply one meteorite that caused the mass extinction. Heavy volcanic activity in western India was sending up huge clouds of gas that would have contributed to climate changes.

Volcanic activity created the Deccan Traps lava beds, which at one point covered more than half of India.

What did the meteorite do?

A huge meteorite smashing into Earth would have created a worldwide cloud of dust and fumes, choking animals and blocking out the Sun's light and warmth. The planet's climate would have changed dramatically, making life impossible for many species.

DINOSAURS AND BIRDS

Early birds

Birds evolved from dromaeosaur-like dinosaurs during the Jurassic Period. The first birds had skeletons like those of *Microraptor* (page 198). Over time, as birds adapted to life in the air, they evolved huge flight muscles and lost their teeth, tails, and claws, making them more lightweight.

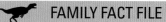
Key features of modern birds
- Feathered body and wings
- Toothless beaks
- Tail bones fused into a stump
- No finger claws or small finger claws
- Deep keel bone on breast to anchor large flight muscles
- Semicircular wrist bone to aid flapping

When
Birds first appeared in the Late Jurassic and have been in the skies ever since.

Modern birds have a toothless beak, but Archaeopteryx *had jaws and teeth typical of a carnivorous dinosaur.*

Very long feathered arms with flight feathers

Archaeopteryx

Confuciusornis
con-FEW-shus-OR-niss

- **When** 130–120 million years ago (Early Cretaceous)
- **Fossil location** China
- **Habitat** Woodlands of Asia
- **Length** 1 ft (0.3 m)
- **Diet** Probably seeds

Confuciusornis was the earliest toothless bird and the first known to have a beak. It also had a stumpy tail like that of modern birds, but it lacked strong flight muscles. Thousands of fossils of *Confuciusornis* have been found in China, and some of the adults have very long tail feathers. These may be male ornaments that were displayed to attract females during courtship.

Archaeopteryx
ar-kee-OP-ter-ix

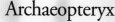

- **When** 150 million years ago (Late Jurassic)
- **Fossil location** Germany
- **Habitat** Forests and lakes of western Europe
- **Length** 1 ft (0.3 m)
- **Diet** Insects, probably reptiles

When the first complete fossil of *Archaeopteryx* was discovered in 1861, scientists were amazed—it looked like a cross between a

dinosaur and a bird. It had a fully feathered tail and wings, yet it also had dromaeosaur-like claws on its hands, bones along its tail, and jaws with teeth instead of a beak. *Archaeopteryx* is the oldest known member of the bird family. It was the size a pigeon and had long flight feathers, but it lacked the powerful muscles needed for flapping flight and was probably more of a glider than a flapper.

◀ THIS FOSSIL *of* Archaeopteryx *was discovered in Germany. Amazingly clear impressions of feathers on the arms and tail are preserved in fine-grained limestone.*

Hesperornis

HESS-per-ORE-niss

- **When** 75 million years ago (Late Cretaceous)
- **Fossil location** USA
- **Habitat** Coastal waters
- **Length** 6 ft (1.8 m)
- **Diet** Fish and squid

Long, slender body

Toothed beak

Tiny wings

Hesperornis was an enormous seabird that had lost the power of flight but become an expert diver. It used its huge feet to push itself through the water as it chased squid and fish, which it caught in a toothed beak. The bones of its hands and forearms had vanished, leaving tiny "wings" that it likely used for steering in water. Like all birds, *Hesperornis* nested on land, but it was probably unable to walk and had to push itself along on its belly.

Vegavis

VAY-gah-viss

- **When** 65 million years ago (Late Cretaceous)
- **Fossil location** Antarctica
- **Habitat** Coast of Antarctica
- **Length** 2 ft (0.6 m)
- **Diet** Water plants

Fossils of *Vegavis*, a relative of ducks and geese, were found in Antarctica in 1992. The discovery was important because it showed that some of today's bird families had already evolved during the age of dinosaurs. *Vegavis* lived in Antarctica when its climate was much less cold than today.

Clawed fingers

Iberomesornis

I-beh-ro-may-SORE-niss

- **When** 135–120 million years ago (Early Cretaceous)
- **Fossil location** Spain
- **Habitat** Woodlands of western Europe
- **Length** 8 in (20 cm)
- **Diet** Probably insects

Iberomesornis was about the size of a finch. It had a stumpy tail and powerful chest muscles, indicating it was a good flyer, and its curved foot claws suggest it perched on trees. But it had features similar to a dinosaur, too, including large claws on its wings.

Backward-pointing toe for perching

Ichthyornis

ICK-thee-OR-niss

- **When** 90–75 million years ago (Late Cretaceous)
- **Fossil location** USA
- **Habitat** Seashores
- **Length** 1 ft (0.3 m)
- **Diet** Fish

Large head

Long beak filled with sharp teeth

Ichthyornis ("fish bird") was a seabird, similar in size and weight to a modern seagull, but its head and beak were much larger. It had a large, keeled breastbone, showing it had powerful breast muscles and was a strong flyer. However, its jaws were packed with small, curved teeth just like those of prehistoric fish-eating lizards called mosasaurs. It may even have fed like one, using its long snout and hooked teeth to snatch fish and other slippery prey from the water. *Ichthyornis* also had webbed feet with short claws.

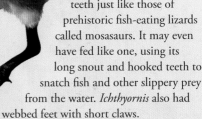

Late birds

Although most dinosaurs disappeared 65 million years ago, birds continued to flourish. During the Cenozoic—the era that followed the age of the dinosaurs—birds evolved into a vast range of new species. Some became masters of the sky or took to the water. Others gave up flying and evolved into huge carnivores, filling the gap that the dinosaurs had left open.

Titanis
tie-TAN-iss

- **When** 5–2 million years ago (Neogene)
- **Fossil location** North and South America
- **Habitat** Grassy plains
- **Height** 8 ft (2 m)
- **Diet** Meat

Also known as a "terror bird," *Titanis* was a gigantic, flightless carnivore as fearsome as a dinosaur. It was twice the weight of a man but much faster, capable of running at up to perhaps 40 mph (65 kph). It used a huge, hooked beak to kill prey and rip open their bodies. *Titanis* lived at the same time as prehistoric humans were beginning to walk on land and spread, but the two never met as *Titanis* lived only in the Americas. Among its prey was the prehistoric horse *Hipparion*.

Dinornis
die-NOR-niss

- **When** 2 million–200 years ago (Neogene)
- **Fossil location** New Zealand
- **Habitat** Plains
- **Height** 12 ft (4 m)
- **Diet** Plants

Twice the height of a man, *Dinornis* (also called the giant moa) was the tallest flightless bird that ever lived. Flocks of *Dinornis* lived in New Zealand until humans settled on the islands about 700 years ago and hunted them to extinction. *Dinornis* belonged to the same bird family (ratites) as the emu, ostrich, and kiwi.

Argentavis
AR-jen-TAY-viss

- **When** 6 million years ago (Neogene)
- **Fossil location** Argentina
- **Habitat** Inland and mountainous areas
- **Wingspan** 26 ft (8 m)
- **Diet** Meat

Enormous wings

Argentavis was the largest bird that ever flew, with a wingspan more than twice that of today's record holder, the wandering albatross. As heavy as a man, it used its vast wings to catch rising air currents and so keep its body aloft, gliding effortlessly as it scanned the landscape for food. Some experts think *Argentavis* was a hunter that could swoop down and snatch prey. Others think it scavenged like a vulture.

Presbyornis
PREZ-bee-OR-niss

Ducklike beak

- **When** 62–55 million years ago (Paleogene)
- **Fossil location** N. America, S. America, Europe
- **Habitat** Lake shores
- **Height** 3 ft (1 m)
- **Diet** Plankton, water plants

Presbyornis looked like a tall duck. Large numbers of fossils, as well as eggs and nests, have been found in sites in North America that were once shallow lakes. Perhaps *Presbyornis* lived in huge flocks by the shore, the birds wading into the shallows to feed, using their beaks to filter food from the water, as ducks do. *Presbyornis* was one of the most successful birds of its time, living for millions of years.

Gastornis

Fifty million years ago, when Europe and North America were covered with lush tropical forests, a giant flightless bird prowled through the undergrowth. *Gastornis* was taller than a man and had a head as large as a horse's. Its beak was gigantic and its bite immensely powerful—but whether it used it to tear flesh, crack bones, or merely munch on leaves remains an unsolved mystery.

Footprint on sandstone
In 2009, a 50-million-year-old footprint made by *Gastornis* was found in a slab of rock in Washington State. To protect the find from rainy weather and fossil thieves, the slab was airlifted in a helicopter to Western Washington University, where it now lies safely.

Gastornis

gas-TORE-niss

- **When** 55–45 million years ago (Paleogene)
- **Fossil location** Europe and N. America
- **Habitat** Tropical and subtropical forests
- **Length** Over 6½ ft (2 m)
- **Diet** Unknown

Discovered in France in 1855, *Gastornis* was named after Gaston Plante, the scientist who found it. A similar bird called *Diatryma* was later found in North America and is now thought to be the same creature. *Gastornis* had large, powerful legs but didn't have the athletic build of a fast runner. Perhaps it was an ambush hunter, hiding in dense forest and waiting for small animals to wander close, before stamping them to death with its giant feet or snatching them in its beak. Some experts think it was a plant-eater and used its beak to crush tough leaves. Others think it was a scavenger that fed on corpses.

▲ MONSTROUS BEAK
Gastornis's huge beak had a slightly hooked tip, like that of a bird of prey. According to some scientists, its bite was strong enough to crack open coconuts and bones. Males and females had similar beaks, so the large size probably didn't evolve for attraction.

Tiny, useless wing

Name game

For more than 100 years, scientists thought *Diatryma* from America and *Gastornis* from Europe were totally different. But then someone realized that the *Gastornis* fossils had been put together incorrectly and they were actually the same bird. Now both are known as *Gastornis*, the older name.

251 million years ago	200		145	65
	Triassic	Jurassic		Cretaceous

MAMMALS

MAMMALS

▲ SINOCONODON *This mammal roamed Early Jurassic China. It was just 12 inches (30 cm) in length and is one of the earliest known mammals. It probably preyed on insects and small reptiles.*

214

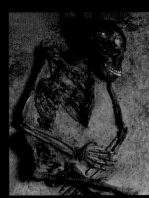

After the dinosaurs perished, mammals took over and became the dominant animals on land. Mammals are hairy, warm-blooded animals that feed their young on milk (such as humans).

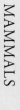

What are mammals?

When the dinosaurs were wiped out, it gave a group of small, warm-blooded animals the chance they needed to thrive. These were the mammals, distinct from other animals largely because they feed their young on milk.

There are now around 5,000 species of mammal.
They are grouped into different families and orders, including:

MARSUPIALS

Marsupials are a group of mammals found in Australasia and the Americas. They give birth to tiny, undeveloped young. Many marsupials have a pouch. The newborn crawls into the pouch to feed on milk and complete its development.

▲ DORIA'S TREE KANGAROO
These unusual climbing kangaroos live in trees.

▶ KOALA *A baby koala will spend more than six months in its mother's pouch.*

▶ GRAY KANGAROO
A kangaroo's pouch faces up but other marsupials have pouches that face down. Young kangaroos are called joeys.

BATS

Bats are the only mammals that can fly (rather than glide). They include the world's smallest mammal, Kitti's hog-nosed bat. Their wings are formed from a double layer of skin.

◀ SMALLEST
Kitti's hog-nosed bat is just 1¼ in (3 cm) long.

▶ GRAY LONG-EARED BAT
Long ears help this bat pick up sounds, leading it to its prey—a moth in this case.

▶ BIGGEST *The Malaysian flying fox is the largest bat, with a wingspan that can reach 5 ft (1.5 m).*

RODENTS

There are more species of rodent than any other mammal. Most rodents are small and many, such as mice, have a long tail. They all have clawed feet, long whiskers, and large gnawing teeth (incisors) at the front of their mouths.

▶ CAPYBARA *This is the world's largest rodent, reaching lengths of up to 4 ft (1.3 m).*

Cape porcupine (well protected by its spines, or quills).

▼ PRAIRIE DOGS *live in burrows that join those of neighbors, forming "towns."*

■ **BRAIN BOX**
All mammals have a large brain relative to their body size. The brain is protected in a hard skull.

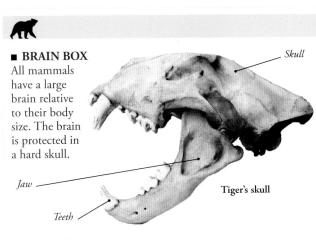

Skull

Jaw

Teeth

Tiger's skull

■ **Hair** Most mammals have hair or fur on their skin to keep them warm.

■ **Young** Rather than laying eggs, most mammals give birth to babies and look after them while they grow and learn.

CARNIVORES

Nearly all the members of this family of mammals are meat-eaters. They all share certain features, such as sharp cheek teeth for slicing flesh. Most are intelligent animals and many are ruthless killers.

Tiger

▶ HYENA
There are four species (types) of hyena, including the striped hyena shown here.

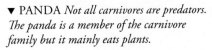

▼ PANDA *Not all carnivores are predators. The panda is a member of the carnivore family but it mainly eats plants.*

HOOFED MAMMALS

Most hoofed mammals walk and run on the tips of their toes on hooves, which are simply large, heavy-duty toenails. This is a large and varied group, and all are herbivores. They are also known as "ungulates." They include deer, zebras, giraffes, and camels.

Zebra

▶ GIRAFFE *The world's tallest mammal can reach more than 17 ft (5 m) in height.*

▼ RED DEER *Many hoofed mammals have horns or antlers. Antlers can grow particularly large on some species of deer.*

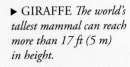

CETACEANS

Although whales and dolphins spend their lives in water, they have to come to the surface to breath air; they have lungs, just like other mammals.

Humpback whale

▲ BOTTLENOSE DOLPHIN *Dolphins are a type of toothed whale. They live in groups.*

▼ SOUTHERN RIGHT WHALE
Some whales, like this one, are filter feeders, sieving plankton from the water through special plates in the mouth.

MAMMALS

Pelycosaurs

Mammals evolved from a group of reptilelike animals called pelycosaurs. The pelycosaurs lived long before even the dinosaurs and for a while were the largest animals on land. They looked more like lizards than mammals, but their link with mammals is clear from a special hole in the skull behind each eye. As in mammals, the jaw muscles passed through this hole, giving these animals a killer bite.

Key features
- Cold-blooded
- Reproduced by laying eggs
- Small brains
- Lizardlike, sprawling legs
- Short claws on toes
- Holes in the skull behind the eyes
- Varied teeth

When
Pelycosaurs first appeared in the Late Carboniferous, 320 million years ago. They died out in the Late Permian, 251 million years ago.

Dimetrodon
die-MET-roe-don

- **When** 280 million years ago (Early Permian)
- **Fossil location** Germany, USA
- **Habitat** Swamps
- **Length** 10 ft (3 m)
- **Diet** Meat

Dimetrodon was the most fearsome predator of its time. It was built like a Komodo dragon, but with a huge "sail" on its back formed from skin wrapped over rods of bone. *Dimetrodon* means "two-sized tooth"—unlike most reptiles, which have teeth that are similar to each other, *Dimetrodon* had teeth of several types, as mammals have. At the front of the mouth were long, daggerlike canines for piercing and grabbing flesh; at the back were smaller, sharp-edged teeth for slicing flesh.

▲ FOSSIL TRACKS *These five-toed footprints may have been left by* Dimetrodon, *one of the most common animals of its time.*

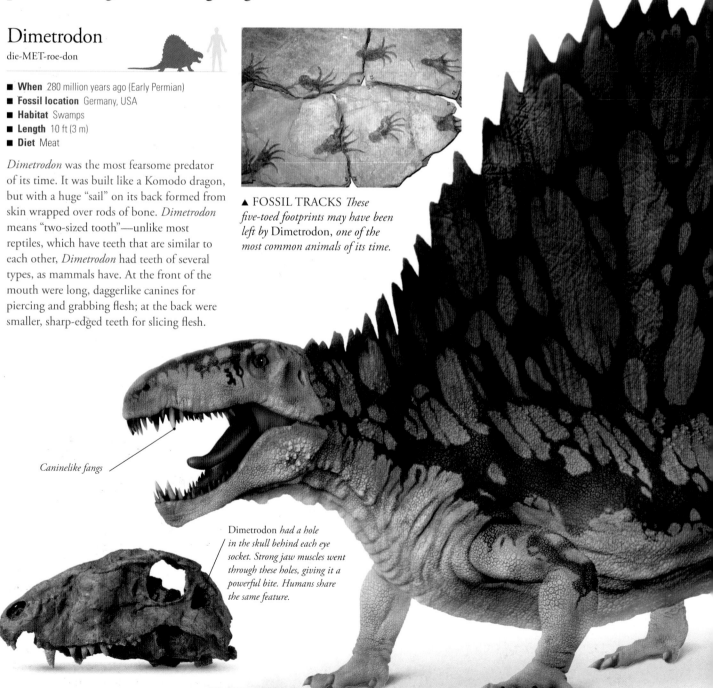

Caninelike fangs

Dimetrodon *had a hole in the skull behind each eye socket. Strong jaw muscles went through these holes, giving it a powerful bite. Humans share the same feature.*

MAMMALS

Ophiacodon
oh-fee-ACK-oh-don

- **When** 310–290 million years ago
(Late Carboniferous–Early Permian)
- **Fossil location** USA
- **Habitat** Swamps
- **Length** 10 ft (3 m)
- **Diet** Fish and small animals

This large predator had a very long skull and huge jaws packed with 170 sharp, pointed teeth. It was built like a crocodile and may even have hunted like a crocodile, lurking in swamps or rivers ready to ambush passing prey. However, *Ophiacodon* is unlikely to have been an underwater hunter, since its tall skull would have been difficult to swing sideways in water, making prey such as fish difficult to catch. On land, *Ophiacodon* walked with its limbs sprawled like a lizard, dragging its tail behind it.

DID YOU KNOW...?

Running along *Dimetrodon*'s back was a spectacular "sail" supported by tall rods of bone that grew from its spine. The sail might have been used to help this cold-blooded creature warm its body. In the early morning, *Dimetrodon* would have been cold and sluggish. Perhaps it basked in the sun, turning its body so the sail caught the sun's rays. Blood flowing through the sail would have spread the warmth through the rest of the body, helping *Dimetrodon* become active.

Sail

Varanops
VA-ran-ops

- **When** 260 million years ago (Late Permian)
- **Fossil location** USA, Russia
- **Habitat** Swamps
- **Length** 3 ft (1 m)
- **Diet** Small animals

Varanops looked like a modern monitor lizard. Compared to other pelycosaurs it was a fast-moving hunter with long legs, well suited to scampering after small animals, which it caught and killed with strong jaws lined with dozens of backward-curved teeth. *Varanops* lived in the Late Permian and was one of the last of the pelycosaurs.

Eothyris
ee-oh-THY-riss

- **When** 280 million years ago (Early Permian)
- **Fossil location** USA
- **Habitat** Swamps
- **Length** Skull 2½ in (6 cm)
- **Diet** Meat

Only a single fossil of *Eothyris* exists: a broad, flat skull that was discovered in 1937. It shows that *Eothyris* probably had a quick, snapping bite. On each side of the upper jaw were two large fangs. The remaining teeth were smaller but sharply pointed, so *Eothyris* was a flesh-eater. A small animal, it perhaps hunted insects or reptiles smaller than itself.

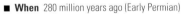

Therapsids

During the Permian Period, the pelycosaurs (see previous page) evolved into more mammal-like animals known as therapsids. Unlike their sprawling, lizardlike ancestors, the therapsids had a more upright build that let them run and breathe more easily, allowing a more active lifestyle. The therapsids were the ancestors of mammals and became increasingly mammal-like over time.

Moschops
MOE-shops

- **When** 255 million years ago (Late Permian)
- **Fossil location** S. Africa
- **Habitat** Forests
- **Length** 8 ft (3 m)
- **Diet** Plants

Moschops was a heavily built plant-eater, about the size of a bear. It had stout legs, a huge, barrel-shaped chest, and a short tail.

The bone in the top of its skull was amazingly thick. Scientists think males may have used their massive skulls as battering rams in contests over mates, as bighorn sheep do today. *Moschops* had wide jaws with short, chisel-like front teeth that met (rather than overlapping) when its mouth closed, allowing it to nip plants precisely.

▼ EARLY HERDS? *Remains of several* Moschops *individuals have been found fossilized together. Perhaps these plant-eaters lived in small herds for protection from predators.*

MAMMALS

Pelanomodon
PEL-an-OH-mow-don

- **When** 255 million years ago (Late Permian)
- **Fossil location** S. Africa
- **Length** 3 ft (1 m)
- **Diet** Plants

Pelanomodon was a member of a large and very successful family of plant-eating therapsids called the dicynodonts (DIE-CYE-no-donts). The dicynodonts used toothless beaks to pluck vegetation, and most had a single pair of tusks. *Pelanomodon* was a stocky, piglike dicynodont that had no tusks. Like other dicynodonts, it could slide its lower jaw forward and backward, which helped it grind the tough plants it ate.

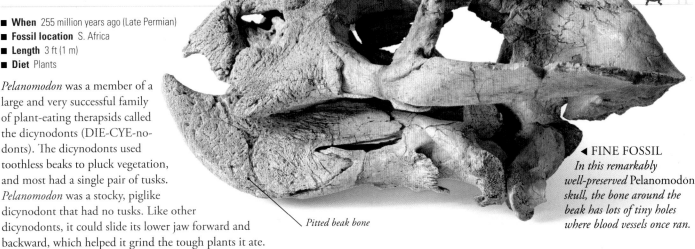

Pitted beak bone

◀ FINE FOSSIL
In this remarkably well-preserved Pelanomodon *skull, the bone around the beak has lots of tiny holes where blood vessels once ran.*

Robertia
roe-BERT-ee-ah

- **When** 255 million years ago (Late Permian)
- **Fossil location** S. Africa
- **Habitat** Woodlands
- **Length** 1 ft (0.4 m)
- **Diet** Plants

The earliest dicynodont known from good fossils is *Robertia*. This small plant-eater was about the size of a domestic cat and had a turtlelike beak, which it used to crop leaves. It had a pair of tusks formed from canine teeth and perhaps used them to dig for roots.

Placerias
plah-SEE-ree-ass

- **When** 220–215 million years ago (Late Triassic)
- **Fossil location** USA
- **Habitat** Flood plains
- **Length** 6–11 ft (2–3 m)
- **Diet** Plants

Placerias was one of the biggest herbivores of its day, weighing about 1,300 lb (600 kg). One of the last large dicynodonts, it lived at the same time as early dinosaurs. Similar in shape and weight to a hippo, it might have wallowed in water, too, and may have used its tusks for fights and social displays as hippos do. A find of 40 skeletons in one place suggests *Placerias* lived in herds.

Broad feet with blunt claws

Sinokannemeyeria
SIGH-no-CAN-eh-my-AIR-ee-ah

- **When** 235 million years ago (Middle Triassic)
- **Fossil location** China
- **Habitat** Woodland
- **Length** 6 ft (2 m)
- **Diet** Tough vegetation, roots

This pig-sized dicynodont had a massive head, a long snout, and a huge belly to house the large intestines needed for digesting rough plant material. Like other dicynodonts, it could move its lower jaw forward and backward to shear and grind tough leaves. Its legs were short and stumpy, with a slightly sprawling gait, suggesting it was not very fast or agile on its feet. But it may have used its powerful forelimbs and small tusks to dig for roots.

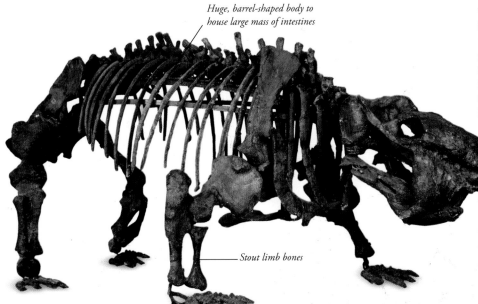

Huge, barrel-shaped body to house large mass of intestines

Stout limb bones

The first mammals

Small and furry, the first mammals looked like mice. They were warm-blooded, which means that their body temperature stayed the same whether it was hot or cold outside. Early mammals lived alongside the dinosaurs but avoided them by hiding in the day and being active only at night, when in the cool, dark air, they chased insects, worms, and other small animals.

Nemegtbaatar

nem-EGT-bat-or

- **When** 65 million years ago (Late Cretaceous)
- **Fossil location** Mongolia
- **Habitat** Woodlands
- **Length** 4 in (10 cm)
- **Diet** Possibly plants

Nemegtbaatar looked a bit like a vole, with a similar short, deep skull, but it wasn't a close relative of voles. It had a wide snout, and its snout bones were riddled with tiny holes for blood vessels. Perhaps the extra blood flow supplied a special gland or a patch of sensitive skin on the top of its head. *Nemegtbaatar* is thought to have been a plant-eater. It had no canine teeth (fangs), and its front teeth (incisors) were large and jutted out, giving it a buck-toothed look.

FAMILY FACT FILE

Key features of mammals
- Females have glands that produce milk
- Body covered with fur or hair
- Ears contain tiny bones that evolved from the jaw bones of ancestors
- Four different types of tooth
- Teeth replaced only once during life

When
The first mammals appeared in the Late Triassic, 200 million years ago.

Teinolophos

TIE-nuh-LOW-fuss

- **When** 125 million years ago (Early Cretaceous)
- **Fossil location** Australia
- **Habitat** Woodlands
- **Length** 4 in (10 cm)
- **Diet** Insects

Only the lower jaw of *Teinolophos* has been found. Even so, scientists are fairly sure this small creature was related to the modern duckbilled platypus, the jaw of which shares key features with that of *Teinolophos*. Most modern mammals give birth to babies, but the duckbilled platypus is one of the few mammals that still lays eggs, as its reptilelike ancestors did. *Teinolophos* was an egg layer, too.

Teinolophos's jaw was tiny but it had a strong bite.

Sinoconodon

SIGH-no-CON-oh-don

- **When** 200 million years ago (Late Triassic)
- **Fossil location** China
- **Habitat** Woodlands
- **Length** 12 in (30 cm)
- **Diet** Omnivorous

Sinoconodon is one of the earliest known mammals. Its ear bones show that it was a mammal, but like a reptile it had teeth that were continuously replaced throughout life. It was about the size of a squirrel and had a slim snout but a strong jaw joint and chin, suggesting a powerful bite—perhaps it preyed on large insects or small reptiles.

▲ HAIRY CREATURE *Fur evolved as a means of keeping the body warm. It allowed early mammals to stay active at night when cold-blooded reptiles had to rest.*

Megazostrodon

MEG-ah-ZO-stroh-don

- **When** 190 million years ago (Early Jurassic)
- **Fossil location** S. Africa
- **Habitat** Woodlands
- **Length** 4 in (10 cm)
- **Diet** Insects

Megazostrodon was built like a shrew, with a slender body and a long snout and tail. Its skeleton was not specialized for any particular lifestyle, but it probably climbed, burrowed, and ran, much like modern rats and shrews. Studies of its braincase indicate it had a relatively large brain and the well-developed hearing and smell of a nocturnal animal (an animal that's active by night). Its teeth suggest a diet of insects. It probably hunted for insects and other small animals at night and hid from danger during daylight hours.

Morganucodon

MORE-gan-oo-CODE-on

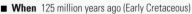

- **When** 210–180 million years ago Late Triassic to Early Jurassic
- **Fossil location** Wales, China, USA
- **Habitat** Woodlands
- **Length** 4 in (9 cm)
- **Diet** Insects

Morganucodon was discovered in Wales, where thousands of fossilized teeth and broken bones were found in a quarry. Later, similar fossils were found as far apart as China, South Africa, and North America, suggesting this creature was common and widespread at the time of the dinosaurs. A tiny, shrewlike animal, it had short legs and a short tail. It probably laid eggs as reptiles do, and its jaw showed a mixture of mammalian and reptilian features.

Eomaia

EE-oh-MY-ah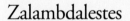

- **When** 125 million years ago (Early Cretaceous)
- **Fossil location** China
- **Habitat** Woodlands
- **Length** 8 in (20 cm)
- **Diet** Insects and other small animals

Only one fossil of *Eomaia* exists but it is beautifully preserved and shows a thick coat of fur as well as features typical of a good climber, such as a very long tail. Studies of the bones show *Eomaia* was more closely related to mammals that give birth to well-developed babies than to egg-layers or marsupials.

Zalambdalestes

ZAH-lam-da-LESS-tease

- **When** 80–70 million years ago (Late Cretaceous)
- **Fossil location** Mongolia
- **Habitat** Woodlands
- **Length** 8 in (20 cm)
- **Diet** Insects

This creature was one of the earliest "placental mammals" (mammals that give birth to well-developed babies). It had a very long, narrow snout and teeth that grew continuously throughout its life, as those of rodents do. Its hindlimbs were longer than its forelimbs, allowing it to hop like a jerboa. Its pointed teeth suggest a diet of insects and maybe seeds.

Flowering plants

It's hard to imagine a world without flowering plants, but today's colorful varieties only began to emerge during the last age of the dinosaurs, the Cretaceous Period.

An old friend
Magnolias color our world today, but they were also familiar to the dinosaurs. They began to appear in the middle of the Cretaceous Period, spreading because they grew quickly, which was a defense against being eaten by dinosaurs.

The beginnings
The earliest flowering plant yet identified is *Archaefructus sinensis* or "ancient fruit," which was small, low growing, and straggly, and not like the colorful plants of today. It dates back around 125 million years.

When did petals appear?
Early flowers lacked petals and when they did first appear, they were tiny. Petals created more variety, as plants began to compete for attention from insect pollinators.

What is pollination?
Most flowering plants don't produce seeds unless a dustlike substance—pollen—is transferred from one flower to another. Pollen can be carried by wind or by animals such as bees, which are rewarded with nectar.

◄ ROBINIA *is a flowering tree native to North America. It is also called a locust.*

It's in the fruit
After being pollinated, a flower produces seeds. To help seeds disperse to new habitats, many plants wrap them in a fruit. Fruits are often sweet and fleshy to attract animals, which eat the fruit and discard the seeds later in droppings.

Grasses
Grasses are flowering plants with tiny flowers that are pollinated by wind. Grasses appeared in the Cretaceous, but grasslands as we know them didn't really become established until around 10 million years ago.

Life in the cold
Flowering plants can survive in hot deserts or on freezing mountaintops. In the land around the North Pole, where the deep soil is frozen solid, trees can't survive but small flowering plants cover the ground, forming a landscape called tundra.

They are everywhere
Today, practically all we eat that isn't meat comes from a flowering plant, while farmed animals, such as cattle, depend on such plants for nourishment. Even our clothes are made from flowering plants, which are used for making linen and cotton.

Many flowering plants burst into bloom in the spring, when insect pollinators become active as the weather warms up. All the plants you can see in this picture are members of the flowering plant family.

MAMMALS

225

Marsupials

The earliest mammals reproduced by laying eggs, but by the Cretaceous Period mammals had evolved new ways of reproducing. The marsupials and their close relatives gave birth to tiny babies that developed outside the mother's body, often in a pouch. Today, most marsupials are found in Australia, but in the past they were very common in South America and Antarctica too.

Thylacosmilus
THIGH-lah-coe-SMILE-us

- **When** 10–2 million years ago (Neogene)
- **Fossil location** S. America
- **Habitat** Woodlands
- **Length** 5 ft (2 m)
- **Diet** Meat

Thylacosmilus looked just like a saber-toothed cat, but it was a close relative of the marsupials. It was the size of a jaguar and built like a cat, but details of its skeleton show it was more like a giant opossum than a member of the cat family. Its huge canine teeth rested on odd-looking bony extensions of its chin, and unlike the teeth of cats they never stopped growing.

FAMILY FACT FILE

Key features of marsupials
- Give birth to tiny, immature babies
- Babies usually develop inside a pouch
- Four pairs of molar teeth
- Furry or hairy body
- Mothers produce milk for young

When
Marsupials first appeared in the Early Cretaceous (about 125 million years ago). Today, there are close to 300 marsupials, including kangaroos, wombats, and koalas.

Diprotodon

die-PRO-toe-don

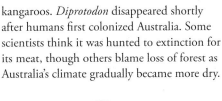

- **When** 2 million–40,000 years ago (Neogene)
- **Fossil location** Australia
- **Habitat** Forest and scrubland
- **Length** 10 ft (3 m)
- **Diet** Plants

Also known as the giant wombat, rhinoceros-sized *Diprotodon* was the largest marsupial known. A plant-eater, it survived on a mixture of rough leaves and grasses and may have lived in herds. Fossils of female *Diprotodons* carrying young reveal that babies' pouches opened toward the rear, unlike the forward-facing pouches of kangaroos. *Diprotodon* disappeared shortly after humans first colonized Australia. Some scientists think it was hunted to extinction for its meat, though others blame loss of forest as Australia's climate gradually became more dry.

Argyrolagus

ar-JYE-roe-LAY-gus

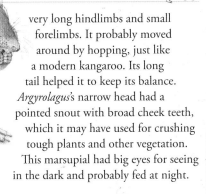

- **When** 23–2 million years ago (Paleogene–Neogene)
- **Fossil location** S. America
- **Habitat** Desert
- **Length** 1 ft (0.4 m)
- **Diet** Plants

Argyrolagus fossils dating back to 53 million years ago have been found in South America. This creature looked like a giant kangaroo rat, with very long hindlimbs and small forelimbs. It probably moved around by hopping, just like a modern kangaroo. Its long tail helped it to keep its balance. *Argyrolagus*'s narrow head had a pointed snout with broad cheek teeth, which it may have used for crushing tough plants and other vegetation. This marsupial had big eyes for seeing in the dark and probably fed at night.

Sinodelphys

SIGH-no-DELF-iss

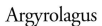
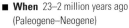

- **When** 125 million years ago (Early Cretaceous)
- **Fossil location** China
- **Habitat** Woodlands
- **Length** 6 in (15 cm)
- **Diet** Insects and worms

Judging by its teeth and by the bones of its wrists and ankles, this chipmunk-sized tree-dweller was closely related to the first marsupials, although it wasn't a marsupial itself. The single fossil, found in China in 2003, is well preserved and shows tufts of hair around the bones. *Sinodelphys* was a good climber, with flexible ankle bones—it could rotate its feet backward to climb down trees. It probably scurried around among the branches—safe from predators—chasing after insects.

▲ **KILLER TEETH** *Two long, saber-shaped teeth pointed downward from* Thylacosmilus's *upper jaw. They were protected by tooth guards made of bone.*

Thylacine

Most large extinct animals are known only from fossils. The thylacine, or Tasmanian tiger, is one of the few that was photographed and even filmed before it vanished. This fascinating animal was a marsupial (a pouched mammal) that evolved the shape, appearance, and lifestyle of a wolf. Thylacines once lived throughout New Guinea, Australia, and Tasmania. The last one died in a zoo in 1936.

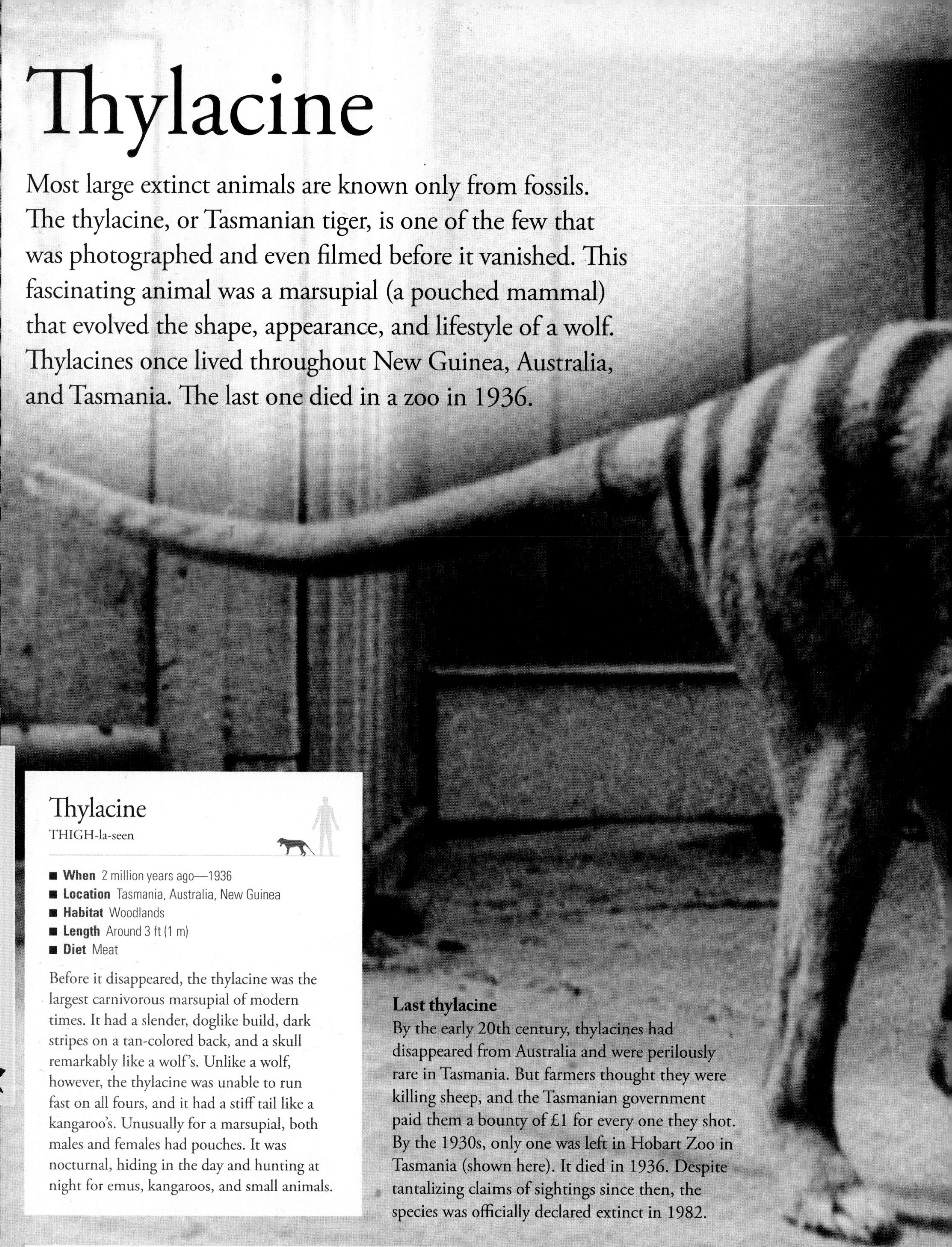

Thylacine

THIGH-la-seen

- **When** 2 million years ago—1936
- **Location** Tasmania, Australia, New Guinea
- **Habitat** Woodlands
- **Length** Around 3 ft (1 m)
- **Diet** Meat

Before it disappeared, the thylacine was the largest carnivorous marsupial of modern times. It had a slender, doglike build, dark stripes on a tan-colored back, and a skull remarkably like a wolf's. Unlike a wolf, however, the thylacine was unable to run fast on all fours, and it had a stiff tail like a kangaroo's. Unusually for a marsupial, both males and females had pouches. It was nocturnal, hiding in the day and hunting at night for emus, kangaroos, and small animals.

Last thylacine

By the early 20th century, thylacines had disappeared from Australia and were perilously rare in Tasmania. But farmers thought they were killing sheep, and the Tasmanian government paid them a bounty of £1 for every one they shot. By the 1930s, only one was left in Hobart Zoo in Tasmania (shown here). It died in 1936. Despite tantalizing claims of sightings since then, the species was officially declared extinct in 1982.

4.6 billion years ago	542 million years ago	488		444		416		359	299
Precambrian Eon		Cambrian		Ordovician		Silurian		Devonian	Carboniferous

LIVING RELATIVE

The Tasmanian devil is one of the closest living relatives of the thylacine. This cat-sized carnivore is named for its blood-curdling scream and is famous for having an immensely powerful bite that can crush bones. It eats every bit of a carcass—bone, skin, feet, and all. When alarmed, it gives out a foul odor to drive away enemies.

▲ ROCK PAINTINGS *made by the aboriginal people of Australia show that thylacines were once widespread on the Australian mainland.*

Permian	Triassic	Jurassic	Cretaceous	Paleogene	Neogene
	251	200	145	65	23	Now

Insect-eaters and relatives

Many early mammals were not carnivores or herbivores but insectivores, surviving on a diet of insects, worms, snails, and other small animals. They had excellent senses of smell and hearing, but often poor vision. They either made burrows in the ground or lived among the trees. Shy and secretive, many were nocturnal, hunting at night when it was safe to venture out.

Leptictidium
LEP-tick-TID-ee-um

- **When** 40 million years ago (Paleogene)
- **Fossil location** Europe
- **Habitat** Woodlands
- **Length** 3 ft (1 m)
- **Diet** Insects and other small animals

Leptictidium had enormous hind legs and might have hopped around like a miniature kangaroo, although it could probably scamper on all fours, too. Studies of its skull suggest it had a long, trunklike nose like that of an elephant shrew. It would have used this to sniff out insects and other small animals. Fossilized stomach contents show it fed not only on insects but also on lizards and small mammals.

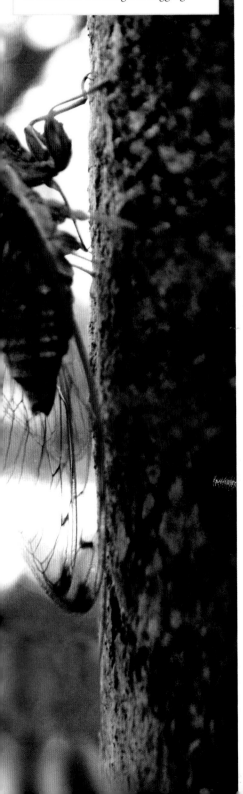

FAMILY FACT FILE

Many different types of mammal feed on insects. Although these insect-eaters share some key features, they aren't closely related and don't make up a true animal family.

Key features

- Coats of fur or hair
- Pointed snouts
- Short legs
- Claws for climbing and digging

Glyptodon
GLIP-toe-don

- **When** 2 million–10,000 years ago (Neogene)
- **Fossil location** S. America
- **Habitat** Swamps
- **Length** 6½ ft (2 m)
- **Diet** Plants

Glyptodon was a giant relative of today's armadillos, but unlike an armadillo it ate plants rather than insects. It was an enormous animal, weighing as much as a small car. Its armor was made up of more than a thousand small, bony plates arranged like tiles over its back and tail. It had a small, helmetlike head and flat-topped teeth for grinding tough leaves.

LIVING RELATIVE

Like their ancient relative *Glyptodon*, armadillos have armor made up of bony plates to protect themselves from predators. Baby armadillos are born with soft shells, which harden as they grow. The three-banded armadillo can roll into a ball to protect its soft underbelly; other armadillo species drop to the ground and pull in their legs.

Eurotamandua
YOU-row-ta-MAN-doo-ah

- **When** 50–40 million years ago (Early Paleogene)
- **Fossil location** Germany
- **Habitat** Woodlands
- **Length** 3 ft (1 m)
- **Diet** Ants and termites

Eurotamandua was a close relative of modern pangolins. Pangolins have no teeth and feed by ripping open ant and termite nests with their claws and collecting insects with a long, sticky tongue. *Eurotamandua* had no teeth but had a long snout and probably a long tongue, too. It also had a flexible, muscular tail with which it might have gripped branches while climbing.

Deinogalerix
DIE-no-GAL-eh-rix

- **When** 10–5 million years ago (Late Neogene)
- **Fossil location** Italy
- **Habitat** Woodlands
- **Length** 2 ft (0.5 m)
- **Diet** Probably insects and dead meat

Although its name means "terrible hedgehog," *Deinogalerix* did not have spines like its modern relatives. Instead, its body was covered with hair. With its long, conical snout, small pointed ears, and a tapering tail, it looked more like a giant rat than a hedgehog. *Deinogalerix* perhaps fed on large insects such as beetles and crickets, but it may also have eaten birds and small mammals, as well as scavenging meat from carcasses. Rather than chasing after prey, it probably rooted through the undergrowth, snapping at any small animal it came across before the victim had time to escape.

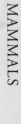

231

Icaronycteris

Prehistoric bats such as *Icaronycteris* were not very different from the ones found today. They even hunted in the same manner—flying around in the night skies and swooping over places where plenty of insects gathered, such as among the trees or above lakes. Some scientists suggest that these early bats flew at night to escape the clutches of predatory birds that hunted during the day.

DID YOU KNOW...?

Icaronycteris is named after Icarus, the son of the ancient Greek craftsman Daedalus. According to Greek myth, Icarus and his father escaped from prison on wings attached by wax. Icarus flew too close to the Sun. The wax melted, and he plunged to his death in the sea below.

MAMMALS

4.6 billion years ago	542 million years ago	488	444	416	359	299	251
Precambrian Eon	Cambrian	Ordovician	Silurian	Devonian	Carboniferous	Permian

Icaronycteris
ICK-ah-roe-NICK-teh-riss

- **When** 55–50 million years ago (Paleogene)
- **Fossil location** USA
- **Habitat** Woodlands of N. America
- **Length** 1 ft (0.3 m)
- **Diet** Insects

We know *Icaronycteris* was a night-flying bat that caught prey in midair because moth scales have been found in the stomach of one fossil. To catch moths at night, modern bats send out pulses of sound and use the echoes to "see" in the dark (echolocation). The structure of *Icaronycteris*'s inner ear suggests it was able to use echolocation, too.

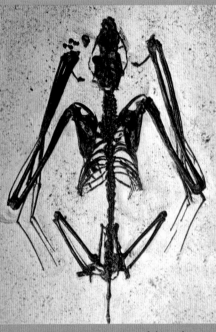

▲ ICARONYCTERIS *is one of the earliest known bats. Unlike some modern bats, its long tail was not connected to its hindlimbs by a flap of skin. However, it did sleep hanging upside down from a tree branch or a cave roof.*

LIVING RELATIVE

Bats are the only true flying mammals. They have membranes of skin between their arms and fingers, which have evolved into long wings. Some bats, such as this fruit bat, or flying fox, feed on fruit instead of insects.

200	145	65	23	Now
Triassic	Jurassic	Cretaceous	Paleogene	Neogene

Cats and hyenas

Prehistoric cats were just as ferocious as their modern cousins and sometimes a lot bigger. Like modern cats, they had powerful, muscular bodies and sharp teeth for slashing flesh. Cats and hyenas share a common ancestor, and early species show features of both types of animal. The group includes some of the most efficient killers on the planet.

Smilodon
SMILE-oh-don

- ■ **When** 5 million to 10,000 years ago (Neogene)
- ■ **Fossil location** N. America and S. America
- ■ **Habitat** Plains
- ■ **Length** 6 ft (1.8 m)
- ■ **Diet** Meat

Smilodon was one of more than 100 species of saber-toothed cat that scientists have discovered. It was a heavy, muscular animal and a predator to be reckoned with, able to wrestle victims to the ground before tearing open their throats. Despite their size, *Smilodon*'s teeth weren't strong enough to bite through the back of the neck, as a lion's can, and would break if they hit bone. *Smilodon* hunted a variety of prey, including bears, horses, and young mammoths. Fossils have been found together, suggesting it lived and hunted in packs as lions do.

Eye socket

◄ SABER TOOTH
Smilodon's *canine teeth were more than 10 in (25 cm) long including the root. Like sabers (short swords), they were curved and had extremely sharp edges.*

Canine tooth with sawlike rear edge

MAMMALS

Dinofelis

DIE-no-FEE-liss

- **When** 5–1 million years ago (Neogene)
- **Fossil location** Africa, Europe, Asia, N. America
- **Habitat** Woodlands
- **Length** 5 ft (2 m)
- **Diet** Meat

Dinofelis ("terrible cat") was about the same size as modern forest-dwelling cats, such as leopards and jaguars. Like these cats, it may even have had a spotted or striped coat that helped it to remain hidden in the undergrowth while it kept a lookout for prey. *Dinofelis* stalked its prey in the forest, hiding behind trees before ambushing victims. Its prominent front teeth were shorter and less flattened than those of other saber-toothed cats but were just as deadly. In Africa, its bones have been found near the sites of early humans, which suggests that it may have preyed on them, too.

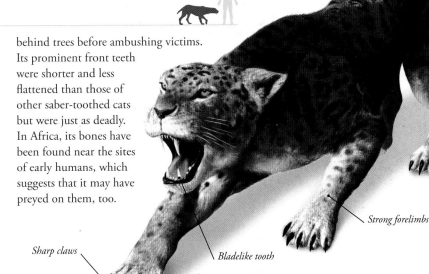

Strong forelimbs

Sharp claws

Bladelike tooth

Cave hyena

cave high-EE-na

- **When** 2 million–10,000 years ago (Neogene)
- **Fossil location** Europe, Asia
- **Habitat** Grassland
- **Length** 5 ft (2 m)
- **Diet** Meat

A hunter and scavenger, the cave hyena fed on wild horses, woolly rhinos, deer, and humans in ice age Europe and Asia. Recent tests of DNA from fossils show it was the same species as the modern African spotted hyena (*Crocuta crocuta*), but larger and with longer legs.

Canine tooth

Ictitherium

ICK-tee-theeri-um

- **When** 13–5 million years ago (Neogene)
- **Fossil location** Europe, Asia, Africa
- **Habitat** Plains
- **Length** 4 ft (1.2 m)
- **Diet** Insects

Ictitherium was an early member of the hyena family. However, with its long body and short legs, it looked more like a civet (a tree-climbing, nocturnal mammal) than a modern hyena. It was probably an insect-eater, but may have also fed on small mammals and lizards.

Machairodus

mah-CARE-oh-duss

- **When** 12 million–125,000 years ago (Neogene)
- **Fossil location** N. America, Africa, Europe, Asia
- **Habitat** Woodlands, grassland
- **Length** 5 ft (2 m)
- **Diet** Meat

Large and ferocious, *Machairodus* was a saber-toothed cat, although its canines were shaped more like a knife blade than those of *Smilodon*. Like most early cats, it was an ambush predator, since its legs were too short to sustain a long chase. Species that evolved later and lived on the plains had longer front limbs, which shows that they were traveling farther to hunt and were running after their prey.

FAMILY FACT FILE

Key features
- Sharp teeth
- Powerful jaws and neck muscles
- Strong forelimbs
- Clawed feet

When

The first catlike mammals lived about 35 million years ago, in the Paleogene Period. They evolved into the family of modern cats that include lions and jaguars.

Ice age!

Imagine a world in which ice extends farther than the Arctic and Antarctic—a world in which ice sheets cover large chunks of North America, Europe, and Asia. At times, much of the Earth's surface has been covered by sheets of ice. These periods of Earth's history are known as its ice ages, with glaciers a prominent feature.

▲ AN EARLY VIEW *A nineteenth century artwork by a Swedish geologist and naturalist, Oswald Heer, provided an unrealistic picture of large mammals, including mammoths and deer, surviving at the edges of the last ice age. In reality, these mammals lived on steppes (grasslands).*

WHAT IS A GLACIER?

A glacier is a slow-moving river of ice, forced to move downhill by its weight. It can be enormous. In an ice age, Earth's temperature varies, with glaciers pushing forward over land during the cold periods (known as glacial periods) and retreating in warmer periods (interglacial periods).

Arctic Ocean

Human migration

Asia

North America

Pacific Ocean

Snowball Earth

Over millions of years, Earth has moved from warm periods to cold periods and back to warm periods. Scientists don't know what triggers an ice age, but think it has something to do with gradual changes in the Earth's orbit around the Sun over millions of years.

During the most severe ice ages, Earth was entirely covered in ice.

An unusual route opens

During an ice age, sea levels fall by as much as 300 ft (100 m) as water becomes locked up on land as ice, instead of flowing out to sea in rivers. As the sea falls, new land appears, sometimes forming a bridge between continents or islands. During the last ice age, land bridges joined Britain to Europe, New Guinea to Australia, and Siberia to Alaska, allowing people to cross from Asia to North America.

Glacial boulders are known as "erratics." Some are small, but they can also be huge.

Clues from the past

When an ice age ends and glaciers disappear, they leave behind lots of clues that the land was once buried under ice. Glaciers carve away land as they flow, forming deep, U-shaped valleys. When they melt, they leave behind huge boulders, called erratics, often made from a type of rock not found locally.

Ice age

Today

DID YOU KNOW?

Modern humans emerged during the last ice age, living south of the ice sheets. There were also big mammals known as megafauna, including:

■ Woolly mammoths
■ Woolly rhinos
■ Cave bears
■ Cave lions
■ Giant beavers

Many of the large mammals became extinct just after modern humans arrived.

A blanket of ice

At the peak of the last ice age, some 20,000 years ago, large areas of northern Europe were covered by ice, as well as Greenland and Iceland and parts of the Atlantic Ocean. Europe's mountain ranges—the Alps, the Pyrenees, the Urals, and the Carpathians—were also covered in ice.

▲ ICE SHEET
Northern Europe was covered by a gigantic ice sheet during the last ice age.

Caniforms

This family of mostly carnivorous mammals includes dogs, bears, foxes, raccoons, weasels, and—perhaps surprisingly—seals, sea lions, and walruses, which evolved from bearlike ancestors. Caniform means "dog-shaped," but early caniforms were tree-climbing animals that resembled pine martens. As they colonized the ground they evolved into more dog- and then bearlike forms.

Canis dirus
CAY-niss DIE-russ

- **When** 2 million–10,000 years ago (Late Pleistocene)
- **Fossil location** Canada, USA, Mexico
- **Habitat** Plains
- **Length** 5 ft (1.5 m)
- **Diet** Meat

Canis dirus ("dire wolf") was a large animal with much stronger jaws and bigger teeth than modern wolves. Its limbs were shorter than those of its cousin the gray wolf, so it probably spent more time scavenging than hunting. The dire wolf died out in the last ice age, possibly because of the extinction of the large herbivores on which it fed. Thousands of fossils have been found in La Brea tar pits in California (see page 240), suggesting it was a pack hunter.

FAMILY FACT FILE

Key features
- Long snouts
- Four shearing teeth at front of jaw (carnassials)
- Walked on all fours
- Most were unable to retract (pull back) their claws into a protective sheath, as cats can do.

When
They first appeared in the Paleogene Period (about 55 million years ago), and still exist today.

Arctodus

ARK-toe-duss

- **When** 2 million–10,000 years ago (Late Pleistocene)
- **Fossil location** Canada, USA, Mexico
- **Habitat** Mountains and woodlands
- **Length** 10 ft (3 m)
- **Diet** Omnivorous

This huge predator was the largest bear ever known. When it reared up on its hindlimbs, it was more than twice the height of a man. *Arctodus* charged at prey such as deer, bison, and horses, outrunning them on its long legs. It also ate plant foods and probably scavenged on carcasses, too.

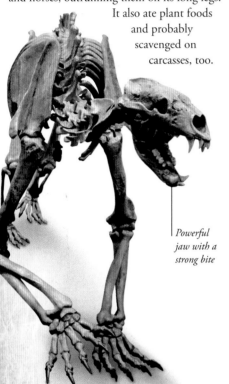

Powerful jaw with a strong bite

Amphicyon

am-fee-SIGH-on

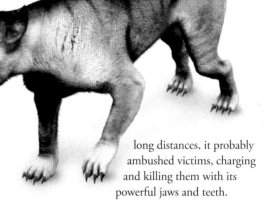

- **When** 30–20 million years ago (Neogene)
- **Fossil location** N. America, Spain, Germany, France
- **Habitat** Plains
- **Length** 6½ ft (2 m)
- **Diet** Omnivorous

Also called a bear-dog, *Amphicyon* looked like a cross between a dog and a bear. But its large build—it was the size of a modern grizzly bear—and diet of plants and meat made it more like a bear than a dog. It had wolflike teeth, powerful limbs, and a long tail. Since it was too heavily built to chase prey over long distances, it probably ambushed victims, charging and killing them with its powerful jaws and teeth.

Enaliarctos

en-AL-ee-ARK-toss

- **When** 20 million years ago (Neogene)
- **Fossil location** USA
- **Habitat** Coasts
- **Length** 3 ft (1 m)
- **Diet** Fish, meat, shellfish

Enaliarctos was one of the earliest members of the pinniped family, which includes seals, sea lions, and walruses. It seems to have divided its time between water and land, rather like a modern sea lion does. With its webbed feet and flippers, *Enaliarctos* swam easily through water, although it was more clumsy on land. Its large eyes helped it to see in deep water, and it had specialized inner ears for hearing underwater. Its teeth were well suited to slicing through flesh, and it probably returned to the shore to eat the fish or shellfish it caught.

Miacis

me-AH-kiss

- **When** 55 million years ago (Paleogene)
- **Fossil location** Europe, N. America
- **Habitat** Tropical forests
- **Length** 1 ft (0.3 m)
- **Diet** Small mammals, reptiles, birds

Miacis was a member of the family from which all modern carnivorous mammals evolved. A small animal about the size of a weasel, it had a similarly slender body and short legs. *Miacis* lived high up in trees, using its agile limbs to climb. Its long tail helped it balance as it leaped from branch to branch. It probably hunted smaller animals, such as small mammals and reptiles, using its sharp teeth to tear off flesh in a scissorlike action. It might also have eaten eggs and fruit. Its vision, though good, was not as sharp as that of modern dogs.

▶ SURE-FOOTED
The needle-sharp claws on Miacis's toes helped it to hold onto trees as it climbed.

A sticky end

Thirty-eight thousand years ago, a pack of saber-toothed cats were pursuing a weak mammoth. The mammoth stumbled into what it thought was a shallow pool, and found itself trapped in sticky tar. The cats were soon trapped, too. Hunted and hunters died. They had fallen into a massive tar pit.

LA BREA

Thousands of fossilized animal bones have been found at the La Brea Tar Pits in Los Angeles, many dating back to the last ice age. There are also huge quantities of fossilized plants and insects—altogether these pits have provided a fascinating view of life in the Los Angeles area some 38,000 years ago.

Many of the species found at La Brea are still there today, including the California condor.

🐻 DID YOU KNOW?

A tar pit is more correctly known as an asphalt pit (asphalt is naturally occurring, whereas tar is made by people). It is a place where asphalt leaks to the ground's surface. Asphalt pits have proved valuable in studying ecosystems that existed thousands of years ago because of the animals caught and preserved in them.

▲WHAT A MAMMOTH FIND! *More than 60 species of mammal have been found at La Brea, including some fine specimens of mammoths. A special museum houses the finds.*

MORE PREDATORS THAN PREY?

One interesting fact shown by the fossils at La Brea is that more than 90 percent of the mammals are carnivores. Why? Perhaps it's because if a single herbivore became trapped, its struggles would draw predators and scavengers hoping for an easy meal, who in turn became trapped.

▲ SKULLS *More than 4,000 dire wolves have been discovered in La Brea tar pits. Dire wolves became extinct some 10,000 years ago.*

Altogether, more than **3.5 million specimens** have been recovered from La Brea, representing nearly **650 species** of plant and animal.

 FACT FILE

All these animals have been found at La Brea.

Herbivores
- Mammoth
- American mastodon
- Ground sloth
- Shasta ground sloth
- Ancient bison
- American camel
- Stilt-legged llama
- Horse
- Pronghorn
- Tar-pit pronghorn
- California tapir
- Elk (wapiti)
- Deer

Carnivores
- Short-faced bear
- Brown bear
- Black bear
- American lion
- Saber-toothed cat (Smilodon)
- Jaguar
- American cheetah
- Cougar
- Dire wolf
- Gray wolf
- Coyote
- Weasel

Birds
- California condor
- Eagle
- Hawk
- Falcon
- Vulture
- Sandhill crane
- Canada goose
- Mallard duck
- Night heron
- La Brea stork
- Grebe
- Cormorant
- Magpie
- Great horned owl
- La Brea owl
- Greater roadrunner
- Band-tailed pigeon
- Curlew
- California quail

Reptiles, amphibians, and fish
- Kingsnake
- Garter snake
- Pond turtle
- Rainbow trout
- Rattlesnake
- Salamander
- Three-spined stickleback
- Tree frog
- Toad

MAMMALS

241

Rabbits and rodents

Rodents—which include rats, mice, and squirrels—were as plentiful in prehistoric times as they are today. Rabbits, too, hopped and jumped across the landscape in much the same way as their modern descendants. Although most were small herbivores, some species grew to a scarily large size.

Castoroides
CASS-tore-OY-deez

- **When** 3 million–10,000 years ago (Neogene)
- **Fossil location** N. America
- **Habitat** Lakes, ponds, swamps
- **Length** 10 ft (3 m)
- **Diet** Plants

Also known as the giant beaver, *Castoroides* was about the size of a black bear and was one of the largest rodents ever to have lived. Modern beavers have chisel-like front teeth, but *Castoroides*'s teeth were broad and large. It had shorter hindlimbs, but its tail was longer and narrower. Like modern beavers, it lived in or near water and perhaps built small dams and dome-shaped lodges (beaver homes).

20,000-year-old fossil tooth of a giant beaver.

Palaeocastor
PAY-lee-oh-CASS-tor

- **When** 25 million years ago (Paleogene)
- **Fossil location** USA, Japan
- **Habitat** Woodlands
- **Length** 15 in (38 cm)
- **Diet** Plants

Palaeocastor was a much smaller and earlier beaver than *Castoroides*. This land-dwelling animal dug deep burrows with its front teeth rather than building dams and lodges. Fossilized burrows with *Palaeocastor* skeletons and tooth marks on the walls were found in 1891. These famous burrows were called "devil's corkscrews" because of their narrow, spiral shape.

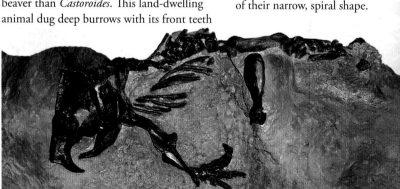

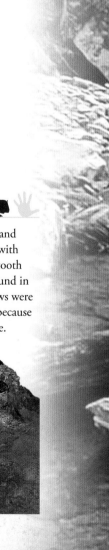

FAMILY FACT FILE

Key features
- Rodents have four special incisor teeth that are used for gnawing; rabbits have eight.
- Furry coats
- Clawed toes

When
They first appeared in the Paleogene Period (about 65 million years ago) and still exist today.

Eomys

EE-oh-miss

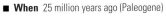

- **When** 25 million years ago (Paleogene)
- **Fossil location** France, Germany, Spain, Turkey
- **Habitat** Woodlands
- **Length** 10 in (25 cm)
- **Diet** Plants

This small rodent could glide through the air. Many *Eomys* skeletons have been found, showing that it had a long skin membrane between its front and back legs, rather like that of a modern flying squirrel. *Eomys* is thought to be a close relative of gophers and pocket mice that exist today.

Palaeolagus

PAY-lee-oh-LAG-us

- **When** 33–23 million years ago (Late Paleogene)
- **Fossil location** USA
- **Habitat** Plains and woodlands
- **Length** 10 in (25 cm)
- **Diet** Grass

Palaeolagus is one of the oldest known fossil rabbits. It had long, pointed ears and a slightly longer tail than modern animals. Its hindlimbs were shorter than those of living rabbits, which suggests that it scampered like a squirrel rather than hopping. It had two pairs of upper teeth to nibble on grass and other plants.

Skull

Short hindlimbs

Ceratogaulus

seh-RAT-oh-GAWL-us

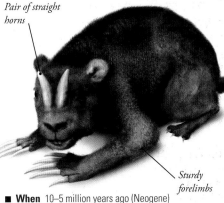

Pair of straight horns

Sturdy forelimbs

- **When** 10–5 million years ago (Neogene)
- **Fossil location** Canada, USA
- **Habitat** Woodlands
- **Length** 12 in (30 cm)
- **Diet** Plants

Known as the horned gopher, *Ceratogaulus* is the smallest mammal known to have had horns and one of the only horned rodents. Scientists once thought that it used its horns for digging, but their position on the skull makes this unlikely. Both sexes had horns, so they were probably used for defense rather than mating displays. *Ceratogaulus* lived in burrows that it dug with its large claws. Its eyes were small and its vision was probably poor.

MAMMALS

Hoofed mammals

Hooves are simply enlarged toenails that support
an animal's weight and help it walk on hard ground.
All hoofed mammals evolved from ancestors with
five toes, but over time some toes withered away,
leaving just one, two, or three main hooves per foot.
Early hoofed mammals were as small as cats, but later
species grew to a huge size on a diet of grass or leaves.

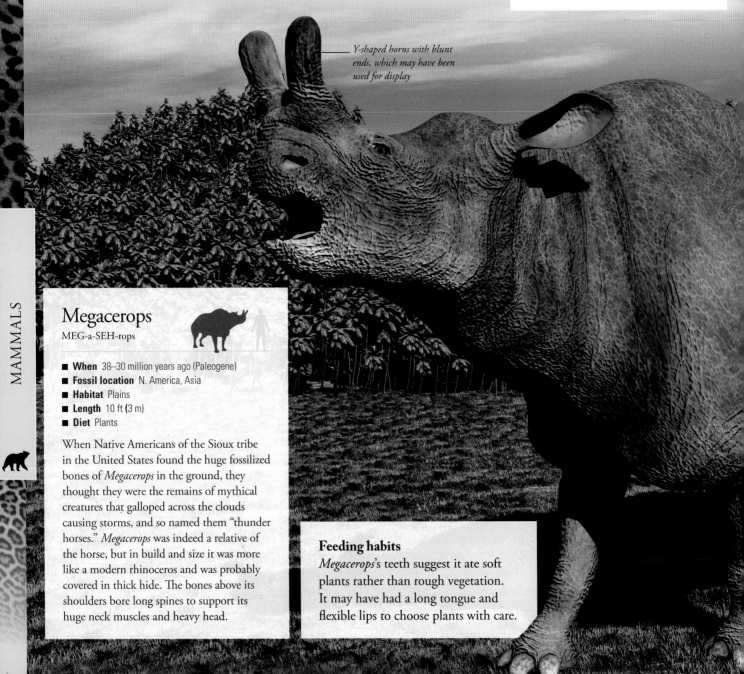

Y-shaped horns with blunt ends, which may have been used for display

Megacerops
MEG-a-SEH-rops

- **When** 38–30 million years ago (Paleogene)
- **Fossil location** N. America, Asia
- **Habitat** Plains
- **Length** 10 ft (3 m)
- **Diet** Plants

When Native Americans of the Sioux tribe in the United States found the huge fossilized bones of *Megacerops* in the ground, they thought they were the remains of mythical creatures that galloped across the clouds causing storms, and so named them "thunder horses." *Megacerops* was indeed a relative of the horse, but in build and size it was more like a modern rhinoceros and was probably covered in thick hide. The bones above its shoulders bore long spines to support its huge neck muscles and heavy head.

Feeding habits
Megacerops's teeth suggest it ate soft plants rather than rough vegetation. It may have had a long tongue and flexible lips to choose plants with care.

Uintatherium

WIN-tah-THEE-ree-um

- **When** 45–40 million years ago (Paleogene)
- **Fossil location** N. America, Asia
- **Habitat** Plains
- **Length** 10 ft (3 m)
- **Diet** Plants

Large, blunt horns

Tusklike teeth

Uintatherium was another rhinoceros-like mammal, with a large, barrel-shaped body. Its skull was large and flat, but its brain was very small. On its head were three pairs of horns covered in skin, with the biggest horns at the back. Male *Uintatheriums* had larger horns than females, which suggests that they used them for display or for fighting other males. The animal's great weight and short legs suggest it usually moved slowly, although it may have been capable of short bursts of speed.

Phenacodus

fen-ACK-oh-duss

- **When** 55–45 million years ago (Paleogene)
- **Fossil location** N. America, Europe
- **Habitat** Grasslands, open woodlands
- **Length** 3 ft (1 m)
- **Diet** Grass

Like horses, *Phenacodus* had a skeleton well suited to running. In fact, experts once thought it was an ancestor of the horse. It had longer, more flexible legs than other primitive hoofed mammals and carried most of its weight on its three middle toes. Its large, squarish teeth were ideal for grinding up tough vegetation.

Phenacodus may have had a striped or spotted coat to blend in with woodland undergrowth and help it hide from predators.

Long, flexible tail

Five toes, each ending in a blunt claw

Mesoreodon

ME-zoe-REE-oh-don

- **When** 23 million years ago (Paleogene)
- **Fossil location** USA
- **Habitat** Deserts, prairies
- **Length** 3 ft (1 m)
- **Diet** Plants

Mesoreodon was a sheep-sized hoofed mammal with big eyes. One fossil was found with its voicebox preserved. Studies of the voicebox reveal that *Mesoreodon* could make loud, hooting sounds like modern howler monkeys—perhaps to frighten predators and warn members of its herd. It had sharp canine teeth that were probably used to defend against attacks, or for display. The teeth at the back of the mouth had crescent-shaped edges, suitable for chewing low-growing plants.

MAMMALS

Leptomeryx

Herds of tiny, deerlike mammals known as *Leptomeryx* fed in the forests and grasslands of North America for more than 13 million years. *Leptomeryx* was not much bigger than a hare and probably just as nimble, darting around on its tiny hooves in the undergrowth. This little plant-eater flourished in huge numbers and was probably an easy snack for predators of the time.

Leptomeryx

LEP-toe-MERRIX

- **When** 38–25 million years ago (Paleogene)
- **Fossil location** USA
- **Habitat** Grasslands
- **Length** 1 ft (0.3 m)
- **Diet** Mostly plants

Leptomeryx was a ruminant—a hoofed mammal that brings up food from its stomach to chew a second time. During the period in which it lived, the climate changed and grasslands replaced forest. Fossils show that the teeth of *Leptomeryx* became stronger at the same time—perhaps it was evolving to live on rougher foods such as grass, which contains tiny flecks of glass to protect itself from herbivores. *Leptomeryx* was built like a deer but had no antlers, although males had small tusks formed from their canine teeth.

4.6 billion years ago	542 million years ago	488		444		416		359
Precambrian Eon	Cambrian		Ordovician		Silurian		Devonian	Carboniferous

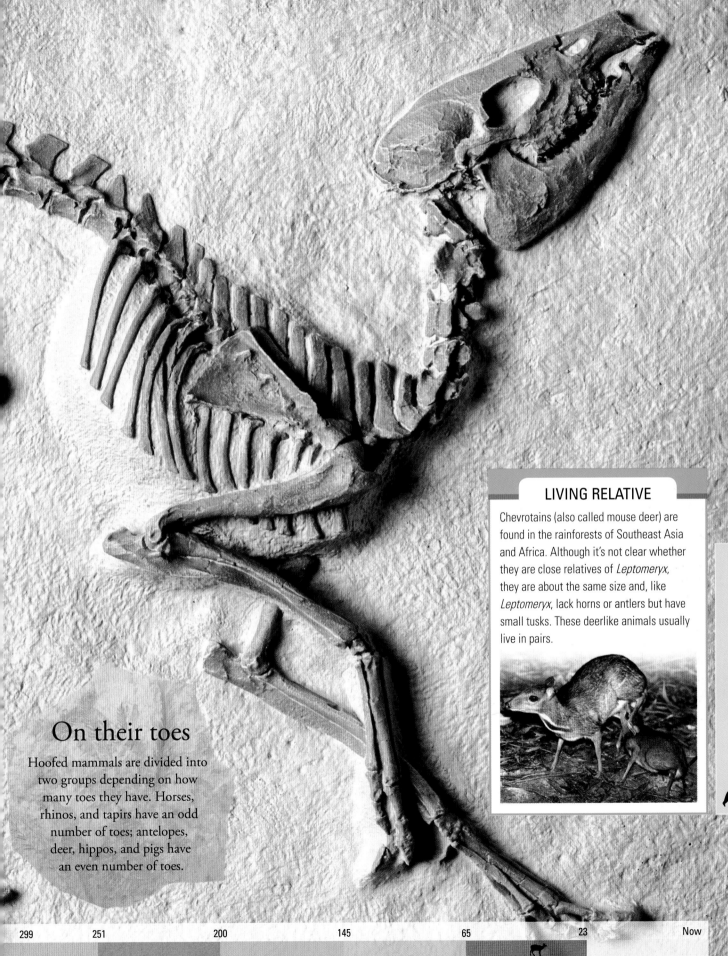

LIVING RELATIVE

Chevrotains (also called mouse deer) are found in the rainforests of Southeast Asia and Africa. Although it's not clear whether they are close relatives of *Leptomeryx*, they are about the same size and, like *Leptomeryx*, lack horns or antlers but have small tusks. These deerlike animals usually live in pairs.

On their toes

Hoofed mammals are divided into two groups depending on how many toes they have. Horses, rhinos, and tapirs have an odd number of toes; antelopes, deer, hippos, and pigs have an even number of toes.

299	251	200	145	65	23	Now
Permian	Triassic	Jurassic	Cretaceous	Paleogene	Neogene	

Macrauchenia

Seven million years ago, this odd-looking herbivore was common on the plains of South America. It looked like a mixture of different animals, with a body like a horse's, a long neck like a camel's, and perhaps even a short trunk. *Macrauchenia* belonged to an extinct family of hoofed mammals that existed only in South America and Antarctica.

DID YOU KNOW...?

When he was in his twenties, the English scientist Charles Darwin spent two years traveling around the world on the ship HMS *Beagle*. He came across many exotic plants and animals. In 1834, on a stopover in Argentina, South America, he found a half skeleton of what appeared to be some kind of prehistoric camel or llama. In fact, it was the first fossil of *Macrauchenia*.

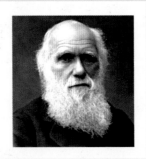

4.6 billion years ago	542 million years ago	488	444	416	359	299
Precambrian Eon		Cambrian	Ordovician	Silurian	Devonian	Carboniferous

Macrauchenia

mack-row-KAY-nee-ah

- **When** 7 million–20,000 years ago (Neogene)
- **Fossil location** S. America
- **Habitat** Grasslands
- **Length** 10 ft (3 m)
- **Diet** Leaves and grass

Macrauchenia's nostrils were high up on its skull, between the eyes, leading some experts to suggest that it had a short trunk. Its long neck would have allowed it to feed on trees as well as grazing on the ground. Short thigh bones imply it was not a fast runner, but its leg bones were arranged in such a way as to allow it to twist and turn when running, helping it outfox predators such as the saber-toothed cat *Smilodon*.

The snout may have looked like a short trunk.

251	200	145	65	23	Now
Permian	Triassic	Jurassic	Cretaceous	Paleogene	Neogene

Horses

The earliest horses were small, leaf-eating mammals that lived in forests. Around 20 million years ago, Earth's climate changed and grasslands began to replace forests. Horses moved to the open plains and adapted to a diet of grass. They grew larger and their legs became longer, making them swifter on their feet. Hundreds of different prehistoric horse species have been found all over the world. They show that the evolution of the horse was like a tree, with many dead ends.

Hipparion

hip-AH-ree-on

- **When** 23–2 million years ago (Neogene)
- **Fossil location** N. America, Europe, Asia, Africa
- **Habitat** Grasslands, plains
- **Length** 5 ft (2 m)
- **Diet** Leaves and grass

With its long muzzle and slender legs, the lightly built *Hipparion* resembled a modern pony. Unlike horses today, which have only one toe on each foot, it had three. Its full weight was borne on its large middle toe, which ended in a hoof. The other toes did not touch the ground, so the feet sprung off the ground quickly, helping the animal to run faster.

▲ GRASS-EATER *Hipparion* *lived on grassy plains. Horses never fully evolved the ability to digest grass. As a result, their manure is full of undigested stalks.*

FAMILY FACT FILE

Key features
- Long, narrow heads
- Long necks
- Slender legs
- Large teeth
- Hoofed feet, with odd numbers of toes (some had one toe, others three)

When
Horses first appeared in the Paleogene Period, 54 million years ago.

Merychippus

MEH-ree-KIP-us

- **When** 17–10 million years ago (Neogene)
- **Fossil location** USA, Mexico
- **Habitat** Plains
- **Length** 3 ft (1 m)
- **Diet** Grass

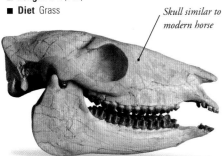

Skull similar to modern horse

Merychippus was the first horse thought to have fed only on grass, unlike its leaf-eating ancestors. It was also the first to have a head similar to a modern horse's, with a long muzzle, deep jaws, and eyes set on either side of its head. Its neck was long, so it was able to graze on grass comfortably. *Merychippus* lived in large herds, traveling long distances to feed. It could run fast on its long legs, even breaking into a gallop when chased by predators.

Protorohippus

PRO-tore-oh-HIP-us

Teeth

- **When** 52–45 million years ago (Paleogene)
- **Fossil location** USA
- **Habitat** Woodlands
- **Length** 1 ft (0.3 m)
- **Diet** Plants

One of the earliest known horses, tiny *Protorohippus* was a forest-dwelling animal that perhaps lived on its own or in pairs, mostly eating leaves rather than grass. It had very short limbs, with hind legs slightly longer than its fore legs, which suggests that it was a good jumper. Of its three toes, the middle one was enlarged and carried the weight of the animal.

Pliohippus

PLY-oh-HIP-us

- **When** 12–2 million years ago (Neogene)
- **Fossil location** USA
- **Habitat** Plains
- **Length** 3 ft (1 m)
- **Diet** Plants

Until recently, scientists thought *Pliohippus* was the ancestor of modern horses, partly because it walked on single-toed feet. However, it had curved teeth (other horses had straight teeth) and strange depressions on its face. With its long, slender limbs, *Pliohippus* was built for speed.

Equus

ECK-wuss

- **When** 4 million years ago to now (Neogene)
- **Fossil location** Worldwide
- **Habitat** Plains and grasslands
- **Length** 9 ft (3 m)
- **Diet** Grass

The name *Equus* includes all modern horses, from racehorses and domestic donkeys to wild zebras. Outside Africa, wild horses are now rare. *Equus* horses clearly show the much bigger brains that are typical of later mammals. Medium to large in size, they have long heads and long, maned necks. They can run fast, especially when threatened, and live in herds.

Mesohippus

MEE-zoe-HIP-us

- **When** 40–30 million years ago (Paleogene)
- **Fossil location** USA
- **Habitat** Woodlands
- **Length** 2 ft (0.5 m)
- **Diet** Plants

Mesohippus ("middle horse") had features of both early and later horses. Like modern horses, it had a long snout with a gap between its front and back teeth. A fast runner, its long, slender legs resembled those of today's horses, except that *Mesohippus*'s feet had three toes. It probably fed on bushes and trees, chewing the leaves with teeth smaller than those of grass-eating horses.

Long, slender legs

One-toed foot

LIVING RELATIVE

Modern horses are large, fast-running mammals with slender legs ending in single-toed, hoofed feet. They have long heads, long tails, and manes of hair on the neck. Today, there are more than 400 breeds of domestic horse but only seven wild species, including zebras and onagers.

Chalicotherium

Chalicotherium was a bizarre hoofed mammal that looked like a cross between a horse and a gorilla. Its front hooves had evolved into massive, hooklike claws, which it probably used to pull branches down from trees so it could reach the leaves. When not on the move, *Chalicotherium* sat on its haunches feeding. It may also have been able to rear up on its hind legs to reach the highest branches. Its odd-toed feet show that it was a distant relative of horses and rhinos.

Chalicotherium
CHA-lih-co-THEE-ree-um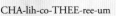

- **When** 15–5 million years ago (Neogene)
- **Fossil location** Europe, Asia, Africa
- **Habitat** Plains
- **Length** 6½ ft (2 m)
- **Diet** Plants

Taller than a grizzly bear, this animal had a horselike head, long, clawed forelimbs, and stout hind legs that bore its immense body weight. When fossils of its claws were first discovered, scientists thought it was a type of carnivore. Further research showed it was actually a plant-eating mammal that first appeared during the Neogene Period, 15 million years ago.

4.6 billion years ago	542 million years ago	488	444	416	359
Precambrian Eon	Cambrian	Ordovician	Silurian	Devonian	Carboniferous

Pebble beast

Chalicotherium means "pebble beast." The animal was so named because the first fossil teeth looked like pebbles. When *Chalicotherium* became an adult, it shed the teeth at the front of its mouth, leaving only fleshy lips and gums to strip leaves from branches. Mouthfuls of leaves were then ground to a pulp with teeth at the back of the mouth.

◀ KNUCKLE WALKER *This animal's front legs were much longer than its hind legs. Each front leg ended in long, curved claws, which meant that* Chalicotherium *couldn't place its foot flat on the ground. So, it probably shuffled along on its knuckles, just like gorillas do today.*

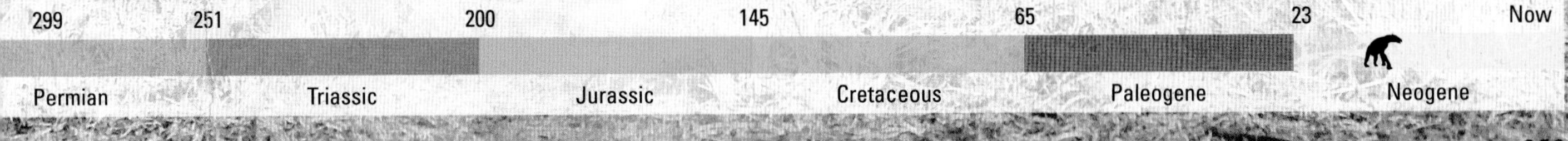

299	251	200	145	65	23	Now
Permian	Triassic	Jurassic	Cretaceous	Paleogene		Neogene

Rhinoceroses

Today there are only five or six species of rhinoceros, all fairly similar. In prehistoric times the rhino family was much more varied, its members ranging from dog-sized animals to giants as tall as trees and heavier than any other land mammals. Some prehistoric rhinos were long-legged hornless animals built like horses for speed; others were short and fat and wallowed in water like hippos.

Paraceratherium
PARRA-serra-THEER-ee-um

- **When** 33–23 million years ago (Late Paleogene–Early Neogene)
- **Fossil location** Pakistan, Kazakhstan, India, Mongolia, China
- **Habitat** Plains
- **Length** 26 ft (8 m)
- **Diet** Plants

As big as a killer whale, this early hornless rhinoceros was the largest land mammal of all time. Its immense size and long neck allowed it feed on treetops, as giraffes do today. Its long, flexible lips could wrap around branches and strip the leaves off.

Teleoceras
TEE-lee-oh-SEE-rass

- **When** 17–4 million years ago
- **Fossil location** USA
- **Habitat** Plains
- **Length** 13 ft (4 m)
- **Diet** Grass

Hundreds of complete skeletons of *Teleoceras* were found at Ashfall Fossil Beds in Nebraska (see next page). The animals died after choking on ash from a volcanic eruption 10 million years ago. *Teleoceras* was a large rhinoceros with a small, conical horn on its nose. But with its long, bulky body and stumpy legs, it looked more like a hippo than a rhino. Fossils have been found in ancient river and pond deposits, suggesting it wallowed in water a bit like a hippo, too.

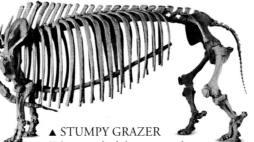

▲ STUMPY GRAZER
Teleoceras *had short stumpy legs and a barrel-shaped body. Its tall teeth were well suited to chewing grass, and fossilized grass seeds found in the throat of several skeletons show that grass was its main source of food.*

FAMILY FACT FILE

Key features
- Large size
- Most had horns made from keratin (the same material that nails are made of)
- Large teeth for chewing leaves or grass
- Feet with hooves

When
Rhinoceroses first appeared in the Paleogene Period.

Coelodonta
SEE-low-DON-tah

- **When** 3 million–10,000 years ago (Late Neogene)
- **Fossil location** Europe, Asia
- **Habitat** Plains
- **Length** 12 ft (4 m)
- **Diet** Grass

Also called the woolly rhino, *Coelodonta* had a thick coat of long, shaggy hair that protected it from the cold. It lived in Europe and Asia during the last ice age, and we know what it looked like thanks to frozen bodies found buried in icy ground (permafrost) and prehistoric cave paintings left by Stone Age people. About the size of a modern white rhino, its body was massive, with short, stocky limbs. On its snout was a pair of huge horns, each of a different size—the front horn was as long as 3 ft (1 m) in males. *Coelodonta* was a grazer, probably grinding mouthfuls of grass and other plants after tugging them out of the ground.

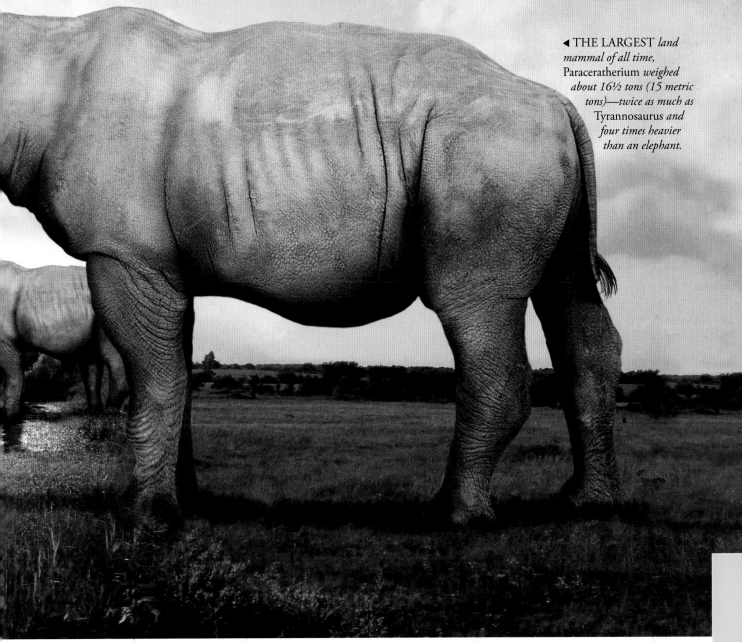

◄ THE LARGEST *land mammal of all time,* Paraceratherium *weighed about 16½ tons (15 metric tons)—twice as much as* Tyrannosaurus *and four times heavier than an elephant.*

Elasmotherium

ell-AZZ-moe-THEER-ee-um

- **When** 2 million–126,000 years ago or later
- **Fossil location** Asia
- **Habitat** Plains
- **Length** 20 ft (6 m)
- **Diet** Grass

Elasmotherium was a large rhinoceros, weighing about 3 tons, that lived until ice age times and may have been hunted by early people. Its huge, single horn has inspired theories that this animal was the source of the unicorn myth, although it probably vanished too early in history to be remembered even in folk tales. With legs longer than a modern rhino's, *Elasmotherium* may have been quicker on its feet. Its teeth were large and flat-topped—adapted to a diet of grass and small plants, which it perhaps tore from the ground by swinging its head.

Subhyracodon

sub-high-RACK-oh-don

- **When** 33–25 million years ago (Late Paleogene)
- **Fossil location** USA
- **Habitat** Plains
- **Length** 9 ft (3 m)
- **Diet** Plants

This cow-sized rhinoceros had no horns and was not heavily armored like modern rhinoceroses. Instead, *Subhyrocodon* relied on its long, slender legs to flee from danger. Its teeth had sharp crests, well-suited to mashing leaves from trees and bushes.

255

Ashfall fossil beds

Twelve million years ago a volcano erupted in North America, spreading a thick blanket of powdered glass (volcanic ash) and killing many prehistoric animals. The animals lay undisturbed until 1971. Welcome to the Ashfall Fossil Beds!

A RARE FIND

Hundreds of well-preserved mammal skeletons were found at Ashfall Fossil Beds in northeastern Nebraska, many complete, which is incredibly rare. Some of the animals survived the volcano's first eruption, but ash came to lie about 1–2 ft (50 cm) deep, and gradually filled their lungs as they attempted to graze. Ash is made up of tiny shards of glass—the animals didn't stand a chance.

Barrel-bodied rhinoceros
(*Teleoceras*)

▼ THESE RHINOS *were among hundreds that died in agony after choking on volcanic dust. So many perished that the site has been called "rhino Pompeii."*

TAKE A LOOK

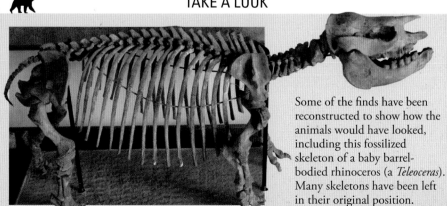

Some of the finds have been reconstructed to show how the animals would have looked, including this fossilized skeleton of a baby barrel-bodied rhinoceros (a *Teleoceras*). Many skeletons have been left in their original position.

FACT FILE

■ Fossils of 17 different vertebrate species, including 12 mammal species, have been found at Ashfall Fossil Beds.
■ They include rhinos, horses, camels, deer, dogs, and birds, all beautifully preserved.
■ The site was discovered when a rhino skull was seen poking out of a gully on the edge of a cornfield.
■ The site is now a protected state park. Special walkways allow visitors to walk over the beds and watch paleontologists at work in the summer.

Elephants and relatives

The three living species of elephant are the largest land animals today. But elephants weren't always so huge. The earliest known species was just 2 ft (60 cm) tall—the size of a cat. Over time they grew larger and their trunks and tusks grew longer, giving rise to an extraordinary range of giant mammals.

Deinotherium
DIE-no-THEER-ee-um

- **When** 10 million to 10,000 years ago (Neogene)
- **Fossil location** Europe, Africa, Asia
- **Habitat** Woodlands
- **Height** 16 ft (5 m) tall at the shoulder
- **Diet** Plants

The third largest land mammal that ever lived, *Deinotherium* was slightly larger than a modern African elephant. Its trunk was much shorter than a modern elephant's, and it had backward-curving tusks that grew from the lower jaw. It might have used the tusks to dig up roots, strip bark, or pull down branches to reach the leaves.

Large skull

Curved tusks growing from the lower jaw

FAMILY FACT FILE

Key features
- Almost all early elephants had trunks
- Mostly naked, wrinkled skin
- Most had tusks
- Columnlike legs

When
The first elephants appeared in the Paleogene Period (about 40 million years ago).

Short trunk

Gomphotherium

GOM-foe-THEE-ree-um

- **When** 15–5 million years ago (Neogene)
- **Fossil location** N. America, Europe, Asia, Africa
- **Habitat** Swamps
- **Height** 10 ft (3 m) tall at the shoulder
- **Diet** Plants

Gomphotherium had two pairs of tusks—one pair extending from its upper jaw, and another smaller, shovel-shaped pair growing out of its lower jaw. The larger tusks were probably used for fighting and display, and the smaller ones to scrape up plants and strip tree bark.

Moeritherium

MEH-ree-THEER-ee-um

- **When** 37–30 million years ago (Paleogene)
- **Fossil location** Egypt
- **Habitat** Swamps
- **Length** 10 ft (3 m)
- **Diet** Plants

Platybelodon

PLAT-ee-BELL-oh-don

- **When** 10–6 million years ago (Neogene)
- **Fossil location** N. America, Africa, Asia, Europe
- **Habitat** Plains
- **Height** 10 ft (3 m) tall at the shoulder
- **Diet** Plants

Arsinoitherium

AR-sin-oh-ee-THEER-ee-um

- **When** 35–30 million years ago (Paleogene)
- **Fossil location** Africa
- **Habitat** Plains
- **Height** 6 ft (2 m) tall at the shoulder
- **Diet** Plants

Arsinoitherium belonged to an extinct family of mammals that was related to the elephant family, but it was not an elephant. It had no trunk and looked like a rhino, with two huge horns on its snout that were likely used by males for display or fights over females. _Arsinoitherium_'s hind legs were crooked and perhaps better suited to a life wallowing in water than walking on land.

Moeritherium was a close cousin of the elephant family and had the beginnings of a trunk. It was much smaller than modern elephants and had a long body with very short legs. It perhaps lived like a hippo, wallowing in lakes and rivers and feeding on water plants, using its flexible lips to grasp stems. The large teeth in both its upper and lower jaws formed small tusks that jutted out of its mouth.

Arsinoitherium's huge double horn was hollow.

The lower tusks of _Platybelodon_ ("shovel tusker") were flat and close together, forming a shovel—perhaps used to scoop up plants from water or marshes. Wear marks on the lower tusks show that it also used its tusks as blades to slice across branches. Like modern elephants, _Platybelodon_ had columnlike legs supporting its body. It also had fatty pads under its feet that helped to bear its massive weight.

Woolly mammoth

Majestic mammoths once roamed in herds across the ice age plains of North America, Europe, and Asia. Mammoths were closely related to modern elephants—in fact, studies of frozen mammoths found in Siberia show their DNA was almost identical to that of living elephants. There were eight species of mammoth, of which the most famous is the woolly mammoth, which died out only 3,700 years ago.

Hair grew up to 3 ft (90 cm) long

4.6 billion years ago	542 million years ago	488		444		416		359
Precambrian Eon		Cambrian		Ordovician		Silurian		Devonian	Carboniferous

Woolly mammoth

WULL-ee MAMM-oth

- **When** 5 million–3,700 years ago (Neogene)
- **Fossil location** N. America, Europe, Asia, Africa
- **Habitat** Plains
- **Length** 16 ft (5 m)

Long, shaggy hair with fine wool underneath covered the body of the woolly mammoth. Most adult woolly mammoths were slightly bigger than African elephants, but 6½ ft (2 m) tall "dwarf woolly mammoths" have also been found on an Arctic island. Adults had a distinct camel-like hump on the shoulders and enormous, curved tusks. Mammoths lived in Ice age grasslands and had ridged teeth for chewing tough grass and other small plants. Studies of woolly mammoth DNA reveal they were more closely related to the Asian elephant than the African species.

Hind leg shorter than front leg

Tusk

▲ SNOW SHOVEL *Mammoths may have used their tusks to scrape away snow and ice when feeding. Males probably also used their tusks to impress females.*

▲ BONE HUTS *Prehistoric people built oval or rounded huts from mammoth bones and tusks. About 30 clusters of these huts have been found in eastern Europe.*

LIVING RELATIVE

When an Asian elephant is born, its body is covered with thick, brownish-red hair, similar to the shaggy coat of its relative the woolly mammoth. However, since the Asian elephant lives in a warm, tropical climate, it sheds its hair as it grows older. Most adults have only sparse hairy patches. African elephants have even less hair.

MAMMALS

299	251	200	145	65	23	Now
Permian	Triassic	Jurassic	Cretaceous	Paleogene	Neogene	

Lyuba, the baby mammoth

In 2007, a Siberian caribou-herder came across a remarkably well preserved, frozen baby mammoth. Lyuba (Lee-OO-bah), as the mammoth came to be known (after the herder's wife), is thought to have died around 40,000 years ago. She is the best specimen of a mammoth ever found.

▲ LYUBA *was found in Russia's Arctic Yamal Peninsula, shown by a dot on the map.*

 DID YOU KNOW?

- Lyuba is small. She is just 4 ft long by 3 ft wide (1.2 m x 90 cm).
- Scientists believe Lyuba was about 30 days old when she died.
- The mammoth may have died from suffocation after being trapped in mud.
- Lyuba had "milk tusks"—small tusks that fall out before the adult tusks grow.

Scientists discovered a store of fat cells at the back of Lyuba's neck, which would have been used to provide energy for keeping the baby mammoth warm in its cold surroundings.

▶ HIDDEN CLUES *By studying the place in which Lyuba was found, the team concluded that her body had been exposed for a year before its discovery.*

Lyuba was so well preserved that scientists even found milk that she'd suckled from her mother in her stomach.

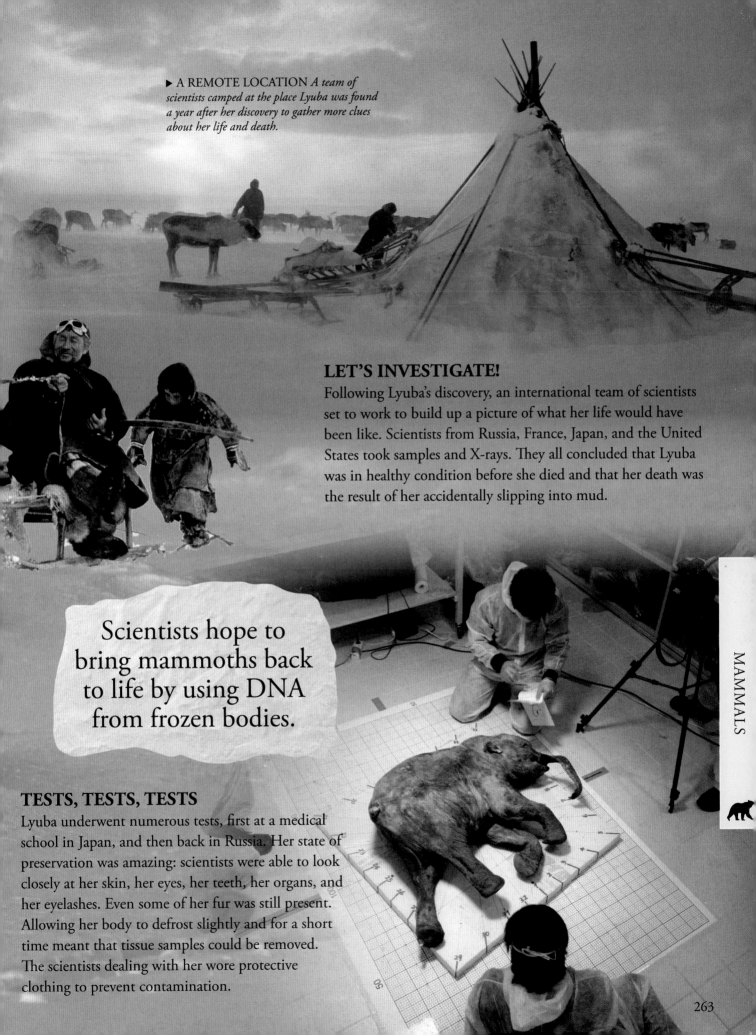

▶ A REMOTE LOCATION *A team of scientists camped at the place Lyuba was found a year after her discovery to gather more clues about her life and death.*

LET'S INVESTIGATE!

Following Lyuba's discovery, an international team of scientists set to work to build up a picture of what her life would have been like. Scientists from Russia, France, Japan, and the United States took samples and X-rays. They all concluded that Lyuba was in healthy condition before she died and that her death was the result of her accidentally slipping into mud.

Scientists hope to bring mammoths back to life by using DNA from frozen bodies.

TESTS, TESTS, TESTS

Lyuba underwent numerous tests, first at a medical school in Japan, and then back in Russia. Her state of preservation was amazing: scientists were able to look closely at her skin, her eyes, her teeth, her organs, and her eyelashes. Even some of her fur was still present. Allowing her body to defrost slightly and for a short time meant that tissue samples could be removed. The scientists dealing with her wore protective clothing to prevent contamination.

Megatherium

Also called the giant sloth, *Megatherium* was a close cousin of modern tree sloths, but this prehistoric beast was as big as an elephant and lived on the ground. Fossilized dung shows it was a herbivore that ate dozens of different kinds of plant. It normally walked on all fours but could also rear up on its hindlimbs to reach high branches, which it pulled down with its claws. *Megatherium* vanished soon after humans first reached the Americas, perhaps hunted to extinction.

▲ MOST Megatherium *fossils have been found in the pampas, a grassy area in South America. This bone was among a find of 12 animals revealed when a drought caused a river in Argentina to dry up.*

4.6 billion years ago	542 million years ago	488	444	416	359	299	251
Precambrian Eon	Cambrian	Ordovician	Silurian	Devonian	Carboniferous	Permian	

Megatherium

meg-ah-THEER-ee-um

- **When** 5 million–10,000 years ago (Late Neogene)
- **Fossil location** S. America
- **Habitat** Woodlands
- **Length** 20 ft (6 m)
- **Diet** Plants

When *Megatherium* walked upright it was almost twice the height of an elephant. It was covered with thick, shaggy hair, under which were bony plates that formed a kind of armor. The teeth were blunt for mashing leaves, but some experts think *Megatherium* may have also used its claws to scavenge on dead meat or even kill for food.

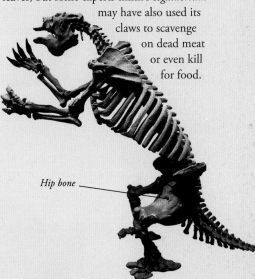

Hip bone

▼ MEGA CLAWS Megatherium *had enormous, curved claws that it used to grasp branches and fight predators. It could not place its feet flat on the ground—instead, it walked on the sides of its feet, with the claws turned inward.*

▲ MEGATHERIUM'S *hip bones were especially strong. They supported the weight of the huge body when the animal stood upright. The stout tail also helped, acting as a prop.*

LIVING RELATIVE

Modern sloths appear to be the laziest animals on Earth, sleeping up to 18 hours a day and moving with amazing slowness when awake. Unlike *Megatherium*, today's sloths spend their lives hanging upside down from trees. They cling to branches with long arms and hooked claws, even sleeping and eating upside down.

Three-toed sloth, Panama

200	145	65	23	Now
Triassic	Jurassic	Cretaceous	Paleogene	Neogene

Deer, giraffes, and camels

Around 20 million years ago, Earth's forests began to shrink as a new habitat—grassland—took over. This change encouraged the spread of plant-eating hoofed mammals, many of which had special stomachs able to digest grass and other rough plant foods. Such plant-eaters became very successful, and many species evolved, including not only the deer, giraffes, and camels on these pages but also sheep, goats, cattle, buffalo, llamas, antelope, and hippos.

Gigantic antlers

Powerful back legs for running quickly

Megaloceros

MEG-ah-LOSS-er-oss

- **When** 5 million–7,700 years ago (Late Neogene)
- **Fossil location** Eurasia
- **Habitat** Plains
- **Length** 10 ft (3 m)
- **Diet** Plants

One of the largest deer ever known, *Megaloceros* was about the size of a modern moose. The male had the most enormous antlers of all time—from tip to tip, they measured more than the total body length of a tiger. It used its antlers for display to attract females, as well as to scare off rival males. Like other deer, it shed its antlers every year. *Megaloceros* was hunted by primitive humans, big cats, and wolves, and died out 7,700 years ago.

FAMILY FACT FILE

Key features
- After swallowing food, deer, giraffes, and camels bring it up from the stomach to chew a second time.
- Three or four stomach chambers
- Head often bears horns or antlers
- Feet have even number of hoofed toes (except camels, which don't have hooves)

When
Even-toed hoofed mammals appeared about 54 million years ago, became widespread and common about 20 million years ago, and still exist.

Giraffokeryx

jee-RAFF-oh-CARE-icks

- **When** 16–5 million years ago (Neogene)
- **Fossil location** Asia, Europe, Africa
- **Habitat** Grasslands
- **Length** 5¼ ft (1.6 m)
- **Diet** Plants

Today, there are only two living members of the giraffe family: the giraffe and the okapi. In the past there were many more, including *Giraffokeryx*. It had two pairs of pointed, furry horns—one pair on its head and another on its snout. At the back of its jaws were ridged teeth, well suited to grinding tough plants.

▲ LONG TONGUE
Giraffokeryx probably had a long, flexible tongue to select the tastiest leaves.

Cranioceras

CRAY-knee-OSS-eh-rass

- **When** 20–5 million years ago (Neogene)
- **Fossil location** N. America
- **Habitat** Woodlands
- **Length** 3 ft (1 m)
- **Diet** Leaves

A hoofed, cud-chewing mammal, *Cranioceras* was a close relative of early deer and giraffes. Males had two short, straight horns over their eyes and a thick, blunt horn that curved up at the back of the head. Injuries on fossilized horns suggest they were used in fights over mates or territories.

▼ THE HORNS of *Cranioceras may have been more like the fur-covered horns of giraffes than the bony antlers of deer.*

Two-toed feet, ideal for running at speed

Aepycamelus

AY-peeh-CAM-ell-us

- **When** 15–5 million years ago (Neogene)
- **Fossil location** USA
- **Habitat** Woodlands and grasslands
- **Length** 11 ft (3 m)
- **Diet** Plants

Aepycamelus was a camel but looked a little like a giraffe—it was very tall, with a long neck. It could run fast on its long legs, each of which had two hoofed toes with broad pads underneath. Like all camels and giraffes, it walked by swinging its left legs together and then its right legs, a style of walking known as "pacing." It probably fed on leaves more than grass.

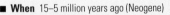
Long, slender neck

Stenomylus

STEN-oh-MILE-us

- **When** 25–16 million years ago (Late Paleogene–Early Neogene)
- **Fossil location** USA
- **Habitat** Grasslands
- **Size** 2 ft (60 cm) tall
- **Diet** Grass

Stenomylus was a small camel. Its neck, legs, and body were delicate and slender, more like those of a gazelle than a modern camel. Unlike modern camels, *Stenomylus* walked on tiptoe. It had huge molar teeth with very deep roots. These must have been used for chewing very tough or gritty plants, as fossilized teeth show signs of extreme wear during the life of the animal.

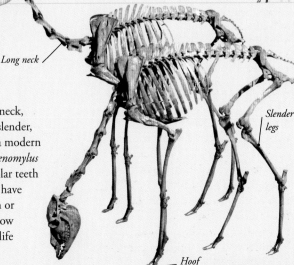

Long neck

Slender legs

Hoof

Forward-facing horns

What the heck?
In the 1920s, two German brothers, Heinz and Lutz Heck, tried to breed the aurochs back into existence. The brothers found breeds of domestic cow with aurochs-like qualities, such as the large-horned highland cattle of Scotland and the fierce fighting bulls of Spain. By crossing the breeds, they produced a new variety—heck cattle—that looks like a small aurochs.

Aurochs

The docile cattle seen on farms today are descendants of a much wilder, fiercer, and bigger ancestor: the aurochs. Now extinct in the wild, the aurochs once roamed in herds across Europe and Asia. Stone Age people hunted these fearsome animals and made paintings of them in caves, such as the one shown on this page. Wild aurochs survived in Europe until 1627, when the last animal was killed in Poland.

Forward-facing horns

Aurochs skeleton

Aurochs
OR-ocks

- **When** 2 million–500 years ago
- **Fossil location** Europe, Africa, Asia
- **Habitat** Forests
- **Length** 9 ft (2.7 m)
- **Diet** Grass, fruit, and plants

Much larger than a domestic cow, the aurochs weighed about a ton and had a very powerful, muscular neck and shoulders, and huge, curved, forward-facing horns. Long feet and high ankles made it a fast runner, and it could also swim short distances. Males may have had a black coat and females a reddish-brown one. Both had a pale stripe along the spine.

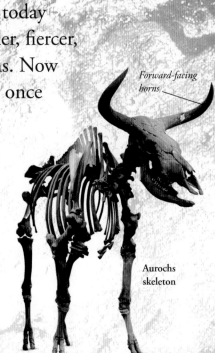

4.6 billion years ago	542 million years ago	488	444	416	359
Precambrian Eon	Cambrian	Ordovician	Silurian	Devonian	Carboniferous

MAMMALS

299	251	200	145	65	23	Now
Permian	Triassic	Jurassic	Cretaceous	Paleogene	Neogene	

In September 1940, four teenage boys set out to try and find a secret passageway rumored to exist near their French village. What they discovered was a cave system decorated with hundreds of paintings of prehistoric animals. They'd found the 17,000-year-old Lascaux cave paintings, now famous the world over.

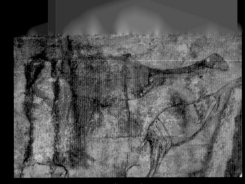

▲ KILLER BIRDS *This rock art in northern Australia is thought to be more than 40,000 years old. It shows two giant, flesh-eating, flightless birds known as* Genyornis. *Nearby are paintings of giant prehistoric kangaroos and Tasmanian tigers.*

ICE AGE HERDS

Lascaux was painted during the ice age, when northern Europe was buried under sheets of ice but France was a treeless, windswept tundra, crossed by huge herds of wild animals. The people who painted the cave were hunters, but, oddly, they didn't paint their favorite prey—caribou.

◀ ON THE RUN *Stags (left) and horses are among the most common animals in Lascaux. Many appear to be moving, as though running in herds. Such animals migrated across the tundra during the last ice age, just as caribou do today.*

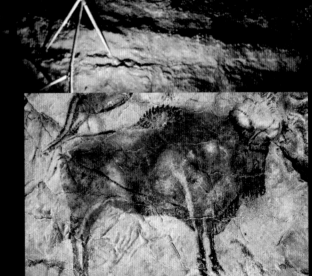

Beautiful bison

Cave painters used a mineral called red ocher to color many of the animals. This picture shows a European bison, a species that later disappeared from western Europe but is now being reintroduced.

▶ LASCAUX ANIMALS
The Lascaux animals include prehistoric species that no longer exist, such as mammoths and the aurochs (the wild ancestor of the domestic cow, shown below with huge horns). There are also lions, bison, hundreds of horses, stags, one bear, and one rhino.

Predators

Lascaux is just one of several painted caves found in France and Spain. Chauvet Cave in southern France contains paintings up to 30,000 years old and features predators such as lions, hyenas, panthers, and bears, as well as mammoths and rhinos.

▲ LIONS *were among the animals painted at Chauvet Cave in France. Now found only in Africa and Asia, lions lived throughout Europe in prehistoric times.*

▲ HAND ART *Prehistoric artists created handprints by placing a hand on the cave wall and spitting red ocher all over it.*

Andrewsarchus

When people mention "hoofed mammals," we normally think of plant-eaters like deer and sheep. But, millions of years ago, some hoofed mammals were bloodthirsty carnivores. The most terrifying of all was probably *Andrewsarchus*, a gigantic predator that prowled the plains of Mongolia. Only one good fossil of *Andrewsarchus* has been found: an enormous skull measuring 33 in (83 cm) in length. Though scientists can't be sure, the huge skull suggests the animal may have been twice as big as a grizzly bear, making it the largest carnivorous land mammal of all time.

Andrewsarchus
ANN-droo-SAR-kuss

- **When** 45–35 million years ago (Paleogene)
- **Fossil location** Mongolia
- **Habitat** Plains of Central Asia
- **Length** 13 ft (4 m)
- **Diet** Meat

Andrewsarchus may have looked like a giant wolf or bear. It had a long snout and immensely powerful jaws, with long, pointed canine teeth at the front for piercing flesh, and blunter teeth at the rear that may have been used to crush bones. Like a bear, it may also have eaten plant foods and scavenged from carcasses—its sheer size would have been enough to scare other predators away from their kills. Some scientists think *Andrewsarchus* is a close relative of whales, since they share a similar jaw structure.

4.6 billion years ago	542 million years ago	488		444		416		359
Precambrian Eon		Cambrian	Ordovician		Silurian		Devonian	Carboniferous

Andrewsarchus is named after Roy Chapman Andrews (1884–1960), an American explorer and fossil hunter. Andrews led many expeditions to the Gobi Desert in Mongolia in the 1920s, where he discovered the dinosaurs *Velociraptor* and *Protoceratops* and the first known dinosaur eggs (see pages 192–193). In 1923, he found a partial skull of *Andrewsarchus*—the only fossil, along with a few bones, that has been found. This priceless fossil is now on display at the American Museum of Natural History, in New York City.

Roy Chapman Andrews with dinosaur eggs in the Gobi Desert

MAMMALS

299	251	200	145	65	23	Now
Permian	Triassic	Jurassic	Cretaceous	Paleogene	Neogene	

Whales in the making

All land animals evolved from sea-dwelling ancestors that left the water and adapted to life on land. Whales are one of several groups of animals that then did the reverse and went back to the sea. They evolved from hoofed land mammals and are distantly related to cows and pigs, while their closest living land relative is the hippopotamus!

THE WALKING WHALE

Ambulocetus, an early member of the whale family, lived more than 50 million years ago. A bit like an otter, it was equally at home on land and in water. Its front feet had small hooves for walking on land, while its back feet served to propel it through the water. Its name means "walking whale."

CLOSE COUSINS

The theory that whales are related to hippopotamuses was first suggested in 1870, but most scientists dismissed it as unlikely. More recently, careful comparison of whale DNA and hippo DNA has shown that hippos probably are the closest living relatives of whales.

▶ HIPPOS *spend much of their lives in water but are less aquatic than whales.*

THE FAMILY TREE

Scientists haven't found enough fossils to trace the evolution of whales in full. However, a handful of fascinating discoveries from different parts of the whale family tree give us snapshots of evolution in action, with later species ever-better adapted to life in water as their limbs evolved into flippers and their nostrils moved backward to become blowholes.

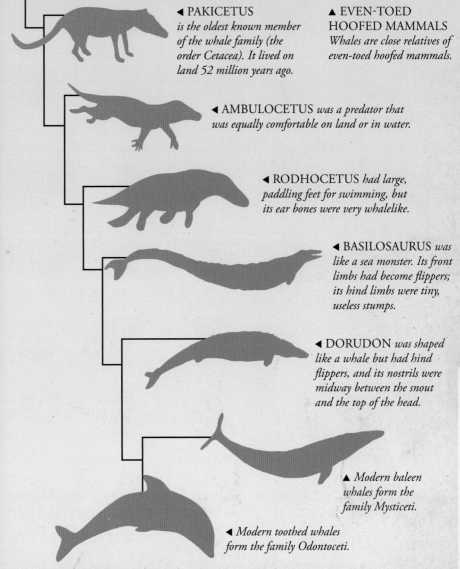

◀ PAKICETUS *is the oldest known member of the whale family (the order Cetacea). It lived on land 52 million years ago.*

▲ EVEN-TOED HOOFED MAMMALS *Whales are close relatives of even-toed hoofed mammals.*

◀ AMBULOCETUS *was a predator that was equally comfortable on land or in water.*

◀ RODHOCETUS *had large, paddling feet for swimming, but its ear bones were very whalelike.*

◀ BASILOSAURUS *was like a sea monster. Its front limbs had become flippers; its hind limbs were tiny, useless stumps.*

◀ DORUDON *was shaped like a whale but had hind flippers, and its nostrils were midway between the snout and the top of the head.*

▲ *Modern baleen whales form the family Mysticeti.*

◀ *Modern toothed whales form the family Odontoceti.*

WHALES TODAY

There are now more than 100 species of whale and dolphin. They are divided into two main types: toothed whales, which hunt fish, and baleen whales, which use plates of bristles in the mouth to sift small animals from the water. The humpback whale (right) is a type of baleen whale.

Primates

The primates are a family of mostly tree-dwelling animals that includes monkeys, apes, and ourselves. The first primates were small, squirrel-like animals that scampered around in the trees about the same time that the dinosaurs died out. Once the dinosaurs were gone, primates evolved into many new species, becoming larger and more intelligent over time.

Darwinius
dar-WIN-ee-us

- **When** 47 million years ago (Paleogene)
- **Fossil location** Germany
- **Habitat** Woodlands of western Europe
- **Length** 2 ft (0.6 m)
- **Diet** Fruit and plants

Only one fossil of *Darwinius* has been found: a skeleton, nicknamed "Ida," so beautifully preserved that soft fur can be seen all over the body (left). Even Ida's last meal of leaves and fruit was preserved in her stomach. *Darwinius* looked like a lemur. An agile climber, it had "opposable thumbs," which means that its thumbs moved the opposite way to the fingers, allowing it to grasp branches and handle food.

FAMILY FACT FILE

Key features
- Large brains
- Most had forward-facing eyes
- Grasping hands and feet
- Most had nails, not claws

When
The earliest primates appeared about 65 million years ago. Numerous species of primate still exist today.

Sivapithecus

SEE-vah-PITH-eck-uss

- **When** 12–7 million years ago (Neogene)
- **Fossil location** Nepal, Pakistan, Turkey
- **Habitat** Woodlands of Central Asia
- **Length** 5 ft (1.5 m)
- **Diet** Plants

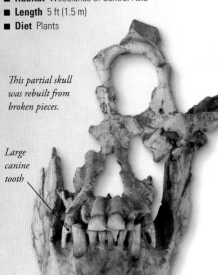

This partial skull was rebuilt from broken pieces.

Large canine tooth

Sivapithecus had the build of a chimpanzee, but its face was more like that of an orangutan, to which it was closely related. It lived in woodland, but scientists think it may have spent much of its time on the ground. It had large molar teeth (rear teeth), suggesting its diet included a lot of tough food such as grass seed gathered on the ground, although it probably also climbed trees for fruit and may have slept in trees at night.

Plesiadapis

PLEEZ-ee-ah-DAP-iss

- **When** 65–60 million years ago (Paleogene)
- **Fossil location** N. America, Europe, and Asia
- **Habitat** Woodlands of N. America, Europe, and Asia
- **Length** 2 ft (0.6 m)
- **Diet** Plants

The oldest known primate is *Plesiadapis*, which looked more like a squirrel than a monkey. It had a bushy tail, a long snout, ratlike incisor teeth for gnawing, and eyes on

the sides of its head for spotting predators. However, the rear teeth of *Plesiadapis* were flat like those of living primates, suggesting its diet included fruit and other soft plant foods.

Gigantopithecus

gi-GAN-toe-PITH-eck-uss

- **When** 9 million–250,000 years ago (Neogene)
- **Fossil location** China, India, and Vietnam
- **Habitat** Woodlands of Asia
- **Length** 9 ft (2.7 m)
- **Diet** Plants

Twice the size of a gorilla, *Gigantopithecus* was the largest ape that ever lived—the King Kong of its day. Some scientists think it may be the source of the Yeti myth. Only teeth and jaws have been found. The pattern of wear suggests it fed on bamboo.

Lower jaw fossil

Dryopithecus

DRY-oh-PITH-eck-uss

- **When** 15–10 million years ago (Neogene)
- **Fossil location** Africa, Europe, and Asia
- **Habitat** Woodlands of Europe, Asia, and Africa
- **Length** 2 ft (0.6 m)
- **Diet** Plants

This primate was about the size of a chimpanzee and spent most of its life up in the trees. It had very long, strong arms, which it used for swinging from branch to branch. Like a chimp, it could also walk on all fours, but rather than walking on the knuckles of its hands as chimps do, it walked with its palms flat on the ground. It had a large brain, but was only a distant relative of human beings.

▲ LONG ARMS
Dryopithecus used long arms to swing under branches like a gibbon.

Eosimias

EE-oh-SIM-ee-uss

- **When** 45–40 million years ago (Paleogene)
- **Fossil location** China
- **Habitat** Woodlands of Asia
- **Length** 2 in (5 cm)
- **Diet** Insects and plants

Eosimias was one of the earliest primates. Unlike the enormous mammals that evolved after the age of dinosaurs, *Eosimias* was like a tiny fur ball and would have easily fit into the palm of a child's hand. Its large eyes may have helped it to spot predators easily, especially at night. It probably fed on nectar and insects.

Australopithecus

Today, all ape species (except for humans) live in forests, but four million years ago things were different. Africa was home to a range of apes that lived on open ground and walked upright as we do. The best known of these walking apes, *Australopithecus*, is probably our own ancestor.

Australopithecus
OSS-tra-low-PITH-ee-cuss

- **When** 4–2 million years ago (Neogene)
- **Fossil location** Africa
- **Habitat** Open woodland, grassland
- **Height** 4–4½ ft (1.2–1.4 m)
- **Diet** Fruit, seeds, roots, insects, small animals

In many ways, *Australopithecus* was like its very close relative the chimpanzee. It had a small, hair-covered body, powerful arms for climbing, and a brain one-third the size of ours. However, its hip bones and feet were like those of modern humans, indicating that *Australopithecus* could walk upright, although less nimbly than we can. Some scientists think *Australopithecus* lived in social groups like those of gorillas, ruled by a single male that was much larger than the females.

▲ HANDS FREE *Walking on only two feet left the arms free for other jobs, such as carrying. This was to be very important later in human evolution, when our ancestors made tools such as hunting weapons.*

SMALL BRAIN

Scientists once thought our ancestors evolved large brains before they mastered the tricky business of walking. But *Australopithecus* proves the opposite was true—it could walk, but its brain was barely larger than a chimp's. This animal didn't have the brainpower needed for language and couldn't talk, although individuals may have whooped and screeched to communicate.

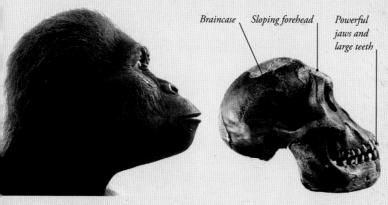

Braincase   Sloping forehead   Powerful jaws and large teeth

▲ THIS RECONSTRUCTION, *based on a skull of* Australopithecus, *shows how apelike it looked. Its small braincase gave it a flat, sloping forehead quite unlike the upright forehead of modern humans.*

In 1975, scientists found fossilized remains of at least 13 *Australopithecus* bodies at the same site in Ethiopia. The find was nicknamed "the first family," although they may have been unrelated victims of predators such as lions.

LANDSCAPE AND FOOD

Today, most apes live in jungles, but *Australopithecus* lived in a more open landscape—a mixture of grassy areas and patches of trees. Its large jaws and thickly enameled molars (back teeth) show it foraged for tough, plant foods like roots and seeds, but like other apes it probably had a very varied diet that included fruit, insects, and perhaps meat.

Footprints from the past

In 1976, scientists found what looked like fossilized human footprints in Tanzania, Africa—but the prints turned out to be 3.6 million years old. They were left by a group of three *Australopithecus* walking over volcanic ash and clearly show that these animals could walk on two feet.

LIVING RELATIVE

The chimpanzee is a very close relative of *Australopithecus*. Chimpanzees sometimes use rocks and sticks as simple tools. They use rocks to crack nuts and sticks to fish termites out of their nests. It's likely that *Australopithecus* also used simple tools like these, but there's little fossil evidence that it could make the kinds of stone tools that the later humans made.

MAMMALS

Homo erectus

Over millions of years, as *Australopithecus* (see previous page) became ever better adapted to life on the ground, it changed and evolved, giving rise to new species that looked much more human. One of the best known is *Homo erectus*—a tall, hairless creature that appeared about two million years ago. *Homo erectus* knew how to make stone tools and perhaps even fires. It spread beyond Africa, reaching deep into Europe and Asia.

Homo erectus
HOE-moe eh-RECK-tuss

- **When** 2–0.1 million years ago (Neogene)
- **Fossil location** Africa, Europe, Asia
- **Habitat** Woodland and grassland
- **Height** 6 ft (1.8 m)
- **Diet** Plant foods and meat

Homo erectus was very similar in size and shape to a modern human, with a tall, athletic body and long legs. The slender build suggests it lived in a hot climate and could sweat to lose heat, which in turn means it was probably hairless. It had a smaller brain than ours, and a flatter forehead and larger jaws and teeth made its face very different, too.

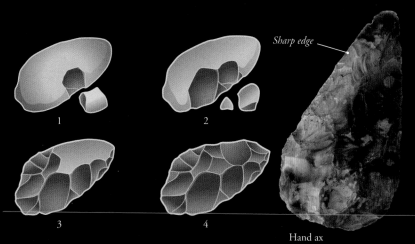

1 2

3 4

Sharp edge

Hand ax

Multipurpose tool

Homo erectus's favorite tool was something called a hand ax. It was made by chipping flakes off a stone (using a heavier rock as a hammer) to make sharp edges on the sides. It was used for all kinds of jobs, from skinning and butchering animals to smashing bones (to release the marrow), and digging for deep roots. Such tools made it much easier for *Homo erectus* to eat meat.

Making fire

Could *Homo erectus* make fire? Scientists don't know for sure. Patches of ash in caves inhabited by *Homo erectus* 400,000 years ago hint that the species could create fire, but the ash might be from wild fires. The mastery of fire was an important step in human history. It allowed our ancestors to cook, making food safer to eat and easier to digest. Fire can also be used to scare predators away, and it provided vital warmth as early humans spread to cold parts of the world.

DID YOU KNOW...?

In 1891, Eugene Dubois, a Dutch scientist, found the first known *Homo erectus* fossil on the island of Java in Indonesia. Dubois thought that humans evolved from apes in Asia rather than Africa, but later discoveries of *Australopithecus* fossils in Africa proved him wrong.

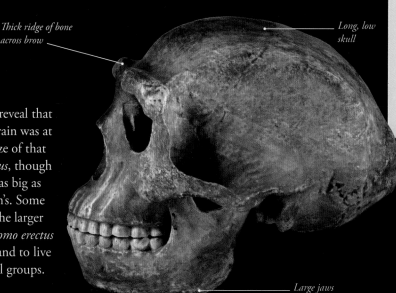

Thick ridge of bone across brow

Long, low skull

Brain size

Fossilized skulls reveal that *Homo erectus*'s brain was at least twice the size of that of *Australopithecus*, though only 70 percent as big as a modern human's. Some scientists think the larger brain allowed *Homo erectus* to use language and to live in complex social groups.

Large jaws and teeth

Neanderthals

During the ice age, Europe was inhabited by a race of physically powerful and intelligent people known as Neanderthals. The Neanderthals had large brains, language, clothing, shelters, fire, tools, and maybe even art—but they were not the same species as us. When our own species finally spread from Africa to Europe 40,000 years ago, the Neanderthals vanished.

Homo neanderthalensis
HOE-moe nee-AN-der-thaw-LEN-siss

- **When** 350,000–30,000 years ago (Neogene)
- **Fossil location** Europe and Asia
- **Habitat** Ice age grasslands and woodlands
- **Height** 5 ft 5 in (1.66 m)
- **Diet** Mainly meat

Neanderthals were shorter, stockier, and far stronger than us. Their compact build helped them cope with the cold environment, and their great strength was needed for hunting wild animals as big as mammoths, although they probably scavenged for meat, too. Their brains were at least as big as ours, but their heads were flatter in shape, with a lower, more sloping forehead, a heavy ridge of bone over the eyes, a huge nose, and large jaws that jutted forward.

Central heating

To survive the freezing cold of the Ice age, the Neanderthals used fire to keep their homes warm. They wore clothes made of animal skin and fur, much like Arctic people do today. They may even have lined their beds with rabbit fur to keep themselves snug at night.

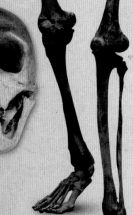

A heavy brow ridge gave Neanderthals a glowering expression.

Numerous chips and scratches suggest the teeth were used as tools.

Tool kit

Like *Homo erectus*, the Neanderthals made stone tools by chipping flakes off a rock to form a sharp edge. Their tools were much more varied than those of *Homo erectus* and included heavy-duty hand axes; smaller, more delicate knives; and spearheads. Neanderthals probably also made tools from wood that have not survived.

Handle

Blade

Blade

Handle

Handle

Hand ax with rounded blade

Hand ax with two blades and point

Stone knife

The Neanderthal voicebox was just like ours, which means Neanderthals could probably speak.

Clues from bones

Scientists have found the remains of around 275 Neanderthals. Wear marks and injuries on the bones reveal that their owners endured great physical stress and often violence. The injuries match those of rodeo riders—perhaps Neanderthals wrestled with the animals they hunted. Some Neanderthal bones bear scratches made by stone tools. Some experts think this means Neanderthals were cannibals. Others think the dead were "defleshed" in religious ceremonies before burial.

Large skull housed a bigger brain

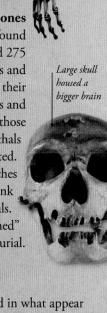

Six feet under

Neanderthal skeletons have been found in what appear to be graves, suggesting that Neanderthals deliberately buried their dead. Unlike later humans, however, they seldom placed sacred or precious objects with the bodies.

Myths and legends

Dinosaurs in the Congo? Abominable snowmen in the mountains? Ever since people began telling stories, there have been tales of fantastic animals. While many are just tall tales about mythical beasts that never existed, some might just have a grain of truth in them—they may be ancient stories from a time when long-lost prehistoric animals still lived.

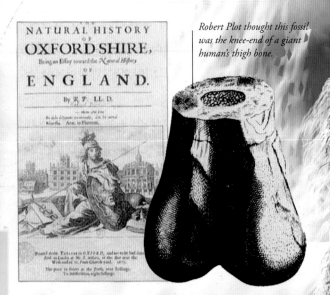

Robert Plot thought this fossil was the knee-end of a giant human's thigh bone.

NATURAL HISTORY OF OXFORD-SHIRE, Being an Essay toward the Natural History OF ENGLAND. By R. P. LL. D.

WHAT'S THAT?

The first dinosaur was not correctly identified until the 1800s—until then, people had no idea what fossils were. A famous description and picture of what was later identified as a dinosaur bone was published in 1677 by the English naturalist Robert Plot. He claimed it was part of the thigh bone of a human giant.

Half human, half ape

From Sasquatch (Bigfoot) in North America to the Yeti in the Himalayas and Orang Pendek in Sumatra, tales of mysterious ape-men are common around the world. Some scientists believe the origin of these old stories might lie in the distant past, when humans spread from Africa to other parts of the world and came across our living "hominin" relatives, including Neanderthals and *Homo erectus*.

Caveman versus dinosaur

In old movies such as 1966's *One Million Years B.C.*, cavemen are shown battling with dinosaurs. This is impossible—dinosaurs vanished at least 63 million years before cavemen existed. And dinosaurs didn't stand with their tails on the ground, as old movies, toys, books, and pictures often show them.

Serpents' heads

Ammonite fossils are the source of many legends. According to English folklore, they are serpents that have been turned to stone—hence their old name, "snakestones." Sometimes the head of a serpent was carved on an ammonite fossil.

The gigantic eggs of elephant birds can still be found in Madagascar.

A living dinosaur?

The mokèlé-mbèmbé is a legendary creature likened to a sauropod dinosaur and said to live in the Congo River basin. In some ways it is similar to the Loch Ness monster (see page 102).

(see page 102)

The elephant bird

Sinbad the Sailor was a fictional Arab sailor whose adventures took him to magical lands. In one story he is carried away in the claws of a gigantic bird. This tale may have been inspired by the elephant bird of Madagascar, a giant flightless bird that lived until the 1600s and was probably known to Arab sailors.

A horned horse?

Some people think the legend of the unicorn might be based on ancient folk tales about the extinct rhino *Elasmotherium* (see page 255), which had an enormous single horn.

(see page 255)

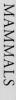
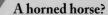

Modern humans

Fossil evidence and studies of our genes show that our own species—*Homo sapiens*—evolved in Africa some 200,000 years ago. Around 60,000 years ago, modern humans spread from Africa to new continents, taking with them tools, art, and a way of life more advanced than anything seen before. As our species spread, other more primitive humans and many large mammal species vanished—perhaps victims of our success.

▲ BURIAL ORNAMENTS
This 24,000-year-old skeleton of a young man was found in a cave in Italy, adorned with a hat and a necklace made of shells.

Homo sapiens

HOE-moe SAP-ee-enz

- **When** 200,000 years ago to now (Neogene)
- **Fossil location** Worldwide, except for Antarctica and some remote islands
- **Habitat** Nearly all land habitats
- **Height** 6 ft (1.8 m)

Compared to other apes and primitive humans, *Homo sapiens* has a small, flat face; a high forehead; a huge, balloon-shaped braincase; small brow ridges; and a prominent chin. Most importantly, our species has a large and complex brain. Intelligence allowed our ancestors to devise ingenious new hunting tools, build shelters, make clothes, and harness fire. Language allowed them to pool knowledge and share skills. Early *Homo sapiens* lived in complex societies in which people looked after their sick and left offerings in graves—a sign they believed in an afterlife.

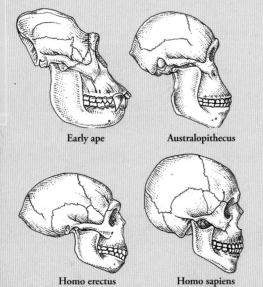

Early ape

Australopithecus

Homo erectus

Homo sapiens

Carved tools

Early *Homo sapiens* was a much more skillful toolmaker than other hominins (human relatives). As early as 73,000 years ago, humans in southern Africa were carving finely made tools from bone and making jewelry from shells. By 18,000 years ago, humans in Europe were using bone, ivory, and caribou antlers to make spear throwers, harpoons, and even needles. Many of these were engraved with artistic designs, such as animal heads.

Spear thrower

Harpoons

Spear points

Bone and antler tools from ice age Europe

Needle

▲ THE BUSHMEN *of southern Africa follow a way of life known as hunter-gathering. Instead of keeping livestock for food or growing crops, their gather all their food from the wild. All early* Homo sapiens *were hunter-gatherers, too. This way of life did not begin to die out until farming began about 8,000 years ago.*

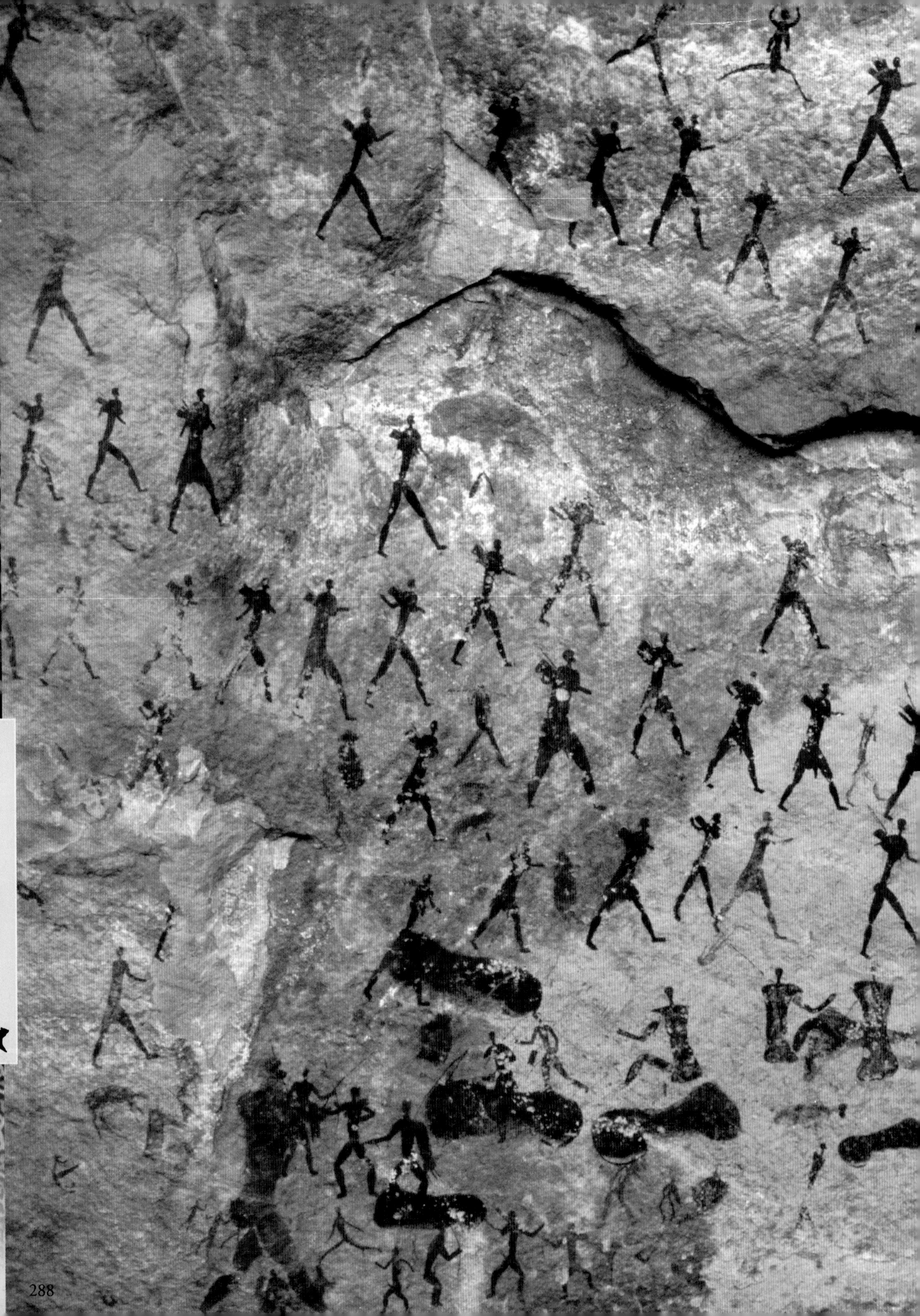

BUSHMAN ROCK ART

The rock art of the native people of southern Africa
(Bushmen) was made in the same way as the ancient
cave paintings of ice-age France (see page 270), but
Bushman rock art is only a few hundred years old.
It shows magical ceremonies such as dances in which
healers are at work.

Glossary

Adaptation A feature of an animal that evolved in response to its environment or way or life. The long neck of a giraffe, for instance, is an adaptation that helps it reach treetops.

Algae Primitive plants and plant-like organisms that grow in wet conditions.

Amber The fossil form of a sticky resin made by certain trees. Perfectly preserved insects and other organisms have been found in amber.

Ammonites Prehistoric sea creatures with coiled, chambered shells. Ammonites were relatives of octopuses and squids.

Amphibian A type of cold-blooded vertebrate, such as frog or newt. Most amphibians develop from larvae that live in water and breathe through gills, becoming land-dwelling adults that breathe air through lungs.

Ancestor An animal or plant species from which a more recent species has evolved.

Angiosperms A scientific term for flowering plants. This group includes broad-leaved trees and grasses.

Ankylosaurs Four-legged, armoured, plant-eating dinosaurs with bony plates that covered the neck, shoulders, and back.

Archosaurs A major group of reptiles that originated in the Triassic Period. It includes dinosaurs, pterosaurs, and crocodylomorphs.

Arthropods Invertebrates with segmented bodies and a hard outer covering (exoskeleton). Extinct arthropods include trilobites and eurypterids. Living ones include insects and spiders.

Aurochs An extinct variety of wild cattle that was the ancestor of modern cattle.

Australopithecus A prehistoric member of the human family that may be a direct ancestor of modern humans. *Australopithecus* looked like a chimpanzee but walked upright like a human.

Bivalves Aquatic animals such as clams and oysters that live in a hinged shell. The two halves of the shell are usually mirror images of each other.

Bony fish (Osteichthyans) Fish with a skeleton made of bone. Some fish, such as sharks, have a skeleton made of cartilage rather than bone and are classed as cartilaginous fish.

Burgess Shale Formation A site in British Columbia, Canada, where many important Cambrian fossils were discovered. Among the 130 species identified are sponges, jellyfish, worms, and arthropods.

Cambrian The first period of the Palaeozoic Era, from 542 to 488 million years ago. This was when most of the main invertebrate groups appeared in the fossil record.

Camouflage Colours or patterns on an animal's skin or fur that help it to blend with its surroundings and hide.

Carboniferous The fifth period of the Palaeozoic Era, from 359 to 299 million years ago. During this period, forests covered the land and were inhabited by insects and four-legged vertebrates (tetrapods), including the first amphibians and the first reptiles.

Carnivore An animal that eats meat. The term carnivore can also refer to a specific family of mammals (the order Carnivora).

Cartilage A firm, rubber-like tissue that is part of the skeleton of vertebrates. In fish such as sharks, the entire skeleton is made of cartilage.

Cephalopod Sea creatures with big eyes and a well-developed head surrounded by a ring of tentacles. Examples include octopuses, squid, cuttlefish, and ammonites.

Ceratopsians Two-legged and four-legged, plant-eating dinosaurs with a deep beak and a bony frill at the rear of the skull. They include the horned dinosaurs.

Chelicerate A type of invertebrate with special mouthparts called chelicerae that are used as pincers or fangs. Modern examples include spiders and scorpions.

Cold-blooded An animal is described as cold-blooded if its body temperature rises and falls along with the outside temperature. Animals that maintain a constant body temperature are described as warm-blooded.

Cretaceous The last period of the Mesozoic Era, from 145 to 65 million years ago.

Crinoids (sea lilies) Plant-shaped sea creatures with feathery arms that live anchored to the sea floor by long stalks. They are related to starfish and sea urchins.

Crocodylomorphs A group of reptiles that includes crocodiles, alligators, and their many extinct relatives. Crocodylomorphs appeared at about the same time as the dinosaurs and were once much more varied than today.

Crustaceans A large and varied group of arthropods, most of which live in water. Living examples include crabs, shrimps, and woodlice.

Cycads Palm-like, seed-bearing plants that are topped by a crown of fern-like leaves. They may be short and shrub-like, or grow as high as 20 m (65 ft).

Descendant An animal or plant species that evolved from an early species (its ancestor).

Devonian period The fourth period of the Palaeozoic Era, from 416 to 350 million years ago. The Devonian is also called the "age of fish". During this period, tetrapods (four-legged vertebrates) evolved from fish.

Digit A finger, thumb, or toe.

Dinosaurs A large group of archosaurs with upright limbs. Dinosaurs were the dominant land animals for 160 million years.

DNA Deoxyribonucleic acid, a chemical whose molecules carry genetic instructions from one generation to the next in nearly all organisms. (See Genes.) The complex double-helix structure of DNA was discovered in the 1950s.

Domesticated Bred to be tame. Cows, sheep, and dogs are examples of domestic animals.

Dromaeosaurs A group of bird-like, two-legged, carnivorous dinosaurs. Most grew no longer than 2 m (6 ft). Dromaeosaurs lived in all northern continents.

Echinoderms Marine invertebrates with a hard, chalky skeleton and a five-rayed symmetry. They evolved during the Cambrian Period and include starfish, sea lilies, sea cucumbers, and sea urchins.

Ediacaran biota Fossil organisms named after those found in the Ediacaran Hills of Australia. The sea-dwelling, soft-bodied organisms lived about 550 million years ago and were some of the earliest animals.

Embryo An animal or plant in an early stage of development from an egg or a seed.

Environment The natural surroundings in which an animal or plant lives.

Era A very long unit of time. Eras are divided into shorter units called periods. The Mesozoic Era, for example, is divided into the Triassic, Jurassic, and Cretaceous periods.

Eurypterids (sea scorpions) An extinct group of large arthropods related to modern scorpions. Eurypterids lived in the sea and freshwater habitats during the Palaeozoic Era. Some grew more than 2 m (6 ft 6 in) long.

Evolution The gradual change of animal or plant species over long periods of time. Evolution is driven mainly by a process called natural selection.

Excavation Digging out and removing fossils or other objects from the ground.

Exoskeleton An external skeleton. Animals such as crabs have an exoskeleton. In contract, humans have an internal skeleton.

Extinction The dying-out of a plant or animal species. Extinction can happen naturally as a result of competition between species, changes in the environment, or natural disasters (such as an asteroid striking Earth).

Fossil The ancient remains or imprint of a prehistoric organism preserved in rock.

Fossilization The process by which dead organisms turn into fossils. Fossilization often involves replacement of the original organism with rock minerals.

Gastropods A class of invertebrates made up of snails, slugs, and their many aquatic relatives, such as cowries and limpets.

Genes Chemical instructions encoded in the DNA molecule. Genes control the way all organisms grow and develop. They are passed on from parents to their young.

Gondwana A vast prehistoric supercontinent that included South America, Africa, Antarctica, Australia, and India. Gondwana existed from Precambrian times until the Jurassic Period, when these lands began to move apart.

Habitat The place where a plant or animal lives naturally.

Hadrosaurids (duck-billed dinosaurs) A family of plant-eating dinosaur species with duck-like beaks that lived during the Cretaceous Period.

Hagfish (Agnathan) A kind of living jawless fish.

Herbivore An animal that eats plants.

Hominins The family of apes that includes humans and our closest relatives.

Homo erectus A prehistoric member of the human family that lived from 2 million years ago to 100,000 years ago. *Homo erectus* evolved in Africa but spread to Asia.

Homo sapiens The scientific name for modern human (our own species).

Hybrid The offspring of parents from two different species.

Ichthyosaurs Prehistoric marine reptiles that resembled dolphins or fish.

Iguanodontians Large, plant-eating ornithopod dinosaurs that were common in the Early Cretaceous.

Invertebrates Animals without backbones.

Jawless fish (Agnathans) A class of primitive vertebrates that flourished mainly in Early Palaeozoic times. They include extinct groups and the living hagfish and lampreys.

Jurassic The middle period in the Mesozoic Era, from 200 to 145 million years ago. During the Jurassic Period, dinosaurs dominated the land, the first birds evolved, and mammals began to diversify.

Juvenile A young animal.

Kin Family – individuals that are genetically related.

Lamprey A type of living jawless fish with a round, sucker-like mouth.

Lungfish A type of fish that has both gills and lungs and can breathe in water and air. Lungfish appeared in the Devonian Period.

Mammals Warm-blooded, hairy vertebrates that secrete milk and suckle their young. Living mammals range from tiny shrews to the blue whale (the largest creature ever) and occupy a great variety of habitats. Mammals originated in the Triassic Period.

Marine Belonging to the sea (particularly animals or plants).

Marsupial A type of mammal with a pouch in which the young develop. Living examples include kangaroos and wallabies. Marsupials survive only in Australasia and the Americas.

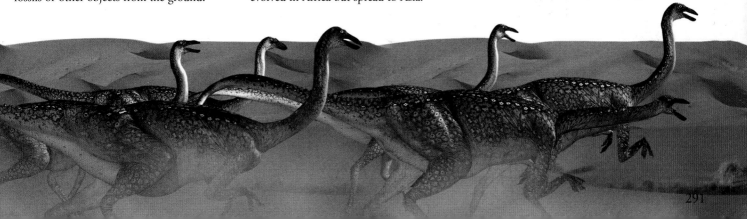

Mastodons An extinct group of large mammals with trunks, tusks, and thick hair. They were related to the elephants.

Meganeura A kind of giant dragonfly (more correctly called a griffinfly) that lived in the Carboniferous Period. *Meganeura* was possibly the largest insect ever found on Earth.

Metamorphosis A major change in an organism when it take on its adult form. The change from caterpillar to butterfly is an example of metamorphosis.

Migration A long-distance journey undertaken by animals moving to new homes. Many birds migrate in autumn in order to spend winter in warmer countries.

Molluscs A large group of invertebrate species that includes slugs, snails, clams, octopuses, and squids. Many molluscs produce hard shells that fossilize easily, making mollusc fossils common.

Mosasaurs Giant, sea-dwelling lizards that lived during the Cretaceous Period. They were fierce predators with slender bodies, long snouts, and flipper-like limbs.

Natural selection The natural "weeding out" of animals and plant that drives evolution.

Neanderthal (*Homo neanderthalensis*) An extinct species of hominin that is very closely related to our own species. Neanderthals lived in Europe and Asia during the last ice age.

Neogene The period of history from 23 million years ago to today. The Neogene Period is divided into the Miocene, Pliocene, Pleistocene, and Holocene epochs.

Nocturnal Awake and active during the night. Nocturnal animals include owls, bats, and cats.

Nothosaurs A group of large, sea-dwelling reptiles that lived in the Triassic Period. Nothosaurs resembled seals and came ashore to breed.

Omnivore An animal that eats both plant and animal food. Examples include pigs, rats, and human beings.

Ordovician The second period in the Palaeozoic Era, from 488 to 444 million years ago. All animals known from this time lived in water.

Ornithischians (bird-hipped dinosaurs) One of two major divisions into which the dinosaur family tree is split (see also Saurischians). Ornithischians were plant eaters with beaked mouths.

Ornithomimids (ostrich dinosaurs) Tall, slender, bird-like dinosaurs that were built like ostriches. They were the fastest animals on land in the Cretaceous Period.

Paleogene The first period in the Cenozoic Era, from 65 to 23 million years ago. The Paleogene is divided into the Paleocene, Eocene, and Oligocene epochs.

Palaeontology The scientific study of fossil plants and animals.

Pampas Treeless, grass-covered plains in South America.

Pangaea A supercontinent that formed at the end of the Palaeozoic Era. Pangaea contained nearly all of Earth's land and stretched from the North Pole to the South Pole.

Pelvis The part of an animal's skeleton that forms the hips.

Pelycosaurs A group of large, reptile-like animals that lived before the age of the dinosaurs. Scientists believe that mammals evolved from these creatures.

Period A very long unit of time, lasting million of years. The Jurassic is a period.

Permafrost Permanently frozen ground found in places such as northern Canada and Siberia. Although the surface thaws out and becomes boggy in summer, the deeper soil remains frozen solid.

Permian The last period of the Palaeozoic Era, from 299 to 251 million years ago. The end of the Permian saw a worldwide mass extinction in which most animal species were wiped out.

Placentals Mammals whose unborn young are nourished by a special organ called a placenta. Placental mammals have replaced marsupials in most parts of the world.

Placoderm (armoured fish) A class of prehistoric fish that had body armour formed from plates of bone. They flourished in the Devonian Period.

Plesiosaurs Large, prehistoric marine reptiles that swam with flipper-shaped limbs. Many had enormously long necks and tiny heads. Others (called pliosaurs) had short necks and huge heads with powerful, fang-lined jaws.

Precambrian The great span of time lasting from Earth's formation 4.6 billion years ago to the start of the Cambrian Period 542 million years ago. For most of the Precambrian, the only forms of life were microscopic, single-celled organisms that lived in water.

Predator An animal that hunts, kills, and eats other animals.

Preservation Keeping something, for example a fossil, free from harm or decay.

Prey An animal that is hunted, killed, and eaten by a predator.

Primates The group of mammals that includes lemurs, monkeys, apes, and humans.

Primitive At an early stage of evolution.

Pterosaurs Huge flying reptiles that lived during the age of the dinosaurs. The wings of pterosaurs consisted of sheets of skin stretched between the limbs.

Ray-finned fish (Actinopterygii) A major class of fish that includes about 25,000 of today's fish species and many prehistoric species. Ray-finned fish have fins consisting of skin stretched over a fan of thin bones.

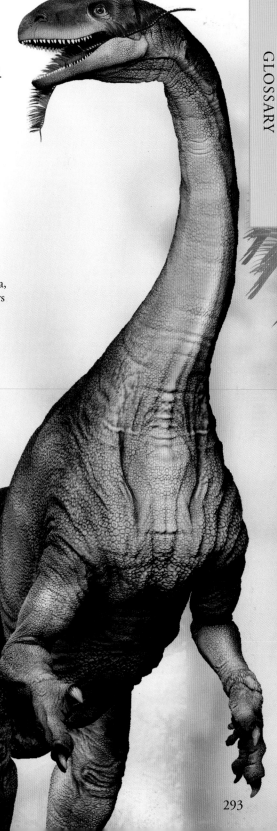

Rays (Batoidea) A group of flat-bodied, cartilaginous fish related to sharks. Examples include stingrays and manta rays.

Reptile A cold-blooded animal with scaly skin that typically lives on land and reproduces by laying eggs. Lizards, snakes, turtles, crocodiles, and dinosaurs are reptiles.

Rodents A group of mostly small mammals that includes mice, rats, squirrels, and porcupines. Rodents have sharp front teeth used for gnawing nuts and seeds.

Saurischians (lizard-hipped dinosaurs) One of the two major divisions into which the dinosaur family tree is split (see also Ornithischians). All meat-eating dinosaurs were saurischians.

Sauropods Gigantic, long-necked, plant-eating, saurischian dinosaurs. The sauropods included the largest animals ever to walk on Earth.

Savanna Tropical grassland. Savannas are often dotted with trees or patches of woodland.

Scutes Bony plates with a horny covering set in the skin of certain reptiles to protect them from the teeth and claws of enemies.

Sediment Material deposited by wind, water, or ice. Sediments such as sand, silt, and mud build up on the sea floor and are eventually turned into rock (sedimentary rock).

Sedimentary rock The type of rock in which fossils are found.

Silurian The third period in the Palaeozoic Era, from 444 to 416 million years ago.

Skull The head's bony framework that protects the brain, eyes, ears, and nasal passages.

Species A type of animal of plant. Examples of species include lions, human beings, and apple trees. Individual in a species can breed with each other.

Spinosaurids A family of huge dinosaurs of the Cretaceous Period that had sail-like structures on their backs.

Stegosaurs Four-legged, plant-eating dinosaurs with two rows of tall bony plates and/or spines running down the back.

Supercontinent A prehistoric landmass containing two or more major continental plates. Examples include Gondwana and Pangaea.

Tetrapod A vertebrate with four limbs (arms, legs, or wings). All amphibians, reptiles, mammals, and birds are tetrapods. Snakes are also tetrapods because they evolved from ancestors with four limbs.

Therizinosaurs A group of bizarre-looking dinosaurs that lived in the Cretaceous Period. Therizinosaurs were tall with small heads, stumpy feet, and pot bellies.

Theropods A large branch of the dinosaur family tree made up mostly of predators. Theropods typically had sharp teeth and claws. They ranged from hen-sized creatures to the colossal *Tyrannosaurus*.

Titanosaurs Very large, four-legged, plant-eating dinosaurs. The titanosaurs were sauropods and included perhaps the largest land animals ever.

Triassic The first period in the Mesozoic Era, from 251 to 200 million years ago. Dinosaurs emerged in the Triassic Period.

Trilobites Prehistoric sea creatures with external skeletons divided lengthwise into three lobes. Variations in the shape and features of trilobite fossils are an accurate indicator of the age of the sedimentary rocks in which they are found.

Vertebrae The linked bones forming the backbone of a vertebrate animal.

Vertebrates Animals with an internal bony or cartilaginous skeleton including a skull and a backbone. Fish, amphibians, reptiles, birds, and mammals are all vertebrates.

Warm-blooded Animals that maintain a constant internal body temperature are described as warm-blooded. Mammals and birds are warm-blooded, whereas fish and reptiles are cold-blooded.

Wingspan The distance from the tip of one wing to the tip of the other when both wings are outstretched.

Index

295

Acknowledgements

Dorling Kindersley would like to thank Madhavi Singh for proofreading and Poppy Joslin for design assistance.

The publisher would also like to thank the following for their kind permission to reproduce their photographs (Key: a-above; b-below/bottom; c-center; f-far; l-left; r-right; t-top).

1 Getty Images: Iconica / Philip and Karen Smith (background). **2 Alamy Images:** Phil Degginger (4). **Corbis:** Frans Lanting (1); Science Faction / Norbert Wu (6). **Dorling Kindersley:** Colin Keates / courtesy of the Natural History Museum, London (2); Barrie Watts (7). **3 Ardea:** Pat Morris (5/l). **Corbis:** Frans Lanting (3/r); Paul Souders (8/r). **Dorling Kindersley:** Jon Hughes (7/r, 2/l). **Getty Images:** AFP (2/r); Stone / Howard Grey (5/r); WireImage / Frank Mullen (4/l). **Science Photo Library:** (1/l); Richard Bizley (1/r); Christian Darkin (4/r); Mark Garlick (7/l). **4 Ardea:** Pat Morris (bl). **Getty Images:** Stone / Howard Grey (clb). **Science Photo Library:** Christian Darkin (br). **4-5 Dorling Kindersley:** Andy Crawford / courtesy of the Royal Tyrrell Museum of Palaeontology, Alberta, Canada. **5 Dorling Kindersley:** Andrew Nelmerm / courtesy of the Royal British Columbia Museum, Victoria, Canada (bl). **Getty Images:** AFP (br). **6-7 Alamy Images:** Phil Degginger. **7 Dorling Kindersley:** Colin Keates / courtesy of the Natural History Museum, London (tc). **8 Corbis:** Arctic-Images (t). **9 Alamy Images:** AF Archive (cla). **Corbis:** Frans Lanting (br); Bernd Vogel (t); George Steinmetz (cra); Visuals Unlimited / Dr. Terry Beveridge (crb). **11 Corbis:** The Gallery Collection (tl). **Dorling Kindersley:** Colin Keates / courtesy of the Natural History Museum, London (cra). **12 Corbis:** Douglas Peebles (bl). **Getty Images:** Science Faction Jewels / Louie Psihoyos (tr). **14 Science Photo Library:** Richard Bizley (cr); Walter Myers (tr). **16 Dorling Kindersley:** Colin Keates / courtesy of the Natural History Museum, London (t, bl). **17 Corbis:** Sygma / Didier Dutheil (tr). **Dorling Kindersley:** Barrie Watts (bl). **18-19 Getty Images:** Science Faction Jewels / Louie Psihoyos. **20 Corbis:** Sygma / Didier Dutheil (l, br). **Science Photo Library:** Ted Kinsman (tr). **21 Corbis:** Sygma / Didier Dutheil (tl, tr, cra, crb, br). **22-23 Harry Wilson. . :** (main illustration). **23 Corbis:** Momatiuk - Eastcott (crb). **Photolibrary:** OSF / Robert Tyrrell (br). **24 Getty Images:** Stone / Howard Grey (l/sidebar). **24-25 Ardea:** Pat Morris. **25 Ardea:** John T. Fowler (cr). **26 Alamy Images:** Nicholas Bird (bc); H. Lansdown (br). **Corbis:** Frank Krahmer (bl); Science Faction / Norbert Wu (cla). **27 Alamy Images:** WaterFrame (br). **Corbis:** Gary Bell (bc); Science Faction / Stephen Frink (clb); Stephen Frink (cr); Paul Edmondson (bl). **Getty Images:** Minden Pictures / Foto Natura / Ingo Arndt (tl). **28 Corbis:** Frans Lanting (bl). **29 J. Gehling,**

South Australian Museum: (tr). **30 Alamy Images:** Kevin Schafer (br). **Getty Images:** National Geographic / O. Louis Mazzatenta (c). **31 Science Photo Library:** Alan Sirulnikoff (cr). **32 courtesy of the Smithsonian Institution:** (cl). **35 Natural History Museum, London:** (br). **37 Ardea:** Francois Gohier (cl). **Dorling Kindersley:** Harry Taylor / courtesy of the Royal Museum of Scotland, Edinburgh (bl). **41 Getty Images:** Comstock Images (tr). **43 Corbis:** Jeffrey L. Rotman (br); Visuals Unlimited / Wim van Egmond (tr). **45 Dorling Kindersley:** Colin Keates / courtesy of the Natural History Museum, London (tr). **Corbis:** Frank Lane Picture Agency / Douglas P. Wilson (cb); Visuals Unlimited / Ken Lucas (tl). **46-47 Alamy Images:** Kate Rose / Peabody Museum, New Haven, Connecticut. **46 Natural History Museum, London:** (bl). **47**

Corbis: Michael & Patricia Fogden (br). **Prof. J.W. Schneider/TU Bergakademie Freiberg:** (tr). **48 Alamy Images:** John T. Fowler (tr). **Corbis:** Tom Bean (bl). **Science Photo Library:** Noah Poritz (t). **50-51 naturepl.com:** Jean E. Roche. **51 Dorling Kindersley:** Frank Greenaway / courtesy of the Natural History Museum, London (br). **52-53 Getty Images:** Stone / Howard Grey. **54 Natural History Museum, London:** Graham Cripps. **55 akg-images:** Gilles Mermet (tr). **NHPA / Photoshot:** Ken Griffiths (br). **57 Getty Images:** The Image Bank / Philippe Bourseiller (br). **58-59 Ardea:** John Cancalosi (c). **58 Alamy Images:** Danita Delimont (c); Scenics & Science (r). **60 Dorling Kindersley:** Colin Keates / courtesy of the Natural History Museum, London (cra/Giant cerith). **Getty Images:** Mike Kemp (bl/snail). **62 Dorling Kindersley:** Harry Taylor / courtesy of the Royal Museum of Scotland, Edinburgh (sidebar). **63 Dorling Kindersley:** Harry Taylor / courtesy of the Royal Museum of Scotland, Edinburgh (cl). **Photolibrary:**

Oxford Scientific (OSF) / David M. Dennis (c). **64 Corbis:** All Canada Photos / Ron Erwin (bc); Frans Lanting (br). **65 Ardea:** Ken Lucas (ca). **Dorling Kindersley:** Andy Crawford / courtesy of the Royal Tyrrell Museum of Palaeontology, Alberta, Canada (tr); David Peart (br). **66 Alamy Images:** blickwinkel (br). **67 Dorling Kindersley:** Harry Taylor / courtesy of the Royal Museum of Scotland, Edinburgh (tr); Harry Taylor / courtesy of the Hunterian Museum (University of Glasgow) (bl). **68 Alamy Images:** All Canada Photos / Royal Tyrrell Museum, Drumheller, Alta, Canada (c). **70 Dorling Kindersley:** Colin Keates / courtesy of the Natural History Museum, London (b). **71 Dorling Kindersley:** Colin Keates / courtesy of the Natural History Museum, London (tl, crb). **Science Photo Library:** Christian Darkin (b). **73 Corbis:** Layne Kennedy (tr); Louie Psihoyos (br).

75 Corbis: Visuals Unlimited (b). **Dorling Kindersley:** Neil Fletcher (c) Oxford University Museum of Natural History (cr); Harry Taylor / courtesy of the Royal Museum of Scotland, Edinburgh (cl); Colin Keates / courtesy of the Natural History Museum, London (tr). **77 Alamy Images:** PetStockBoys (tl). **Dorling Kindersley:** Harry Taylor / courtesy of the Natural History Museum, London (tr). **79 Dorling Kindersley:** Colin Keates / courtesy of the Natural History Museum, London (tr). **Getty Images:** Taxi / Peter Scoones (br). **81 Alamy Images:** B. Christopher (bl). **Corbis:** Gallo Images / Anthony Bannister (tr). **Dorling Kindersley:** Jan van der Voort (crb). **Dr Howard Falcon-Lang:** (br). **82 Alamy Images:** WaterFrame (cl). **83 Dorling Kindersley:** Steve Gorton / Richard Hammond - modelmaker / courtesy of Oxford University Museum of Natural History (c); Colin Keates / courtesy of the Natural History Museum, London (tl). **84 Science Photo Library:** Visuals Unlimited / Ken Lucas (t). **86**

Alamy Images: Realimage (tl). **87 Alamy Images:** botanikfoto / Steffen Hauser (clb). **Dorling Kindersley:** Colin Keates / courtesy of the Natural History Museum, London (tc). **88 Corbis:** Arctic-Images (l). **89 Corbis:** Science Faction / Louie Psihoyos (tr). **92 Corbis:** Sygma / Vo Trung Dung (b/background). **95 Photolibrary:** Oxford Scientific (OSF) / David M. Dennis (cl). **96-97 Corbis:** Mark A. Johnson (background). **96 Luigi Chiesa:** (bl). **98 Corbis:** Kevin Schafer (b). **98-99 Dorling Kindersley:** (c) David Peart (background). **102-103 Science Photo Library:** John Foster. **102 Corbis:** Sygma / Vo Trung Dung (bl). **103 Science Photo Library:** Victor Habbick Visions (cl). **104 Dorling Kindersley:** David Peart (background). **105 Corbis:** In Pictures / Mike Kemp (br). **107 Getty Images:** AFP / Valery Hache (cl). **108 Natural History Museum, London:** Berislav Krzic (b). **110 Alamy Images:** Pictorial Press Ltd (b). **111 Dorling Kindersley:** Colin Keates / courtesy of the Natural History Museum, London (tr). **Science Photo Library:** (tl); Michael Marten (tc). **Wellcome Images:** Wellcome Library, London (br). **113 Alamy Images:** Kevin Schafer (t). **114-115 Alamy Images:** Paul Kingsley. **114 Dorling Kindersley:** John Downes / John Holmes - modelmaker / courtesy of the Natural History Museum, London (sidebar). **115 Dorling Kindersley:** Colin Keates / courtesy of the Natural History Museum, London (cl). **Science Photo Library:** Joe Tucciarone (cr). **116-117 Corbis:** Michael S. Yamashita. **118 Science Photo Library:** Roger Harris (br). **119 Dorling Kindersley:** Jon Hughes (tl, bl, tr). **120 Dorling Kindersley:** Andy Crawford / courtesy of the Royal Tyrrell Museum of Palaeontology, Alberta, Canada (cl). **122-133 Dorling Kindersley:** Nigel Hicks / courtesy of the Lost Gardens of Heligan (background). **125 Getty Images:** National Geographic Creative / Jeffrey L. Osborn (cl). **126-127 Corbis:** Inspirestock (background). **127 Dorling Kindersley:** Colin Keates / courtesy of the Natural History Museum, London (bl). **Wikipedia, The Free Encyclopedia:** (br). **128 Dorling Kindersley:** Jon Hughes; Colin Keates / courtesy of the Natural History Museum, London (b). **130 Getty Images:** Panoramic Images (t/background). **131 Dorling Kindersley:** Andy Crawford / courtesy of the Royal Tyrrell Museum of Palaeontology, Alberta, Canada (bl); Courtesy of the Royal Tyrrell Museum of Palaeontology, Alberta, Canada (ca). **Natural History Museum, London:** Berislav Krzic (br). **132-133 Corbis:** Louie Psihoyos. **133 Dorling Kindersley:** (c) Rough Guides / Alex Wilson (tr). **U.S. Geological Survey:** (br). **135 Dorling Kindersley:** Lynton Gardiner / courtesy of the American Museum of Natural History (tr, br). **137 Dorling Kindersley:** Lynton Gardiner / courtesy of the American Museum of Natural History (tr, c). **141 Dorling Kindersley:** Tim Ridley / courtesy of the Leicester Museum

(br). **144 Dorling Kindersley:** Peter Minister (c). **145 Dorling Kindersley:** Bruce Cowell / courtesy of Queensland Museum, Brisbane, Australia (t). **146 Corbis:** Rune Hellestad (b). **148 Dorling Kindersley:** Andy Crawford / courtesy of the Institute of Geology and Palaeontology, Tubingen, Germany (cl, tr). **150 Alamy Images:** Fabian Gonzales Editorial (t/background). **Getty Images:** The Image Bank / Don Smith (b/background). **152-153 Dorling Kindersley:** Philippe Giraud (background); Steve Gorton / John Holmes - modelmaker. **153 Dorling Kindersley:** Steve Gorton / Robert L. Braun - modelmaker (t). **157 Corbis:** Cameron Davidson (tr); Louie Psihoyos (bl). **Dorling Kindersley:** Lynton Gardiner / courtesy of the Carnegie Museum of Natural History, Pittsburgh (br). **158-159 Getty Images:** Siri and Jeff Berting (background). **158 Corbis:** Bob Krist (bl). **160 Corbis:** Joson (background). **163 Dorling Kindersley:** Jon Hughes (ca). **Science Photo Library:** Walter Myers (br). **164 Alamy Images:** Alberto Paredes (r). **165 Alamy Images:** Paul Kingsley (br); Tony Waltham / Robert Harding Picture Library Ltd (crb). **Corbis:** Science Faction / Louie Psihoyos (cl). **Dorling Kindersley:** Colin Keates / courtesy of the Natural History Museum, London (tc). **Science Photo Library:** Sinclair Stammers (bl). **169 Corbis:** Louie Psihoyos (cr). **170-171 Corbis:** Aurora Photos / Randall Levensaler Photography (b/background). **171 Dorling Kindersley:** Colin Keates / courtesy of Senckenberg, Forschungsinstitut und Naturmuseum, Frankfurt (r). **172-173 Ardea:** Andrey Zvoznikov (background). **174-175 Getty Images:** Iconica / Philip and Karen Smith (background). **175 Dorling Kindersley:** Jon Hughes (br). **176 Mike Hettwer:** (br). **177 Corbis:** Sygma / Didier Dutheil (bl, bc, br). **178-179 Dorling Kindersley:** Jon Hughes. **179 Dorling Kindersley:** Andy Crawford / courtesy of Staatliches Museum fur Naturkunde Stuttgart (bl); Steve Gorton / Richard Hammond - modelmaker / courtesy of the American Museum of Natural History (br). **181 Ardea:** Francois Gohier (bl). **182-183 Getty Images:** Willard Clay Photography, Inc. (background). **184-185 Corbis:** amanaimages / Mitsushi Okada (background). **185 Dorling Kindersley:** Colin Keates / courtesy of the Natural History Museum, London (tr). **186 Dorling Kindersley:** Andy Crawford / courtesy of the Royal Tyrrell Museum of Palaeontology, Alberta, Canada (tl). **187 Corbis:** Science Faction / Louie Psihoyos (tr). **188-189 Getty Images:** WireImage / Frank Mullen. **189 Corbis:** George Steinmetz (bl, tr, cr, br). **190 Corbis:** Louie Psihoyos (tr). **190-191 Corbis:** Owen Franken (background). **191 Corbis:** Louie Psihoyos (tr). **196 Science Photo Library:** Roger Harris (bl). **197 Dorling Kindersley:** Gary Ombler / (c) Luis Rey - modelmaker (tr). **Getty Images:** Science Faction Jewels / Louie Psihoyos (tc). **198-199 Corbis:** Nick Rains (background). **199 Dorling Kindersley:** Lynton Gardiner (c) Peabody Museum of Natural History, Yale University (tr). **200-201 Getty Images:** Spencer Platt. **201 Science Photo Library:** Christian

Darkin (t). **202-203 Reuters:** Mike Segar. **203 Corbis:** Grant Delin (b). **206 Corbis:** Jonathan Blair (b). **Science Photo Library:** Mark Garlick. **207 Nicholas/http://commons.wikimedia.org/wiki/File:Western-Ghats-Matheran.jpg:** (cr). **Science Photo Library:** Joe Tucciarone (b); D. Van Ravenswaay (tl). **208 Corbis:** Layne Kennedy (bl). **Dorling Kindersley:** Colin Keates / courtesy of the Natural History Museum, London (tl). **209 Dorling Kindersley:** Jon Hughes (br). **210 Dorling Kindersley:** Jon Hughes / Bedrock Studios. **211 Corbis:** National Geographic Society (tr). **Dorling Kindersley:** Jon Hughes (cr). **212 John Scurlock:** (bl). **213 courtesy of the Smithsonian Institution. 214 Dorling Kindersley:** Philip Dowell (sidebar). **215 Dorling Kindersley:** Andrew Nelmerm / courtesy of the Royal British Columbia Museum, Victoria, Canada (bc). **Science Photo Library:** Pascal Goetgheluck (br). **216 Ardea:** Steve Downer (tc). **Corbis:** Frans Lanting (tr); Visuals Unlimited / Thomas Marent (bc); Momatiuk - Eastcott (br). **Getty Images:** AFP / Sam Yeh (cl). **217 Corbis:** Paul Souders (cra); Keren Su (bl). **Dorling Kindersley:** courtesy of the Booth Museum of Natural History, Brighton (tl); Nigel Hicks (bc). **218 Corbis:** Lester V. Bergman (tc). **Dorling Kindersley:** Colin Keates / courtesy of the Natural History Museum, London (bl). **219 Getty Images:** Ken Lucas (cl). **221 Dorling Kindersley:** Harry Taylor / courtesy of York Museums Trust (Yorkshire Museum) (b). **224 Corbis:** Radius Images (r). **Getty Images:** National Geographic / Jonathan Blair (tl). **Science Photo Library:** Maria e Bruno Petriglia (bl). **225 Corbis:** Ecoscene / Wayne Lawler (clb); Karl-Heinz Haenel; Stock Photos / Bruce Peebles (bl, bc); Frans Lanting (tl). **Getty Images:** Stockbyte / Joseph Sohm-Visions of America (cla). **226 Dorling Kindersley:** Lindsey Stock (background). **227 Corbis:** Frans Lanting (bl). **Dorling Kindersley:** Bedrock Studios (tl); Colin Keates / courtesy of the Natural History Museum, London (bl). **228-229 naturepl.com:** Dave Watts. **229 Corbis:** epa / Dave Hunt (t); In Pictures / Barry Lewis (br). **230 Science Photo Library:** Christian Darkin. **231 Getty Images:** Photonica / Theo Allofs (cra). **232 Corbis:** Bob Krist (background). **233 Alamy Images:** blickwinkel (br). **Getty Images:** Ken Lucas (tr). **234 Dorling Kindersley:** Colin Keates / courtesy of the Natural History Museum, London (cl). **235 Dorling Kindersley:** Jon Hughes / Bedrock Studios (tr). **Getty Images:** De Agostini Picture Library (cr). **Science Photo Library:** Mauricio Anton (br). **236-237 Corbis:** Jonathan Andrew. **236 Science Photo Library:** Dr Juerg Alean (tr); Richard Bizley (bl); Gary Hincks (br). **237**

Corbis: David Muench (tr). **Science Photo Library:** Gary Hincks (br, bl). **239 Dorling Kindersley:** Bedrock Studios (b). **240-241 Natural History Museum, London:** Michael R. Long . **240 Alamy Images:** Martin Shields (bl). **241 Alamy Images:** Martin Shields (tl). **Pyry Matikainen. 242 Alamy Images:** Ryan M. Bolton (tl). **Dorling Kindersley:** Jon Hughes (r). **244 Alamy Images:** Elvele Images Ltd. **245 Dorling Kindersley:** Bedrock Studios (cr). **247 Alamy Images:** blickwinkel (br). **248-249 Dorling Kindersley:** Bedrock Studios. **248 Getty Images:** Popperfoto / Bob Thomas (b). **250 Corbis:** Carl & Ann Purcell (background). **Dorling Kindersley. 251 Corbis:** Kevin Schafer (br). **255 Science Photo Library:** Walter Myers (bl). **256-257 Corbis:** Annie Griffiths Belt. **257 Science Photo Library:** Larry Miller (b). **258 Getty Images:** Gallo Images / Ray Ives (r/background). **259 Alamy Images:** vario images GmbH & Co.KG (br). **Dorling Kindersley:** Dave King / courtesy of the Natural History Museum, London (tr, c); Harry Taylor / courtesy of the Natural History Museum, London (bl). **260-261 Science Photo Library:** Christian Darkin. **261 Ardea:** Masahiro Iijima (br). **Photolibrary:** Goran Burenhult; (tr). **262 Alamy Images:** ITAR-TASS Photo Agency (b). **Corbis:** Science Faction / Steven Kazlowski (b/background). **262-263 Alamy Images:** Gerner Thomsen (c). **263 Alamy Images:** Arcticphoto (t). **Getty Images:** AFP / RIA Novosti (bl). **264 Corbis:** Reuters / Marcos Brindicci (bl). **265 Alamy Images:** The Natural History Museum (tr). **Corbis:** Buddy Mays (br). **267 Dorling Kindersley:** Bedrock Studios (cr, bl). **268 Alamy Images:** Niels Poulsen mus (b). **Ardea:** Duncan Usher (tl). **269 Alamy Images:** blickwinkel (tl). **270-271 Getty Images:** National Geographic / Sisse Brimberg. **270 Getty Images:** Stone /

Robert Frerck (br); Time & Life Pictures / Ralph Morse (bl). **Robert Gunn:** (tr). **271 French Ministry of Culture and Communication, Regional Direction for Cultural Affairs - Rhône-Alpes region - Regional department of archaeology:** (bl). **Getty Images:** AFP (br). **274 Getty Images:** Gallo Images / Latitudestock (b). **275 Corbis:** Denis Scott (b). **276 Getty Images:** AFP / Stan Honda. **277 Dorling Kindersley:** Harry Taylor / courtesy of the Natural History Museum, London (tl). **278 Science Photo Library:** Mauricio Anton. **279 Corbis:** Frans Lanting (bl); Sygma / Régis Bossu (t). **naturepl.com:** Karl Ammann (br). **Science Photo Library:** John Reader (tr). **280 Science Photo Library:** Mauricio Anton. **281 Corbis:** Larry Williams (tr). **282 Corbis:** epa / Federico Gambarini. **Dorling Kindersley:** Rough Guides (background). **283 Corbis:** Reuters / Nikola Solic (tl). **Science Photo Library:** Pascal Goetgheluck (bl). **284 Science Photo Library:** Christian Darkin (r). **285 Alamy Images:** Sabena Jane Blackbird (ca). **Corbis:** Frans Lanting (bl); Sygma / Kevin Dufy (cb); Buddy Mays (br). **The Kobal Collection:** Hammer (t). **286-287 Getty Images:** Gallo Images / Andrew Bannister. **288-289 Getty Images:** Gallo Images / Peter Chadwick. **290 Getty Images:** Gallo Images / Peter Chadwick (sidebar). **294 Dorling Kindersley:** Dave King / Jeremy Hunt at Centaur Studios - modelmaker (bl). **300 Dorling Kindersley:** Andy Crawford / courtesy of the Royal Tyrrell Museum of Palaeontology, Alberta, Canada (bl). **302 Dorling Kindersley:** Peter Minister. **304 Corbis:** Frans Lanting.

Jacket images: *Front:* **Alamy Images:** Javier Etcheverry br. **Dorling Kindersley:** Jon Hughes c; Natural History Museum, London fbl / (background). **Science Photo Library:** Chris Butler bl; Tom McHugh fbr. **SuperStock:** imagebroker.net (background). *Back:* **Dorling Kindersley:** Royal British Columbia Museum, Victoria, Canada br; Senckenberg Nature Museum, Frankfurt bl. **Getty Images:** Photographer's Choice / Colin Anderson fbr. **Science Photo Library:** Christian Darkin fbl, t. *Front Flap:* **Dorling Kindersley:** Jon Hughes.

All other images © Dorling Kindersley
For further information see:
www.dkimages.com